Cousins at one remove

Anglo-German Studies 2

Cousins at one remove
Anglo-German Studies 2

edited by

Richard Byrn

Leeds, 1998

Published by Northern Universities Press, an imprint of W.S. Maney & Son Ltd, Hudson Road, Leeds LS9 7DL, UK.
Telephone: +44 (0) 113 249 7481
Fax: +44 (0) 113 248 6983

ISBN: 0 901286 98 2

Printed in Great Britain by W.S. Maney & Son Ltd, Leeds.

The three sonnet translations by Celan are printed with the permission of Suhrkamp Verlag.

The front cover images of Shakespeare and Goethe and of the Town Halls of Munich and Leeds were created by Francis J. Byrn.

Published with the aid of a grant from the Leeds Philosophical & Literary Society.

Contents

To all
British Teachers of German
with thanks

Preface

As its sub-title indicates, this set of essays is a sequel to *Anglo-German Studies* published in 1992 by the Leeds Philosophical and Literary Society. Publication of the present volume by Northern Universities Press has been enabled by a grant from the same Society – to whose Council we express our gratitude.

These two *Anglo-German Studies* volumes are closely connected with the work of the Leeds University MA programme in Anglo-German Cultural Relations. Most of the contributors are, or have been, on the teaching staff of the Leeds University Department of German. The three editors of letters from the Brotherton Library's Bithell Collection are recent graduates of the MA programme – indeed, their preparation of these editions was an integral part of their work for the MA. Our one distinguished 'external' contributor, Joyce Crick, has also served as External Examiner for the Department. Two of the essays (Bridgham's and Crick's) were originally delivered to the Anglo-German Literary Relations Seminar at the annual Conference of University Teachers of German in Great Britain and Ireland. Crick's paper was given as one of a pair describing British productions of Schiller's *Wallenstein*.[1]

Where the nine essays in the 1992 volume explored aspects of the German reception of English literary ideas, the emphasis in the present volume is the other way round. Five of the literary essays here treat the English reception of aspects of German literature. The other two examine aspects of Shakespeare-reception in Germany/Switzerland. The Women's Studies essay reflects the wider cultural aspect of the MA programme, as it treats Josephine Butler's pioneering work to ameliorate the condition of prostitutes in England and the repercussions of her campaign in Germany. Concluding the volume, the edition of three letters from the Bithell Collection brings to public notice again the existence and research potential of that Collection.

The title of this volume, *Cousins at One Remove*, deliberately echoes John Mander's *Our German Cousins* (1974).[2] On the other hand, whilst we admire the scale and purposefulness of that study we have not set out to emulate them – although the context of our work, i.e. a programme on Anglo-German Cultural Relations, does presuppose Mander's wide perspectives. Amongst the purposes which Mander pursued was to discover what 'the "traditional" English view of the Germans' might be, implicitly challenging the verdict of a recently published opinion poll (c.1973) which declared: 'The traditional view of the Germans still remains, with many people thinking them violent, lacking in tolerance, and unfriendly' [p.3]. Mander's conclusion on this count was to disparage the idea that Germans are 'unfriendly', but to concede that English public opinion towards them is unlikely to grow friendlier 'simply by virtue of the healing processes of time'. It has not been the object of any of our contributors, of course, to examine what has become of the 'traditional' English view of the Germans, but, a quarter of a century on, we can only confirm the rightness of Mander's observation – the cartoon image of Germans[3] as published in the British press remains far from amiable.[4]

Another of Mander's tasks was to present a view of recent German history which, differing from that of the immediately preceding generation of historians, was likely to be perceived as 'revisionist' in tone and thus an implicit reproach. His work makes 'one assumption which [...] is lacking in many even of the best books produced by the generation of our seniors [namely] that, no matter how disastrous the course it ran, it was as natural and inevitable that the Germans should develop a national consciousness (though not Nazism!) as it was that the peoples of Spain, France, and England should have done so' [p.6]. For our part, though we sympathise with and accept the reasonableness of Mander's assumption, our essays focus on literary and cultural relations, not political history. We simply note here the further progress of Germany's nation-building 25 years on: the Germanys East and West have been reunited and, by the turn of the new millennium, Berlin will once again be the country's capital – we note also that in these political developments Germany has had the support of all her Western allies (albeit her Eastern neighbours remain uneasy).

But the overriding purpose of Mander's book is to generate understanding – to combat the black imagery of Vansittartism – and this is a purpose which we do share (in common with all conscientious British teachers of German, be they, like us severally, Irish, Scottish, Welsh or English): 'I shall try [...] to examine the emergence of [the Germans'] character through English eyes, and to examine what lessons there may be for the future in this strange, ambivalent tale of mutual misunderstanding. The Germans are not required to love us; nor we to love them. But we are required to understand, if we are to survive' [p.15]. Sharing this presupposition, we trust that the spirit of our essays corresponds wholly to his.

But as teachers we would also go further, for we recognise that 'understanding' is a prerequisite for reconciliation.

For all that Mander's wider purpose was political, however, the main thread of his narrative from 1750 to 1870 is (like ours) the story of literary relations between Britain and Germany. From the panorama of eighteenth and nineteenth century literary contacts which he unfolds, the parts played by Shakespeare, Goethe, Schiller, Kleist, Coleridge and Nietzsche also feature in this volume. (Remarkably enough, Wagner is missing from Mander's work).

Coleridge features here in two essays. Ingo Cornils explores the debt owed by Coleridge to the kindly pastor of St Georgsberg in Ratzeburg – a widower with ten children – in whose home he spent three months around Christmas 1798/9, learning German before moving on to Göttingen. Where biographers generally dwell on the Göttingen months as being of greatest importance for Coleridge's development as a writer, Cornils makes a strong case for the impact of the initial Ratzeburg stay. A century on in time, Joyce Crick describes the impact of two productions of Coleridge's *Wallenstein* translation prepared by William Poel for performance at Oxford (in 1900) and London (1911), also placing them in the wider context of the political developments of that war-clouded pre-First World War period. Here the emphasis is on the play: on how Poel cut it and adapted it for the theatre – 'the place of hope which was his contribution to the larger social and educational reforms of the time'.

The period when Poel was active transects the years of Alfred Orage's weekly *New Age* (1907-22). Adopting a quotation from the 'Nietzscheist' Orage for her title, 'Our wretched German cousins', Diane Milburn provides a generous-spirited and ironically witty survey of British reactions towards Germany and German thinkers in the lead-up to the First World War as reflected in the activities of the Leeds Arts Club and Orage's periodical.

Shakespeare-reception in Germany and Switzerland is represented in two essays. Deploying ample detail and cross-reference, Raymond Hargreaves and Sydney Donald analyze respectively Paul Celan's translations of three of Shakespeare's Sonnets and Dürrenmatt's adaptation of Shakespeare's *King John*. Hargreaves sets out to answer the question: 'Is a text which negates the linguistic premise of the text it purports to translate still a translation, and if so in what sense ?' Donald examines how Dürrenmatt succeeded in transforming a relatively little-known Elizabethan drama into a huge box-office success.

In an essay filled with contemporary and historical allusions, spanning virtually the whole period covered by Mander's book and bringing it up to the present day, Fred Bridgham (translator of Hans Werner Henze's libretto, *The Prince of Homburg*, for performance in 1996) explores the manner in which Schiller, Kleist and Wagner – 'arguably Germany's greatest dramatists' – have been received and continue to be received in Britain.

Prompted by Goethe's confession that it is wickedness, not goodness, which sets his creativity on fire – in which respect Auden declared that Goethe was speaking for all artists – and with Goethe's Mephisto as the point of reference, Richard Byrn reviews the way five modern English writers (D.J. Enright, Robert Nye, Terry Pratchett, Emma Tennant and Fay Weldon) variously evoke the personality of Mephisto in their respective *Faust*-books – might they also have been moved to write by the twitchings of wickedness?

Ingrid Sharp surveys the attempts by nineteenth century social reformers, pre-eminently Josephine Butler in England and Anna Pappritz in Germany, to improve the condition of prostitutes. After 20 years of campaigning Butler and her Abolitionist allies eventually succeeded in persuading Parliament to repeal the deplorably repressive Contagious Diseases Acts. The progress of Abolitionist ideas in Germany, on the other hand, was depressingly negative: 'measured in terms of legislation, the women's campaign had no effect at all.'

The volume's final contribution is a tribute to one of this century's most influential British Teachers of German, Jethro Bithell, whose career was lived out under the shadow of both of those World Wars fought against our German cousins. The letters edited here – from Alfred Mombert (1909), Franz Werfel (1940), and Hans Carossa (1949) – reflect the work Bithell did on three different publications. The latter two letters in particular also reflect the interest which Bithell took in individual 'good' Germans at a time when they were going through great personal difficulties.

If the contributors to this volume were to declare a commonly held position on Anglo-German relations it might well be expressed in the words of Alfred Orage quoted in Milburn's essay: without being blind to pre-First World War German bellicosity Orage nevertheless referred to them as 'reasonable, fallible creatures – much as we are'. This volume's underlying purpose is, thus, to reflect on aspects of the cultural inheritance which the Germans and the English share, despite all mutual animosities from the past – 'cousins', certainly, but perhaps 'at one remove'.

Several people have assisted in the preparation of this volume. Our thanks go to the Keeper of the Brotherton Library Special Collections and his colleagues for their unstinting advice and assistance. Emeritus Professor K.G. Knight's name does not appear as co-editor of this volume, but his encouragement and careful reading of the contents in typescript represent a significant contribution which it is our pleasure to acknowledge. This volume's most careful reader prepared its index – for having checked much more than just references to people and topics we thank Janet Pickering unreservedly. Two other colleagues in particular have assisted with seminal ideas: Frank Lamport (Oxford) and Helen Chambers

(Leeds) – sometimes without knowing it. For the stimulus of such creative ideas scattered generously in conversation we express grateful appreciation.

It is our pleasure here also to acknowledge eight decades-worth of moral and financial support to Leeds-based academic German studies from the Leeds Philosophical and Literary Society. Their sponsorship has included Charles Gough's pioneering *Helmbrecht* edition of 1928, Lionel Thomas' several essays during the 1950s and '60s on aspects of nineteenth century German literature, down to the present two volumes of *Anglo-German Studies* in the 1990s. For scholars in a minority subject-area such assistance is invaluable and it is correspondingly appreciated.

---

[1] The other, by F.J. Lamport, was published as: '*Wallenstein* on the English Stage', in *German Life and Letters*, XLVIII No.2, 1995, pp.124-147.

[2] John Mander, *Our German Cousins. Anglo-German Relations in the 19th and 20th Centuries* (London: Murray, 1974). A great admirer of John Maynard Keynes, Mander states that Keynes' view: 'Without Germany, no Europe; without Europe, no Civilisation' could be the motto of his book too. 'A century ago no one would have doubted the truth of this axiom. There are many today who doubt it all too readily' [p.13].

[3] Harald Husemann, who has assembled a major collection of recent political cartoons reflecting the British image of Germans and *vice versa*, quotes a subversive *Daily Mail* limerick of 1997 as being symptomatic of enduring British attitudes to Europe and the Germans: 'There's nothing more certain or surer // than that the United States of Europa // is a cunning Hun scheme // to fulfil their old dream: // *Eine Volk, Eine Reich, Eine Führer*' (As a linguist and teacher one doesn't know whether to tut-tut more about the rhymes, the sentiments, or the accidence.) – See Husemann's essay 'When William came – if Helmut were to come: fictional and factual europhobia in Britain', forthcoming in S.P. Stark (ed.), *The Novel in Anglo-German Context. Proceedings of the 1997 Leeds Conference* (Reihe: *Internationale Forschungen zur allgemeinen und vergleichenden Literaturwissenschaft*; Amsterdam: Rodopi, 1999).

[4] Mander's review of German national characteristics concludes that English unease towards them arises above all from a sense of their unpredictability. 'Your Frenchman and your Dutchman you may rate as you will; but both are assumed to be *predictable* in their general behaviour, whereas Germans are not – *les incertitudes allemandes*' [p.4].

Schiller, Kleist, Wagner: a Great British Tradition?

FRED BRIDGHAM

I

Even in their own country, the names of Schiller and Kleist, arguably Germany's greatest dramatists, are seldom linked, still less in conjunction with that of Wagner – 'the most outstanding theatrical genius the Germans ever had' (Nietzsche).[1] Only at the turn of this century, when the inevitable decline of Schiller-mania after the 1859 centenary coincided with a triumphant Wagner cult and the rediscovery of Kleist,[2] did the process of critical reassessment appear to register at least some two-way connections. Thus: 'man kann von einer [...] Wagnerschule sprechen, von einer Schillerschule nicht' (Egon Friedell).[3] Or, 'die größte künstlerische Tat seit Goethes Tod, das Musikdrama Richard Wagners und die Bühne von Bayreuth ist die Schöpfung eines Genius, der von Schillers Blut stammt, dessen Name und Töne erklingen müssen, wo man Schiller feiert' (Konrad Burdach).[4] A more polemical note was also struck, especially among those championing 'einen so unendlich echteren Dichter als Schiller, Heinrich v. Kleist' (Carl Bleibtreu),[5] and who consequently juxtaposed 'Goethe und Kleist [...] nicht mehr Goethe und Schiller. Denn Kleist ist Schiller in jedem Betracht unbedingt und weit überlegen' (Heinrich Meyer-Benfrey).[6]

But as these examples also reveal, those who advocate a new perspective most forcefully also tend to start from some traditional assumption of natural affinity or complementariness – here 'Goethe and Schiller' – which they aim to displace. Where such assumptions are less firmly rooted, different configurations may more readily emerge. In Britain, for instance, early reception seems more often to have posed the question 'Goethe or Schiller?' After Carlyle's *Life of Schiller* (1825), in particular, 'an inclusive literary adherence which would find room for both men was not commonly thought of.'[7] Even when 'the immortal Dioscuri, twin stars' were indeed acclaimed, by Edward Bulwer Lytton in 1844, it was on the basis of a reading of Schiller to which few in Germany would have subscribed: he was 'one of Nature's nobleman', or even gentlemen – yes – but hardly one deserving of 'Christian canonization'.[8] The native tradition, in other words, when seen through foreign eyes, is susceptible to curious reinterpretations.

On the other hand, some features of a national culture may come more clearly into focus from a distance, and hitherto unfamiliar constellations become more readily visible. Like most non-Germans, the British have had no difficulty in subsuming our chosen trio of dramatists (they were, of course, much else besides) within the Romantic tradition which Mme de Staël in *De l'Allemagne* (1813) had so persuasively established, and in its progressive rather than its reactionary form promoted, as the essence of contemporary German culture. If the point needed reinforcing, it was masterfully done for what Noel Annan calls 'Our Age' by Isaiah Berlin,[9] who again traces 'this last great convulsion in European thought' to late eighteenth and nineteenth-century Germany. One consequence of such broad categorization, widely accepted in Britain as part of the 'German Renaissance',[10] has perhaps been to obscure the distinction increasingly entrenched in German literary history between Romanticism and Classicism, of which Goethe himself had observed: 'The notion of classical and romantic poetry, which is now spreading all over the world and causing so much controversy and division, originated with myself and Schiller'.[11] A further consequence of viewing the period from, say, the 1790s to as late as the 1910s in terms of the catchall category 'Age of Romanticism', or indeed a reason for doing so, may have been to give tacit credence to the German Romantics' own emphasis on the connectedness of all the arts, particularly the fusion of poetry and music,[12] and ultimately the belief that, as Pater put it, all art aspires to the condition of music.[13] This, in turn, is surely (*pace* Leavis) *the* great tradition in all its acknowledged cumulative continuity – from Haydn and Mozart to Beethoven and Schubert, from Mendelssohn and Schumann to Brahms, from Weber to Liszt and Wagner, and beyond.

The point is vividly illustrated, though also trivialized, if we turn to the British reception of the Schiller and Kleist plays generally considered their best, *Wallenstein* and *Prinz Friedrich von Homburg* – both of them 'classics' in more senses than one. *Wallenstein* did not receive its first fully professional[14] performance in English – albeit in a version reduced by translator Frank Lamport and director Tim Albery from seven hours to three – until 1993, in the Pit at London's Barbican Centre. Reviewers of this production found the play itself 'purest melodrama' [*The Sunday Times,* 19.9.1993]; 'if only Verdi had got round to setting it [...] The scenes between Max Piccolomini and his father have a thrilling operatic quality' [*The Independent,* 17.9.1993]; 'one of the few Schiller plays not yet made into an opera [...] it's quite funny enough already' [*The Observer,* 19.9.1993].

Kleist had to wait almost as long, and to similar effect. *The Prince of Homburg* which reached the Royal National's Cottesloe Theatre in 1982 was 'so drab and plodding, so lacking in any variety of excitement [...] that it must surely have been deliberate' [*The New Statesman,* 30.4.1982], while the play's first professional English production inaugurating Manchester's Royal Exchange in 1976, with Tom Courteney as the Prince, was for *The Sunday Times* 'no more than a standard bit of High Romantic twaddle [...] If only Verdi had made an opera out of it!' [19.9.1976]. As it happens, Hans Werner Henze, with Ingeborg Bachmann, had already turned the play into an opera in 1960, though he had done so only because Luchino Visconti, fresh from the triumph of producing Verdi's *Don Carlos* at Covent Garden in 1958, insisted that he make good this glaring omission in the repertoire. This Henze recalled when his *Prince of Homburg* in turn received its first performance in English at English National Opera in 1996.[15]

As for Kleist's other best-known play, *Der zerbrochene Krug*, Northern Broadsides' hilarious production at the West Yorkshire Playhouse in 1995 (and subsequently at Skipton's unreconstructed cattle market) demonstrated that *The Cracked Pot*, in Blake Morrison's inspired Yorkshire demotic, can come alive without the aid of music in a way that the play's first English outing as *Jug* at Stratford East clearly had not for the critic of *The Times* in 1986, who gained 'the bizarre impression of a Shakespearian sub-plot gone mad', its 'ant-paced story-line' belying the reputation of a piece that is 'even on occasion adduced to testify that the Germans do have a sense of humour after all'.[16]

And in the case of *Don Carlos*, over a century after the first production of Verdi's opera at Covent Garden in 1867,[17] 'what may well be Schiller's best play and is certainly as neglected as any classic need be' was staged at the Cheltenham Everyman in 1975 in what 'seems to be its English première' [*The Observer,* 30.3.1975]. It was seen again at the Lyric, Hammersmith in 1992, though it was another fine northern production, by Nick Hytner in Manchester in 1987, of this 'long play without a single longueur', somewhat condensed by James Maxwell 'in an idiom which is natural, plain and vigorous', with Ian McDiarmid as Philipp, which prompted the most telling critical response: 'I was convinced that one destiny of the Royal Exchange is to rescue Schiller from the opera house' [*The Independent,* 14.9.1987].

But if it is indubitably the opera house which has made Schiller palatable to British audiences, it is still certainly a narrower spectrum here than enjoys him (or for that matter Shakespeare) in German or Italian or French opera houses. Rossini's *Guillaume Tell*, Donizetti's *Maria Stuarda*, Verdi's *Giovanna d'Arco*, *I masnadieri*, *Luisa Miller*, *Don Carlos*, even *Simon Boccanegra* (an oblique glimpse of *Fiesco*), are only the best known adaptations. In the process, plots are rearranged, the most poignant situations highlighted, theatrical effects appropriated, and the text commonly – it may be argued, necessarily – reduced by two thirds or more, then substantially re-written. In traditional opera, as Wagner claimed in his most famous dictum, the music had become the end, while drama, which should be the end, was merely the means.[18] As the author of his own dramas, Wagner wished to restore the balance.[19] This is one of the more interesting levels at which the question 'Wagner or Verdi?' continues to challenge opera *cognoscenti* well able to distinguish libretti loosely based on Schiller from those of Wagner, rather as knowledgable Germans might distinguish Gounod's *Faust* from Goethe's,[20] even to the point of calling the opera *Margarethe*.[21] In order to establish more significant Wagner-Schiller connections we might do better to look at 'the increasing tendency towards the operatic' in Schiller's own late plays – in *Die Jungfrau von Orleans*, for instance (the one play he himself called '*eine romantische Tragödie*'), or the use of the chorus in *Die Braut von Messina*, or the 'opening songs, carefully orchestrated crowd scenes, set-piece encounters and vivid Swiss backcloth' of *Wilhelm Tell* [22] – though at much else besides.

Wagner was keenly aware of Schiller's achievements, though characteristically uninformative in acknowledging their relevance to his own work. His high regard for Kleist, too, is sparingly documented, but again in often unsuspected ways it reflects the composer's prodigious reading and depth of insight. Finally, the creative consequences of Kleist's acute sense of rivalry with Schiller remain largely unexplored.[23]

A brief sketch of some earlier landmarks of Schiller, Kleist and Wagner reception in Britain, outlining the vicissitudes of the rejection or naturalization process, may provide a suitably novel perspective on these claimed connections – tentative evidence for which will be offered mainly from the works themselves.

II

SCHILLER

In Isaiah Berlin's words, Schiller, like his mentor Kant, was 'almost intoxicated' with the idea of freedom and autonomy, though still a 'restrained Romantic' when compared with the 'unbridled Romantics' who followed.[24] It was certainly intoxication rather than restraint which made Coleridge 'tremble like an aspen leaf' in 1794 on reading Tytler's translation of *Die Räuber* (1792),[25] and the play's perceived political subversiveness which Canning wittily parodied as *The Rovers* in his *Anti-Jacobin Review* (1798), shortly before the authors of the *Lyrical Ballads* left for Germany. One of Coleridge's many plans was to translate all of Schiller's works (oddly, though, he shied from a visit to Weimar). Radicalism is also what the British public continued for some time to associate with Schiller, *and* with Coleridge, who was still, to his dismay, perceived as Schiller's champion or disciple long after the Terror in France had extinguished such inflammatory sentiments in them both.[26]

Schiller's early hopes of winning 'das Bürgerrecht auf dem Theater zu Drury Lane' were based on a deep sense of affinity with the freedom-loving British (to which his Lady Milford is eloquent testimony), though they also draw on his indebtedness to Shakespeare, and to the aesthetic thinking of Shaftesbury and Ferguson, Hutcheson and Burke: 'denn ich hoffe, daß meine Arbeiten sich dem Geschmack der englischen Nazion mehr als dem Teutschen nähern, da ich ja ohnehin nach englischen Mustern gebildet bin'.[27] But his ideas on the interplay of aesthetics and ethics failed to get a sympathetic hearing in Britain, where the distinction was fashionably blurred,[28] whereas the *Sturm und Drang* origins of *Die Räuber* could not be overlooked, even in the much-altered, heavily moralizing guise of the play for puritans which finally appeared at the Haymarket in 1800, its 'very loyal sentiments' replacing the 'anarchical notions of the German original'[29] and with a high-sounding title to match, *The Red-Cross Knights*. After the Napoleonic upheaval, a more authentic version of *The Robbers*, one no longer so submissive to anti-Jacobin sensibilities, duly appeared at Sadler's Wells in 1821 – a 'spectacle, that emulates the noblest productions of any time or stage'.[30]

Nor does *Kabale und Liebe* appear to have lost its social-critical edge between 'Monk' Lewis's 'faithful and elegant translation of an excellent play' (1793/94, published as *The Minister* 1797, 2nd ed. 1798) and its appearance at Covent Garden as *The Harper's Daughter* in 1803, where it was criticized for culminating in 'the melancholy catastrophe of suicide'.[31] Meanwhile, Schiller's later plays remained unperformed, though a 'mangled' version of the 1801 translation of *Maria Stuart* was eventually staged at Covent Garden in 1820, incurring – as both Goethe and Schiller had half foreseen – 'the severest accusations of immoral argument, and historical infidelity'.[32]

It was instead the extraordinary cult of Kotzebue, astutely fostered by Sheridan, which chiefly accounted for 'the modern rage/ Of German dramas on the English stage' [33] in the 1790s. When the public had had a surfeit of Kotzebue's sentimental, domestic banalities by 1800, other fashionable aspects of 'Germanico-terrifico-Romance',[34] from its Gothic extremities to its bold sublimities, seem to have been left likewise 'floundering in ridicule'.[35] This was inopportune for Coleridge, who partly in consequence appears to have played down his great *Wallenstein* translation (1800) until the times were more propitious[36] – long after the publication in London of *De l'Allemagne* in 1813 (in both French and English), which established Schiller as the lofty, chaste, idealistic *Dichter-Denker*. By then, however, Coleridge's own interest had moved on from German literature to German metaphysics, though not before Byron helped him get his Schiller-imitation *Osorio* (1797) finally accepted for performance by Sheridan in 1811.[37]

Carlyle, whose pioneering *Life of Schiller* (1825) further promoted the ennoblement of Schiller's character as well as of his works, left unqualified hero-worship to Bulwer Lytton in his introduction to the influential *Poems and Ballads of Schiller* (1844), which traced the alleged metamorphosis of the formerly wild and 'more German' dramatist into the 'more English' poet, his natural manly simplicity 'in unison with English hearts'.[38] Around 1850, there were stagings in London of *Fiesco* and an adaptation of *Kabale und Liebe* entitled *Power and Principle*, as well as a visiting troupe (under the great Eduard Devrient) performing in German *Tell*, *Fiesco*, *Don Carlos*, *Die Braut von Messina* and a dramatized version of 'Das Lied von der Glocke'. Of these productions George Henry Lewes thought *Tell* the best, and *The Robbers* at Drury Lane the following year an 'intolerable absurdity'. Lewes, who appears to have undergone a recent revulsion from Schiller, was nevertheless soon to provide a more balanced account than either Carlyle (who omitted the aesthetics) or Bulwer (who claimed Schiller for Christianity), by recognizing that, like Goethe, Schiller had divorced himself from religious orthodoxy and created his own system 'out of Spinoza, Kant, and the Grecian sages'.[39]

But the German engineers, traders, bankers and post-1848 political émigrés[40] among the crowd which filled the Crystal Palace in 1859 to see a colossal bust of

Schiller unveiled and to listen to Rossini's overture to *William Tell* and hear a choir of a thousand sing Andreas Jakob Romberg's setting of 'Das Lied von der Glocke'[41] will scarcely have wanted to suppress their own dawning national feeling in the name of a lofty universalism.[42] Equally, a more recent tradition of promenade concerts might give cause to doubt how deeply 'Schiller belonged to England and to Englishmen' (*The Athenaeum*)[43]. Ultimately, it was Schiller himself for whom the bell tolled. Carlyle had voiced the crucial perception, in 1831, that Schiller 'looks aloft rather than around',[44] and his own translation of Goethe's *Wilhelm Meister* (1824) – a 'healthy' antidote to *Werther* – had already given the British access to what August Wilhelm Schlegel had singled out as one of the three great events of modern times,[45] – times which by mid-century had seen philosophical fashion swing from transcendental idealism towards the positivistic, the scientific, the materialistic. Lewes's *Life and Works of Goethe* (1855) was the landmark which crowned the long-growing acceptance, indeed the institutionalization of Goethe.[46] When Nietzsche compared Goethe's destiny 'im moralinsauren, altjungfernhaften Deutschland' with that of 'Schiller, der "edle" Schiller, der ihnen mit großen Worten um die Ohren schlug – *der* war nach ihrem Herzen', he had recourse to the rivalry in Wagner's opera between the noble Wolfram and Tannhäuser, fresh from the arms of Venus: 'alle Art "Wartburg" in Deutschland bekreuzte sich vor Goethe. [...] *Diese* Geschichte hat Wagner in Musik gesetzt. Er *erlöst* Goethe [...] ein Gebet rettet ihn, eine höhere Jungfrau *zieht ihn hinan*'.[47] So, too, in Victorian Britain, Goethe was gradually absolved from his association (whether vicariously fictional or actual) with libidinous actresses, adultery, mysticism and paganism,[48] and it was Goethe and Beethoven, not Schiller and Beethoven, who came to embody 'Weimar' when the new threat of 'Potsdam' began to sour Anglo-German relations after 1871.[49]

KLEIST

Kleist's reputation fared very differently. *The Times* recorded the death of 'the celebrated Prussian poet', but this obituary (28.12.1811) is itself the only known contemporary celebration in Britain – if that is the word, for it deplored the manner of his death (a suicide pact) as an 'act of insanity' (mention is also made of 'a number of bottles of wine or rum'). Moreover, it is entirely based on a piece in *Le Moniteur universel*,[50] which may have been one of Mme de Staël's sources, too.[51] She had once written sympathetically about suicide (*Sur l'Influence des Passions*, 1796), but now attacked it as a threat to public morality (*Réflections sur le suicide*, 1811), citing the 'assassinat mutuel' of 'M de K.' and 'Madame de V.' Perhaps her dismissal of the 'untalented' and 'unpatriotic' German poet, can charitably be ascribed to ignorance of all but the circumstances of his death.[52] Their paths had certainly crossed in the salons of Berlin and Dresden – she even contributed a French translation of Schiller's 'Das Siegesfest' to Kleist and Müller's *Phöbus*[53] – yet there is no mention of Kleist in *De l'Allemagne*. After

Napoleon effectively suppressed her book in 1810, she had swept through Austria, Poland, Russia and Sweden before establishing herself, in 1813, at the heart of British social and literary life in Hanover Square,[54] but would appear to have gleaned little if any additional knowledge of her fellow anti-Bonapartist along the way. Such ignorance was to remain the norm.

One exception, however, was M.G. Lewis, author of that benchmark Gothic novel, *The Monk* (1796), who first conveyed something of Kleist's work to Britain with *Mistrust, or Blanche and Osbright*. This, the first of his *Romantic Tales* (1808), is an adaptation of Kleist's *Die Familie Schroffenstein* (1803), a sort of Gothic *Romeo and Juliet*, the original version of which, *Die Familie Ghonorez*, itself borrows significantly from the German translation of *The Monk* (1797).[55] Lewis acknowledges a German source but pleads forgetfulness of the details,[56] while Kleist may have switched his setting from Spain to Swabia precisely because it was too close to the Lewis novel[57] – at all events, neither the secretive Kleist nor the endearingly open Lewis appears to have made written mention of the other, or of the little flurry of cross-fertilization between and around them.[58] Just as Schiller's *Ghost-Seer* (1795) and its various continuations by different hands such as *The Armenian* (4 vols., 1800)[59] continued to grip British readers as firmly as instalments of *Der Geisterseher* (1785-89) had already gripped readers of *Thalia*, so *Mistrust* satisfied at least some contemporary taste as a piece of popular Gothic fiction.[60]

The next known mention of Kleist, a decade after the *Times* obituary, was an isolated comment by Coleridge describing *Die Familie Schroffenstein* as 'harsh and branny' – meaning perhaps morally indigestible – continuing: 'and the freedom from sentimentality, for which our friend Tieck gives him so much credit, [is] too evidently a matter of purpose'.[61] What better guide, now, than Coleridge's friend, fellow-Shakespearean, would-be collaborator, and present editor of Kleist's works,[62] Ludwig Tieck? – except that Tieck's enthusiasm for a British staging of *Schroffenstein* is somewhat at odds with Kleist's own dismissal of the play as 'eine elende Scharteke'.[63] Although it was popularized from Hamburg to Vienna by the industrious bowdleriser Franz Ignaz Holbein,[64] and eventually came into its own with the Theatre of the Absurd, readers of Stephen Vizinczey's eloquent bicentenary tribute to Kleist in *The Times* have still not had an opportunity to judge whether 'this masterpiece, superior to Shakespeare in its concept' (notably the 'undressing scene') will 'help pack the theatres in the third century of Kleist's immortal life'.[65] Tieck will certainly have sent Coleridge a copy of *Homburg*, too, but there is no indication that the one Englishman who was ostensibly best equipped to appreciate, say, Homburg's vision of immortality through his reborn sense of moral duty (a central Kantian issue)[66] – if less likely to applaud the play's covert (though recently topical) political dimension[67] – ever read it.

Not until the late 1820s did the mental fog over the Channel lift, and with it the import restrictions on foreign books. In his *German Romance* (1827), Carlyle writes of Kleist as 'a noble-minded and ill-fated man of genius, whom the mismanagement of a too impetuous and feeling heart has since driven to suicide', which seems apt – until he places him as a contemporary of Klopstock and Lessing and it emerges that he means Ewald von Kleist: this was to be a common confusion.[68] None of the other main Germanophiles took up Kleist: neither Scott, De Quincey, Crabb Robinson nor Lockhart. On the contrary: the latter pressed Robert Pearse Gillies, formerly the celebrated 'Germanist of *Blackwoods'*, for more by and on Schiller.[69] But Gillies did give Tieck's Kleist edition prominent coverage in his pioneering (if unoriginal) essay 'The Works of Henry Kleist' in the new *Foreign Quarterly Review* (1828),[70] using what he had (imperfectly) gathered from Tieck's preface to describe the writer's character: 'his genius more or less paralysed by a degree of irritability, impatience and hypochondriacal gloom, such as has seldom been equalled'. The 'lamentably tame' *Homburg* with 'faulty dialogue' reflects the author's 'capricious', 'dreamy', 'lamed genius' (only the battle and briefing scenes escape censure).[71]

This pathological diagnosis and its effect on the reception of Kleist's works was to be a recurrent feature of the British *Kleistbild*, while Kleist the patriot and propagandist was totally unknown – even to Gillies, as can be seen from his complaint that 'none of the great German authors, Goethe in particular, ventured to breathe one syllable of discontent against Napoleon, so long as it was an act of courage to do so'. As for *Michael Kohlhaas*, which Gillies, like later critics, praised at the expense of the dramas, a serviceable translation by John Oxenford in *Tales from the German* (1844)[72] helped make it perhaps the most widely-known Kleist text (ahead of *Homburg* and *Das Käthchen von Heilbronn*[73]). It was hailed by Charles Dilke's progressive *Athenaeum*, against a background of Chartist unrest, as 'a service to moral progress [...] illustrating the sentiment of justice in the human bosom; showing how dearer it is than liberty or life, and how, when withheld and perverted by the public tribunals, it reverts to individual responsibility'.[74] In stark contrast, there was a terrible warning to be had from the hero's 'moral insanity' in a new translation which appeared in the Tory *Dublin University Magazine* a decade later.[75] Although the Famine had ostensibly broken Irish nationalism, 'tenant protection societies' had begun to threaten subversion, and this heavily-cut version of the story pointedly contrived to vindicate both the figure of religious (Protestant) authority, Luther, and the secular establishment, while excising the double-statehood theme as uncomfortably close to the political relationship between England and Ireland. A text – however bowdlerized – which allows of such divergent readings is clearly alive.

Luther was also Carlyle's prime exemplar of 'the Priest as Hero' (a topic which, one imagines, was anathema to the anti-clericalism of both Schiller and Kleist), whereas the King as Hero with whom he had been 'decidedly growing in love' since his *Heroes and Hero-worship* lectures (1840) was Frederick the Great.[76] Some 300 pages into the first volume of the *History of Frederick II of Prussia* (1858) – a 'Whig' interpretation of the rise of the Hohenzollerns for which 'In Staub mit allen Feinden Brandenburgs!' would have been an entirely appropriate motto – Carlyle introduces us to Friedrich Wilhelm, the Great Elector[77]:

> What the Teutsch Ritters strove for in vain, and lost their existence striving for, the shifty Kurfürst has now got: Ducal Prussia, which is also called East Prussia, is now a free sovereignty, – and will become as 'Royal' as the other Polish part. Or perhaps even more so, in the course of time!

The Elector has just won the Battle of Fehrbellin (meaning, we learn, 'Ferry across the Beleen'), and

> there are many histories of him, but they are not comfortable to read. He also has wanted a sacred poet; and found only a bewildering Dryasdust.[78]

Carlyle's book may have fostered pro-Prussian sentiment in Britain,[79] and titles such as *Carlyle and Hitler* point to subsequent controversy over when a 'doctrine of heroes' becomes 'praise of despots',[80] but the biography of Frederick evidently did not do for Kleist what Carlyle had done for Schiller, his 'representative man', in 1825, and Lewes for Goethe in 1855. That *Prinz Friedrich von Homburg*, and perhaps its author too, were unknown even to Carlyle, close though he was to such friends and admirers of Kleist as Varnhagen von Ense and Tieck (to whom he indeed talked in Berlin while researching his book on Frederick[81]) is indicative of this continuing blindspot. Soon after German unification, however, readers of Lloyd and Newton's curious volume entitled *Prussia's Representative Man* (1875)[82] had their eyes opened to Kleist the patriotic poet, an exegesis designed to repudiate and replace both Schiller and the greatest of Emerson's *Representative Men* (1850), the cosmopolitan Goethe.[83] Neither German *Klassik* nor *Romantik* are perceived as being in harmony with the *Volk*, but Kleist is shown to have embodied in his own life's struggle and works a key, and ultimately healthy, breakthrough in the evolution of the Prussian *Volk*, which by 1871 had convincingly demonstrated its Darwinian survival as the fittest to lead Bismarck's 'Lesser German' Reich. Besides furnishing new translations of *Kohlhaas* and *Homburg*, the book summarizes aspects of Kleist's character and writing by now commonplace in Germany (notably from Julian Schmidt's introduction to the 1859 *Gesammelte Schriften*) – his soaring ambition and bitter disappointments, acute sensitivity and single-mindedness, and the dry, unadorned, bold, pacy style of his writing. At the same time, it reinterprets lingering criticism of the author's 'weak and sickly, disturbed, suicidal nature' as *Weltschmerz* arising from historical intuition, or of Homburg's 'psychopathological and unstageworthy somnambulism' as Hamlet-like reverie, or of the 'barbarism' of *Die Hermannschlacht* as an anticipation of the Darwinian necessity of Prussian discipline.[84]

In short, this panegyric, however questionable its 'scientific' pretensions, must have created a dawning awareness of those issues which jingoistic appropriation of Kleist in Germany during two world wars has made a contentious constant of Kleist reception ever since.[85] When the German Question was reopened in 1914, he was for many Germans 'our national poet', and, by 1933, 'the prophet of our new world'. A performance of *Homburg*, with Hitler in attendance, after *Anschluß* with Austria had created 'Greater Germany' in 1938, was clearly meant to illustrate the benefits of the *Führerprinzip* – that one must lead and the others obey.[86] True, the founding of the Kleist-Gesellschaft after the First World War[87] had little international resonance initially, but the competing manifestos of the 'intellectuals'[88] prepared the ground for a new *Kulturkampf* in which 'Schiller und Kleist als politische Dichter' were the heavy guns.[89] Hans Fabricius's *Schiller als Kampfgenosse Hitlers* (1932) showed what way the wind was blowing – though Kleist might have proved even more adaptable to his purpose.

Seen from the other side, Lord Vansittart thought it 'worth noting that the first German national hero to make himself a name for treachery was Hermann in the year 9'.[90] In a similar vein, Ronald Gray could point to chapter and verse of 'Kleist's insane and brutal nationalism' in his assessment of *The German Tradition in Literature*[91] and recall that Kleist had indeed (most overtly in *Die Hermannschlacht* and several blood-curdling poems) 'counselled the use of every atrocity, every deliberate lie, to save the Fatherland from foreign domination'.[92] The production which cleansed at least *Homburg* of its immediate post-war stigma emanated from Jean Vilar's Théâtre National Populaire, first for the Avignon Festival in 1951, then in Paris, and eventually an appreciative Hamburg. Far from mere humiliation, chastisement and reintegration in an absolutist system, Gérard Philippe pursued his spiritual journey through alienation from a code devised by 'them', blind fear of death and loss of self-esteem in a fragile world, to Existentialist victory over 'the enemy within' as the Romantic dreamer who vanquishes his inauthenticity. It was this 'Prussian Midsummer Night's Dream under a starry Kantian sky'[93] which convinced Ingeborg Bachmann of the play's anti-militaristic universal appeal. Unfortunately, Philippe was dead (pictured lying in state in his Homburg costume on the front cover of *Paris Match*) before the World Theatre seasons began in London.

WAGNER

Whereas familiarity with the performance history of Schiller and Kleist among British theatre-goers is unlikely to go any deeper than we have seen reflected in recent reviews, Wagner and Wagnerism are widely known to the point of caricature. The penniless Kapellmeister's storm-driven voyage from Riga set the proto-Flying Dutchman down for a first brief visit to London in 1839. There he hoped to discuss adapting Bulwer Lytton's tale of the struggle between corrupt Papal Rome and a tribune of the people: *Rienzi*. The conventional grand opera which Wagner completed in 1840 and which Hans von Bülow memorably dubbed 'Meyerbeer's best opera', still retains strong echoes of Bulwer's interest in Schiller's *Fiesco* and the anti-aristocratic *bürgerliches Trauerspiel*,[94] and points to Wagner's political radicalism and coming revolutionary commitment in 1848/9. When in 1855, a year after the first public performances of his music in London,[95] the now established composer (and political refugee) undertook a four-month conducting stint for the Old Philharmonic, the notorious 'music of the future' (and unconventional conducting) of a 'desperate musical democrat like Herr Wagner'[96] ran up against the Spohr and Mendelssohn-loving musical establishment, but was 'rapturously' welcomed by Queen Victoria and Prince Albert:

> In truth they were the first to speak up for me without disguise: if one reflects that they were dealing with a political outcast, under warrant of arrest for high treason, one will surely think me right to thank the pair of them right heartily.[97]

Had not Albert died in 1861, a performance of *Lohengrin* would have complied with Victoria's request some fifteen years before it was finally staged in 1875.[98] Even so, only in the fateful year 1870, long after the scandal of *Tannhäuser* in Paris and Baudelaire's championship had generated lasting French idolatry, did Covent Garden stage its first Wagner opera, *Der fliegende Holländer*. It was sung in Italian.

By the time of Wagner's third and last visit to London in 1877,[99] the non-royal 'London Germans' (Edward Dannreuther and Francis Hueffer to the fore) had already established a Wagner Society, and the resistance of the *Times* critic John Davison had succumbed to the magic of Bayreuth, though Joseph Bennett's 'Letters from Bayreuth' in the *Daily Telegraph* raised, amid much admiration, the soon-to-be-familiar cry: 'Oh, for a Verdi'.[100] Even George Eliot – 'Your husband does not like Jews', she told Cosima, 'My husband [sic] is a Jew' – was enthralled by both the man and his music and, according to Cosima, 'wept plentifully over the heavenly scene between Siegmund and Brünnhilde'.[101] William Ashton Ellis's quarterly *The Meister* (1888-95) and its propagation of 'the goodness of Wagner's personal character ... and the moral and religious interpretation of his music dramas' [SESSA, p.43] in translation continued to swell the cult. In *The Sanity of Art* (1895) Shaw convincingly rebutted Nordau's notorious attack in *Degeneration* (1893) on Wagner as 'the last mushroom on the dunghill of Romanticism [SESSA, p.53]. While the pilgrimage to Bayreuth was henceforth *de rigueur* for many (though the unconverted doubtless still echo Nietzsche's *mot*: 'bereits bereut'), the first London performances in German of the *Ring*, *Meistersinger* and *Tristan* in 1882 [102] nevertheless proved less immediately accessible than Richter's purely orchestral Wagner concerts, to which 'musical and fashionable London flocked'. 'English people like serious music and like the stage', Hueffer continued, 'but they do not care for serious music on the stage.'[103]

If at least aspects of Kleist lost a natural champion in Carlyle, the same might be said of Wagner. Carlyle's first instance of the Hero as Divinity is Odin – 'the genuine thought of deep, rude, earnest minds [...] how profound the myth of the great Tree Igdrasil'. How *might* 'a moralist seeking to preach a regenerative doctrine to a materialistic and hedonistic age'[104] have been affected by the *Ring*? Or the author of *Sartor Resartus*, that heartfelt celebration of 'the German peaceful in his watch-tower [...] with preparatory blast of cowhorn, emitting his *Höret ihr Herren und lasset's Euch sagen*', by the sublimely comic conclusion to Act II of *Die Meistersinger*, when the Night Watchman, oblivious of all street-fighting *Wahn*, renders the full stanza to restore peace to moonlit Nürnberg?[105] But ultimately the Carlyle whose favourite line, from St John's Gospel, was 'Work while it is called today; for the Night cometh wherein no man can work'[106] could not have welcomed the (albeit ecstatic) Schopenhauerian nihilism of either *Tristan* or the *Ring*.[107] Like so many eminent Victorians, Carlyle was, moreover, tone-deaf. When William Morris received Alfred Forman's translation of *Die Walküre*, his response was unequivocal: 'I look upon it as nothing short of desecration to bring such a tremendous and world-wide subject under the gas-lights of an opera: the most degraded and rococo of all forms of art – the idea of a sandy-haired German tenor tweedledeeing over the unspeakable woes of Sigurd, which even the simplest words are not typical enough to express!'[108] Yet it was not *Sigurd the Volsung*, perhaps conceived by Morris as an anti-*Ring*[109] and certainly acclaimed by Shaw as the greatest epic since Homer,[110] which came to epitomize the heroic life of the bourgeoisie, but Liszt's piano transcriptions of *Tannhäuser* and *Lohengrin*, *The Valkyre* and *Tristan*.

III

Some attempt must now be made to draw these three strands together, however tentatively. Just as early translations/adaptations of Schiller's *Der Geisterseher* and Kleist's *Die Familie Schroffenstein* fed an appetite for the terror and dread of Gothic sensationalism, so the high seriousness of the later Gothic Revival was drawn to the overheated religiosity of Wagner's *Tannhäuser*. Indeed, the story of Wagner's Byronic hero[111] struck some in Dresden as a reactionary and intentionally provocative glorification of Catholicism; even Wagner's *Stammtisch* friend, the architect Gottfried Semper, 'hielt mich für den Repräsentanten einer mittelalterlichen katholicisierenden Richtung, die er oft mit wahrer Wuth bekämpfte'.[112] Yet the Gothic was not obviously subversive in a way that, for a while, *Die Räuber* seemed to be – though the father-disinterring finale of that play is of course as Gothic as, say, the subterranean vehmic court scene which opens *Das Käthchen von Heilbronn*. Wagner, however, was soon to join his revolutionary friend on the '*Semper-Barrikaden*' and thence into exile (they met again in London in 1855). While *Tannhäuser* could be all things to all men,

Victorian and Edwardian England's artists and writers in particular were often hypnotised by its potential for subversion as 'almost [...] a code word for experimentation with forbidden pleasures'[113] – from Swinburne to Maurice Baring, who could still wish in 1924 'that someone should sing the Venusberg song all over England and shatter the walls of Philistinism [...] which would cause their conventions, creeds, prejudices, morals and ideals to come crashing to the ground'.[114]

It was indeed the challenge to tradition and authority issued by the French Revolutionaries and again in the revolutionary year 1848/9 which was taken up by each of our trio, a commitment which the darkly Gothic veneer of some of their early works could not finally conceal. Whatever his subsequent misgivings, the Schiller who was created an honorary French citizen in recognition of his perceived libertarianism continued to test the old order in play after play,

> *das ewig Gestrige,*
> *Was immer war und immer wiederkehrt,*
> *Und morgen gilt, weils heute hat gegolten!'*
> [Wallensteins Tod, ll.208-210]

and to find it wanting. 'Die Ruhe eines Kirchhofs'[115] may claim both Carlos and Posa in Philipp's Spain, but Schiller's audiences knew the historical truth of Posa's prophesies, and had witnessed the end of the French monarchy foreseen by Johanna:

> *von den niedern Hütten, wo dir jetzt*
> *Der Retter ausging, droht geheimnisvoll*
> *Den blutbefleckten Enkeln das Verderben!'*
> [Die Jungfrau von Orleans, ll.2099-2101].

In his one non-tragic work (as it happens, also the one with the most historically distant setting), Schiller directly confronts Kant's widely accepted absolute veto on the right of rebellion, and shows the Swiss throwing off the Austrian yoke 'without an inevitable descent into barbarism' [see SHARPE, pp.308-9], though with *some* necessary bloodshed – an assassination he attempts to justify by contrasting Tell's act with Parricida's.[116]

Like Tell, Michael Kohlhaas also claims the moral legitimation of self-defence, though Luther's rejection of Kohlhaas' arguments plainly echoes Max Piccolomini's rejection of Wallenstein's self-exculpation.[117] Kleist went further in *Die Hermannschlacht*, rejecting Kant's prohibition on *Machtpolitik* as decisively as he had once accepted (and been disoriented by) Kant's epistemological scepticism. Within the Kleist family tradition – which was subsequently to impel Heinrich Ewald von Kleist, with his father's approval, to attempt to assassinate Hitler by a bomb strapped to his body – acts of patriotic 'insanity' against the foreign (in the case of Hitler, Austrian) usurper were a moral duty.[118] Thus, Hermann ruthlessly and single-mindedly subordinates even his humanity to the political task in hand, which is no less than the birth of a nation. Yet even this most transparent anti-French propaganda envisages the war which will unify the fragmented German lands as a 'Krieg für die Menschheit':

> *Wenn [...]*
> *Jemals die ganze Menschheit sich vereint,*
> *So läßt, daß es ein Deutscher führt,*
> *sich denken,*
> *Ein Britt', ein Gallier, oder wer ihr wollt,*
> *Doch nimmer jener Latier'.*[119]

As in *Penthesilea*, or in *Die Marquise von O...*, all's fair in love and war, but in *Homburg* Kleist finally realigns the *Hermannschlacht*'s subordination of people as means to political ends in the more nuanced moral terms of individual responsibility.[120]

For Shaw, the *Ring* was also transparent political allegory (one which he approved, at least up to the end of *Siegfried* – 'Siegfried as Protestant'!), and it has remained a political allegory ever since, however fanciful the meanings superimposed in performance have subsequently become. It is Wagner, rather than Schiller or Kleist, whom many still associate with the triumphalism of German unification (*Kaisermarsch*), though Wagner did not believe – any more than Nietzsche did – in the triumph of German arms as a triumph of contemporary German culture; nor is Sachs's disparagement of 'falscher wälscher Majestät' prophetic of some more authentic German sovereignty in 1871, but rather of the survival, development and flowering of her great tradition: 'die heilige deutsche Kunst'. As befits comedy, Sachs in *Die Meistersinger* finds a way both to acknowledge and to defuse the challenge to tradition and authority, to reconcile the old with the new – to the delight of the people of Nürnberg, and ultimately, too, for their, and our, aesthetic education.

Schillerian categories are equally central to Wagner in his more pervasive heroic-tragic mode, when he takes 'delight in describing his hero as the Freewiller of Necessity, thereby beyond measure exasperating Englishmen with a congenital incapacity for metaphysics.' But even Wagner's English audiences will scarcely have needed Shaw to interpret for them what Wagner 'hesitated to explain for fear of prosecution', namely the world of the *Ring* as a world 'waiting for Man to redeem it from the lame and cramped government of the gods'; or to appreciate that 'the most inevitable dramatic conception of the nineteenth century is that of a perfectly naïve hero upsetting religion, law and order in all directions'.[121] For Shaw, '*Prometheus Unbound* is an English attempt at a *Ring*', and Shelley's Wotan, 'whom he calls Jupiter, is the almighty fiend into whom the Englishman's God had degenerated during two centuries of ignorant Bible worship and shameless commercialism.' Unlike Shelley, however, Wagner 'understood Wotan and pardoned him, [...] making the truth and heroism which overthrow him the children of his inmost heart; and representing him as finally acquiescing in and working for his own supersession and annihilation'.[122]

In comparison with the gods of Shelley and Wagner, the seducer-god of Kleist's comedy *Amphitryon* seems to get off lightly. Goethe, suspecting Romantic Catholicism, perceived 'eine Deutung der Fabel ins Christliche, in die Überschattung der Maria vom Heiligen Geist'.[123] Certainly, Jupiter's annunciation of the birth of a son to Amphitryon ('Dir wird ein Sohn geboren werden,/ Dess' Name Herkules') is an unmistakable biblical echo, yet there can be no question of the birth of a Redeemer where the only 'sin' in question is the god's own lust. Goethe thought the play's dénouement wretched ('klatrig'): 'Der wahre Amphitryon muß es sich gefallen lassen, daß ihm Zeus diese Ehre angetan hat. Sonst ist die Situation der Alkmene peinlich und die des Amphitryon zuletzt grausam.' Yet it is also true that the *deus ex machina* of the play's operatic ending scarcely masks the god's moral – or amoral – discomfiture, for Kleist's focus is precisely on human reaction to divine caprice. He chose not to develop that strand of the myth in which Jupiter (like Wagner's Wotan) takes a mortal woman with whom to create 'one who shall redeem both the gods and mankind',[124] though Jupiter is certainly inspired by Alkmene's constancy (as is Wotan by the unanticipated, human-inspired disobedience of his daughter[125]). Instead, it is Amphitryon who demands satisfaction[126] in the form of a son, and Jupiter who obliges, foretelling that Hercules, after his trials, will be received on Olympus as a god. Coincidentally, Schiller planned to use the same myth to demonstrate 'the triumph of modern over naïve poetry [...] the apotheosis of Hercules, the transition from earth to Olympus, the transformation of Man into God' (letter to Humboldt, 30.11.1795).[127]

Yet the threat to 'religion, law and order' more openly posed by Kleist and Wagner, and most vividly realised in *Kohlhaas* and the *Ring*, remains imbued with Schillerian idealism rather than any movement towards atheistic materialism (Wagner's enthusiasm for Feuerbach's philosophy of the natural, sensual man notwithstanding). *Wallenstein* 'muß nicht gelesen, sondern gelernt werden', Kleist writes to his sister. 'Ich bin begierig, ob Wallenstein den Carlos bei Dir verdrängen wird. Ich bin unentschieden.' And to his fiancée: 'Alles was *Max Piccolomini* sagt, möge [...] für mich gelten, alles was *Thekla* sagt, soll [...] für Dich gelten.' However unfashionable ('Unsre Väter und Mütter und Lehrer schelten immer so erbittert auf die Ideale'), without such ideals 'Posa würde seinen Freund nicht gerettet, und Max nicht in die schwedischen Haufen geritten sein.' In concluding this homily with a sentiment already central to his early 'Lebensplan' – 'was dein erstes Gefühl Dir antwortet, das tue' – Kleist is echoing Thekla's advice to Max ('folge deinem ersten/ Gefühl', *Tod*, li.2338-9), while the nub of his last great play – Homburg's impulsive, unauthorized charge against the Swedish army – is a non-tragic variation on Max's action, informed by the same sentiment. The need for absolute trust to which Kleist draws Ulrike's attention in

Don Carlos ('Elisabeth ehrte die Zwecke Posas, auch ohne sie zu kennen'[128]), and which is such a dominant theme in his own works, in turn shapes the plot of Wagner's *Lohengrin* ('Nie sollst Du mich befragen,/ noch Wissens Sorge tragen,/ woher ich kam der Fahrt,/ noch wie mein Nam' und Art!', III, 3).

As Cosima's diaries show, Wagner's veneration for Schiller was no less ardent than Kleist's – indeed, it seems to have grown, the more unfashionable Schiller once again became after the 1859 centenary. Nor does Wagner appear to have shared Kleist's competitive urge to surpass Schiller, play for play. Only days before his death in Venice, he and Cosima chose *Don Carlos* for their customary evening readings, the Posa/Carlos scene in Act 4 prompting Cosima to remark: 'Ich glaubte, diese Dinge, nun beinahe lächerlich gemacht, würden in der Schätzung der Menschen noch wachsen', and Wagner to reply: 'gewiß, das ist die arische[129] Idealität, das haben wir hervorgebracht.' Even more than *Don Carlos* ('er sagt: Er habe die Reife des Werkes überschätzt früher, jetzt freue er sich der herrlichen Züge'), it is *Wallenstein* to which they repeatedly return, convinced 'daß das Stück – zumal das Verhältnis von Thekla und Max – lange nicht hoch genug gewürdigt sei.' Interestingly though, it is not *Wallensteins Tod* but *Wallensteins Lager* and *Die Piccolomini* which suggest themselves as material for a possible opera in three long acts, the first ending with the arrival in camp of Max escorting Wallenstein's wife and daughter, to the accompaniment of dragoons and march music, and the final act with the great exchange between Octavio and Max at the Terzkys' banquet.[130]

Wagner envisaged the climax to yet another unwritten work, potentially 'ein Pendant zum *Hamlet*', as a similar confrontation between father and son: 'er bedauere, daß nicht Goethe oder Schiller ein Stück über Friedrich den Großen gemacht hätten, von Katte's Hinrichtung an, das Leben in Rheinsberg bis zum Tode seines Vaters und der großen letzten Unterredung zwischen beiden [...] Heinrich Kleist hätte das Zeug dazu gehabt.'[131] No doubt he had *Homburg* in mind, though *Don Carlos* and *Wallenstein* offer similar constellations (insubordination, execution/threat of execution, breach/reconciliation with father/father figure). The working out of large political issues *as* family affairs – a synthesis with which Schiller was notably still wrestling in *Don Carlos* – may be as old as Classical Greek tragedy, but the strikingly recurrent patterns in domestic relationships linking the works of these three German dramatists, not least through multiple Shakespearean echoes, speak to us perhaps as directly today as to nineteenth-century sensibilities.

Most obviously, if unexceptionally, the authority of fathers and father-figures seldom survives its encounter with the younger generation intact: Schiller's Miller and Präsident von Walter, König Philipp, Thibaut d'Arc, Octavio and Wallenstein (whose loss of Max, Wagner argued, far from being subsidiary to the main plot, induces the play's catastrophe[132]) – all are affected, and often diminished or unmasked, by their worldly (in the case of der alte Moor, gullible) opposition to youthful idealism and innocence, whose extinction is tragically underlined by the ultimate survival of an aged Doria or Grossinquisitor. Kleist's Schroffensteiners and Richter Adam undergo a comparable process, as do his Amazonian Oberpriesterin and Kurfürst, not forgetting those dramatis personae *manquées*, the father of the Marquise von O... and the paternalistic authorities seemingly destroyed by the earthquake in Chili, though ironically reanimated in the penultimate twist to that story (for it ends on a chiliastic note), with father slaying son as pitilessly as Piachi slays Nicolo the 'Findling'. Similarly, Wagner's Daland, Landgraf, König Marke, Sachs, Wotan, Gurnemanz – all collide with passionate youth.

Fathers (Thibaut d'Arc, Daland, Wotan) and father-substitutes (Käthchen's foster-father, the Oberpriesterin) disown their daughters, believing them to have been bewitched (Johanna, Senta, Käthchen, Penthesilea, even Telramund's intended child-bride, Elsa) or wilfully errant (Brünnhilde) – a favourite Victorian theme. These women in turn have visions of the men they will love (Käthchen: von Strahl; Senta: Dutchman; Elsa: Lohengrin; Brünnhilde: Siegfried). The three virgin warriors (Johanna, Penthesilea, Brünnhilde) emancipate themselves from their unnatural martial calling, however momentarily (Johanna), and are humanized (in the case of Wotan's daughter, literally made human) through their acts of disobedience inspired by love. But active women such as these, or Venus, or Ortrud, find their counterparts in the passive suffering of a Maria Stuart, Käthchen, Gutrune, Elisabeth or Elsa. One suspects that Kleist's famous observation that Penthesilea and Käthchen 'gehören wie das + und - der Algebra zusammen und sind ein und dasselbe Wesen, nur unter entgegengesetzten Beziehungen gedacht' might hold good for several of the female characters in Schiller and Wagner, too.[133] Sometimes the opposition tends towards caricature, when a Lady Macbeth figure tries to dominate the simple and straightforward heroine: Gräfin Terzky and Thekla, Isabeau and Johanna, Kunigunde and Käthchen, Ortrud and Elsa. (The ultimate such monster is probably Marina in Schiller's *Demetrius* fragment.)

If active disobedience leads to self-knowledge and emancipation (Max, Homburg, Brünnhilde) from erstwhile mentors (Wallenstein, Kurfürst, Wotan), a third person is needed to achieve the interplay of love and power, heroism and death, to full dramatic effect. Hence the archetypal triangular situations in which the young lovers clash with a mature figure of power and prestige – again a dramatic commonplace, but notable here for the noble renunciation of the older man vis-à-vis his younger rival. This – with the overlaid political theme of an arranged dynastic marriage, proposed or already effected – is the thread linking Schiller's Philipp/Carlos/Elisabeth and Wallenstein/Max/Thekla with Kleist's Kurfürst/Homburg/Natalie and Wagner's Marke/Tristan/Isolde. While the philandering protagonists of Kleist's two comedies at best parody the situation (Jupiter/Amphitryon/Alkmene and Adam/Ruprecht/Eva – it is the women who here emerge as moral victors), the cobbler-poet of Wagner's comedy (Sachs/ Walther/ Eva) puts a mellow, life-enhancing gloss on the resignation he ultimately shares with the noble Marke, whose predicament he famously professes to renounce. Each of Wagner's music dramas is constructed on a similar triangular configuration, including Wolfram/Tannhäuser/Elisabeth if we substitute maturity confronting youthful impetuosity for mere age-difference (though the religious dimension in the linked stories of *Parsifal* and *Lohengrin* rather rearranges the co-ordinates – intriguingly so, when we remember that the eponymous heroes are father and son). From the Dutchman/Eric/Senta to Wotan/Siegfried/Brünnhilde, Wagner's preoccupation with redemption through love and renunciation creates at least the sublime artistic effect of transcending Schopenhauerian nihilism. His works 'seemed to offer philosophic and psychic inspiration to late Victorians', Sessa concludes; 'some Wagnerians found the elements with which to revitalize their interest in traditional Christian concepts of love, compassion, and redemption, while others used Wagnerism to restore a spiritual dimension to liberalism or to transcend Darwinism.'[134]

These are some of the perennially topical configurations, long familiar through Wagner, to which English audiences may yet find themselves drawn in the works of Schiller and of Kleist, his two illustrious predecessors. Whether or not English audiences will share Wagner's view that Kleist stood in the same relationship to Schiller as Schubert to Beethoven, or Cosima's view, writing of Schiller, 'daß nach seiner Dichtung nur noch das musikalische Drama möglich war, zu welchem er gleichsam den Übergang bildet',[135] it is time to see them plain and see them whole – not only in operatic adaptations – as they enter 'the third century of their immortal lives.'

Notes and References

[1] 'der größte Mime, das erstaunlichste Theater-Genie, das die Deutschen gehabt haben' – Nietzsche, 'Der Fall Wagner', in *Werke*, ed. Schlechta (Munich, 1969: <*cited as*: NIETZSCHE-*Werke*>) Bd II, p.919. But note Nietzsche's distinction: 'Wagner ist *kein* Dramatiker' in the sense that a Schiller 'oft Blut schwitzt: dem Knoten *Notwendigkeit* zu geben und ebenso der Lösung, so daß beide nur auf eine einzige Art möglich sind, beide den Eindruck der Freiheit machen' (*ibid.* pp.920-21).

[2] So little was known that the centenary of Kleist's birth, for instance, was mistakenly celebrated in 1876 – see Helmut Sembdner (ed.), *Heinrich von Kleists Nachruhm* (Bremen, 1967), documents 313, 342; Dirk Grathoff, *Kleists Geheimnisse* (Opladen, 1993; <*cited as*: GRATHOFF>), p.16. See also in general Mary Howard, *Vom Sonderling zum Klassiker, Hundert Jahre Kleist-Rezeption in Großbritannien* (Berlin, 1990; <*cited as*: HOWARD>).

[3] Egon Friedell, writing in 1909; quoted in N. Oellers, *Schiller – Zeitgenosse aller Epochen. Dokumente zur Wirkungsgeschichte Schillers in Deutschland*, Bd II (Munich, 1976; <*cited as*: OELLERS>), p.244.

[4] OELLERS, p.198.

---

[5] OELLERS, p.176.

[6] Heinrich Meyer-Benfrey, *Das Drama Heinrich von Kleists* (Berlin, 1911-13), p.13.

[7] Frederic Ewen, *The Prestige of Schiller in England 1788-1859* (New York, 1932; <*cited as*: EWEN>), p.148.

[8] EWEN, pp.202-4.

[9] Perhaps most memorably in his broadcast Mellon Lectures, *Some Sources of Romanticism* (1965). Annan credits Berlin with giving 'the truest and most moving of all interpretations of life that my own generation made', *Our Age* (London, 1990; <*cited as:* ANNAN>), p.378.

[10] ANNAN, pp.335-356.

[11] To Eckermann, 21.3.1830. Cf. 'To those outside Germany the use of the term *Klassik* for a period and works with such strong Romantic tendencies can seem somewhat mystifying' [the period 1786-1805; the works *Faust, Wilhelm Meisters Lehrjahre, Die Jungfrau von Orleans, Wilhelm Tell*], Lesley Sharpe, *Friedrich Schiller, Drama, Thought and Politics* (Cambridge, 1991; <*cited as*: SHARPE>), p.315. Nor was there any such gulf before c.1800 – Goethe and Schiller made common cause with the Schlegels, Novalis and Tieck against both Enlightenment moralizing and contemporary popular sentamentalism (*ibid.* pp.319-20). See also Klaus Berghahn, 'Von Weimar nach Versailles', in *Klassiklegende*, ed. Reinhold Grimm & Jost Hermand (Frankfurt/Main, 1971), pp.50-78.

[12] Culminating in Wagner's *Gesamtkunstwerk*, but for his attempt to reestablish (at least theoretically) the primacy of drama over music in *Oper und Drama*, see below and also Michael Tanner, *Wagner* (London, 1996; <*cited as*: TANNER>).

[13] Houston Stewart Chamberlain quotes Kleist's 'merkwürdiges Wort: "Ich betrachte die Musik als die Wurzel aller übrigen Künste" ' in his *Richard Wagner*, [1896] (Munich, 1942), p.276.

[14] i.e. as distinct from the memorable amateur productions staged by William Poel at the turn of the century – see the essay by J. P. Crick later in this volume.

[15] Hans Werner Henze in conversation with the author, who translated the libretto: ENO *Prince of Homburg* Symposium (London, 1996).

[16] *The Times*, 5.6.1986. One must in fairness add that the fate of the German classics in Germany is often no less bizarre – witness the existentially bewildered Adam of Ernst Wendt's 1983 Hamburg production of the *Krug*.

[17] This was also the year of its Paris première.

[18] See TANNER, p.12.

[19] Only in the first work in the canon, *Der fliegende Holländer*, is there clear borrowing from a contemporary source, in this case from Heine, though it is a debt soon ignored after much creative accounting.

[20] As the cosmopolitan musical impresario Fitelberg puts it in Thomas Mann's *Dr Faustus*: 'Wir wissen sehr wohl zwischen Gounods *Faust* und dem von Goethe zu unterscheiden, auch wenn wir französisch sprechen, auch dann [...]' (Frankfurt, 1949), p.406.

[21] See *Kobbé's Complete Opera Book*, ed. Earl of Harewood (London, 1987), p.626.

[22] SHARPE, pp.282, 293.

[23] As Grathoff notes, Paul de Mann (in *Allegories of Reading*) 'hat den Antagonismus zwischen Kleist und Schiller erkannt, der für das Verständnis von Kleists literarischem Werk

von ungleich höherer Bedeutung ist, als es seine gelegentlichen Scharmünzel mit Goethe sind' [GRATHOFF, p.82].

[24] Isaiah Berlin, *Some Sources of Romanticism* (1965).

[25] *The Robbers*, by Alexander Fraser Tytler, Lord Woodhouselee; further translations followed in 1799 and 1801.

[26] For a succinct account of Coleridge and Germany, see Rosemary Ashton, *The German Idea, Four English Writers and the Reception of German Thought 1800-1860* [1980] (Libris, 1994; <*cited as:* ASHTON>), pp.27-35; also EWEN, p.59; also Karl S. Guthke, *Englische Vorromantik und deutscher Sturm und Drang* (Göttingen, 1958; *Palaestra*, Band 223; <*cited as*: GUTHKE>), p.156.

[27] To Reinwald, 22.7.1783; see also William Witte, 'Der Einfluß der britischen Ästhetik auf Schiller', in Klaus L. Berghahn (ed.), *Friedrich Schiller: zur Geschichtlichkeit seines Werkes* (Kronberg/Ts, 1975), pp.309-16.

[28] Mary Howard observes that it was a mark of the literary journalism of the day, 'daß für die Appelle an "taste" keine Differenzierung zwischen ästhetischen und moralischen Gesichtspunkten erforderlich ist' [HOWARD, p.25]. Carlyle judged the *Aesthetic Letters* 'one of the deepest, most compact pieces of reasoning we are anywhere acquainted with', but leaves it at that [EWEN, p.145]. Harrold notes Carlyle's attempt to find in Schiller's aesthetic writings 'greater ethical and metaphysical content than they possess' [C. F. Harrold, *Carlyle and German Thought* (London, 1927), p.253]. For all his identification with Schiller's heroic struggle against constant ill health (Carlyle, too, planned to translate all of Schiller's works – see Fred Kaplan, *Thomas Carlyle, A Biography* (New York, 1983), pp.85, 108, 123), he remained in some ways a Calvinist Scot with little inclination to 'play the game', let alone accept the primacy of the *Spieltrieb*.

[29] *The Monthly Review*; see ASHTON, p.180; EWEN, p.18.

[30] *Theatrical Inquisitor*; see EWEN, p.113.

[31] *The Monthly Review*; Lewis 'endeavoured to keep strictly to the original', unlike Jakob Karl Timäus, whose 'extremely ill executed' effort, *Cabal and Love* (1795), he castigates – see GUTHKE, pp.156-7.

[32] *Theatrical Inquisitor*; see EWEN, p.113. On the fictional encounter of Maria and Elisabeth, cf. Schiller to Goethe: 'Die Situation ist an sich selbst moralisch unmöglich' (3.9.1799); Goethe: 'Mich soll nur wundern, was das Publicum sagen wird, wenn die beiden Huren zusammenkommen und sich ihre Aventüren vorwerfen' (*Briefwechsel*, ed. Meusebach-Grimm, 1980, p.69). See Benno von Wiese, *Friedrich Schiller* (Stuttgart, 1959) p.715.

[33] From an 'Ode on the Prevalence of German Drama' (1800) in the *Gentleman's Magazine* – see John Mander, *Our German Cousins* (London, 1974; <*cited as*: MANDER>), pp.30-31.

[34] – as the *Critical* dubbed *The Bravo*, Lewis's very free adaptation of Heinrich Zschokke's *Abällino*; see GUTHKE, pp.201-12; also MANDER, p.28.

[35] MANDER, p.28.

[36] See ASHTON, pp.33-5.

[37] Now entitled *Remorse*, echoing *Hatred and Remorse* (Sheridan's own hit version of Kotzebue's *Menschenhaß und Reue*), though Coleridge's main debt is to Schiller's *Die Räuber* and to his popular mystery and suspense pot-boiler, *Der Geisterseher*.

[38] See EWEN, pp.200, 208 & 162 (*North British Review*, III, 1845).

[39] In his *Life and Works of Goethe* (1855); see EWEN, pp.215, 243-6.

[40] London's German community in the 1840s was estimated at around 40,000 – see Paul M. Kennedy, *The Rise of the Anglo-German Antagonism 1860-1914*, [1980] (London, 1987; <*cited as*: KENNEDY>), p.109.

[41] See EWEN, p.253; 'Das Lied von der Glocke' was composed in 1809, long before Beethoven incorporated Schiller's 'An die Freude' in his Ninth Symphony (first performance, 1824). 'The success of [Romberg's] setting of Schiller's 'Lied von der Glocke' reached as far as New York; the work was still being performed after 1900' – *The New Grove Dictionary of Music*, ed. Stanley Sadie (London, 1980), vol.16, p.145.

[42] After the *Schiller-Feier* in Vienna, for instance, Grillparzer voiced his suspicion, 'man wolle dabei noch etwas anderes feiern als Schiller, den ausgezeichneten Dichter und Schriftsteller: etwa das deutsche Bewußtsein, die deutsche Einheit, die Kraft und Machtstellung Deutschlands' – see OELLERS, *vol.*I, p.428.

[43] EWEN, p.249

[44] EWEN, p.143.

[45] together with Fichte's *Wissenschaftslehre* (access to which, in whatever language, was restricted) and the French Revolution (an altogether less welcome gift). Wilhelm's self-creation perhaps even provided a (Fichtean) *Anstoß* to Carlyle's own conversion to the 'Everlasting Yea' – however idiosyncratic his understanding of Goethean 'renunciation' – see MANDER, pp.94-5, 104-7; KAPLAN, pp.67-8, 123-4, 468.

[46] (If not yet quite as an *Institut* – Manchester had its Schiller-Anstalt some time before the English Goethe Society was founded in 1866.) See KENNEDY, p.109. For the friendly argument between Bulwer Lytton and Lewes on the respective merits of Schiller and Goethe, see ASHTON, pp.124-6.

[47] 'Der Fall Wagner', in NIETZSCHE-*Werke* II, pp.910-11.

[48] In 1828, a testimonial from Goethe had failed to secure Carlyle the Chair of Moral Philosophy at the University of St Andrews – see KAPLAN, pp.138-9.

[49] See e.g. ANNAN, p.336.

[50] 18.12.1811; see HOWARD, p.30.

[51] Though she will have had more direct contact with the German literary scene through her erstwhile mentor and amanuensis, A. W. Schlegel.

[52] 'M de K.' is also unprincipled, blasphemous, sensation-seeking and a drunkard – in need of 'Dutch' courage to do the deed: 'L'homme qui, prêt à tuer son amie, célèbre un festin avec elle et s'exalte par des chants et des liqueurs, comme s'il craignait le retour des mouvements vrais et raisonnables; cet homme, dis-je, n'a-t-il pas l'air d'un auteur sans génie qui veut produire avec une catastrophe véritable les effets auxquels il ne peut pas atteindre en poésie?' (*Oeuvres Complètes*, vol.I, Paris, 1871, p.190). See also Joachim Maass, *Kleist, A Biography* (London, 1983; <*cited as*: MAASS>), p.295.

[53] MAASS, p.171.

[54] MANDER, pp.44-47.

[55] Friedrich von Oertels, *Der Mönch* (1797). Peter Jansen ('Monk Lewis and Heinrich von Kleist', *Kleist Jahrbuch 1984*, Berlin, 1984, pp.25-55) speculates on reciprocal influence in addition to Lewis's borrowing from Kleist as originally identified by Louis F. Peck (1945) and developed at length by GUTHKE. – See my forthcoming essay 'Kleist and Lewis, give and take' in S.P. Stark (ed.), *The Novel in Anglo-German Context. Proceedings of the 1997 Leeds Conference* (Reihe: *Internationale Forschungen zur allgemeinen und vergleichenden Literaturwissenschaft*; Amsterdam: Rodopi, 1999).

[56] See preface to *Romantic Tales*. Since *Die Familie Schroffenstein* was published anonymously, as was customary with first plays, this might seem plausible, but less so in the light of the close links both Kleist and Lewis had established with the Wieland family and Heinrich Zschokke. – See JANSEN; GUTHKE.

[57] Ludwig Wieland suggested the change, and also arranged for publication by Gessner – see GUTHKE.

[58] The friendship of Kleist, Zschokke and Ludwig Wieland is of course best known through the competition which led to *Der zerbrochene Krug* [GRATHOFF, pp.96-97]. Wieland published a translation of Lewis's *The Castle Spectre* (1804) while Lewis adapted Zschokke's *Abällino* as *The Bravo* [see note 34]. (Kleist's first impression of the original – 'des erbärmlichen Stückes *Abällino*' – predated his acquaintance with Zschokke – see Kleist, *Sämtliche Werke und Briefe*, ed. Helmut Sembdner, 2 vols (Munich, 1984; <*cited as*: KLEIST-*SW*>) vol.2, p.536). Kleist and Lewis both use *Robert Guiscard* material, Kleist in his unfinished and partially destroyed play of that name, much praised by Ludwig Wieland's father, Christoph Martin Wieland, and Lewis in his *Adelgitha*.

[59] See preface to *The Works of Frederick Schiller, Early Dramas and Romances*, trans. Henry G. Bohn (London, 1849). Cf. Bulwer Lytton (1828) 'Such of the Germans [...] as follow the school of Schiller, will often stop as far short of the true boundaries of terror, as the French romanticists would go beyond it [...] Is not the *Ghost-Seer* a successful novel? Does it not afford the highest and most certain testimony of what Schiller could have done as a writer of narrative fiction?' Goethe, Schiller and Hugo must be 'separated from the herd of horror-writers, with whom they had previously been confounded' [EWEN, p.198].

[60] According to *The Gentleman's Magazine* (LXXXIX, February 1809, p.141), no other contemporary author could produce 'pictures equally awful, new and sublime'.

[61] To J. H. Green (1821). Tieck had earlier congratulated Coleridge that his own Schiller-inspired play, *Remorse* [see note 37], 'never loses itself in shallow sentimentality.' The terms of reference are doubtless indebted to Schiller's *Über naive und sentimentalische Dichtung* and to A. W. Schlegel's recent Vienna lectures. See Coleridge, *Collected Letters*, ed. E. L.Griggs, 6 vols (Oxford, 1956-71), vol.3, p.422; vol.5, p.190; vol.6, p.828.

[62] *Hinterlassene Schriften* (1821), *Gesammelte Schriften* (1826). See Kathleen Wheeler, 'Coleridge's Friendship with Ludwig Tieck' in *New Approaches to Coleridge*, ed. Sultana, (London, 1981).

[63] KLEIST-*SW*, vol.2. p.731.

[64] With a happy end, of course; the mutilation to the play also involved cutting the mutilation in the play. See William C. Reeve, *Kleist on Stage, 1804-1987* (Montreal & Kingston, 1993), pp. 8-21.

[65] 26.11.1977; now in Stephen Vizinczey, *Truth and Lies in Literature. Essays and Reviews* (London: Hamish Hamilton, 1986), p.154.

[66] But see ASHTON, pp.43-48, on the vexed question of Coleridge's reading of Kant.

[67] If there are 'zwei große Traditionen' in Kleist reception, the one 'die ihre eigenen politischen, ja militärischen Ziele bei Kleist unvermittelt wiederfindet', the other, ignoring any such dimension, which focuses on 'die Explikation seiner ästhetischen und aufklärerischen Werte', it seems clear to which strand the Coleridge of 1821, anxious to avoid any further identification with 'seditious' German literature, would have belonged – see Wolf Kittler, *Die Geburt des Partisanen aus dem Geist der Poesie* (Freiburg, 1987; <*cited as*: KITTLER>), pp.12-13; see there also for acknowledgement of Richard Samuel's pioneering studies on Kleist's political connections, *passim*.

[68] Engendered no doubt in part by the belated translation of *Die Irin* (1800) and *Der Frühling* (1818) by Ewald von Kleist (who had been killed at Kunersdorf in 1759); see HOWARD, pp.30-32.

[69] Especially Coleridge's *Wallenstein*, translations of *Tell, Don Carlos*, even *Die Braut von Messina*.

[70] vol.2, pp.671-696.

[71] See HOWARD, pp.38-50.

[72] ed. John Oxenford and C. A. Feiling. For the full story, see HOWARD, pp.68-83, to whom I am indebted for many of these details.

[73] That 'evergreen' in Germany inspired five operatic versions, though none by Verdi. For the important publication of *Homburg* and *Kohlhaas* in book form in *Prussia's Representative Man* (1875), see below and note 82. *Käthchen* 'kept the dramatist's work alive on stage throughout the nineteenth century, albeit more often than not in the perverted form of an adaptation (Holbein)', see REEVE, p.139.

[74] 30.11.1844.

[75] 1853; vol.XLI, pp.556-578.

[76] MANDER, p.114. On Carlyle's indebtedness to Fichte for his ideas about the divine mission of the hero as thinker, poet, prophet and king, see HARROLD, p.14. Carlyle was not impressed by the Germany he eventually visited in 1852 to collect material for the biography – see KAPLAN, p.387-392, 397-8.

[77] Readers of Saki, *When William Came* (1913) will recall that the sycophants and mercenary social climbers of a German-occupied England 'in the near future' write works such as *Frederick William, the Great Elector, A Popular Biography*.

[78] *History of Frederick II of Prussia Called Frederick the Great*, vol I, p.294, in Centenary Edition of the *Works of Thomas Carlyle* (London, 1858-1865).

[79] Writing of 'the heroic struggles of Frederick the Great' as depicted by Carlyle, Mander asks: 'did they influence the initial English enthusiasm for the Prussians in 1870? I think they did' [MANDER, p.115]; though when siegeguns were deployed around Paris by the end of 1870, Queen Victoria observed 'that "the English are very fond of Paris", and soon sensed [...] that English opinion was shifting against the Germans' [MANDER, p.194].

[80] In *The New Age*, for instance, where Carlyle's book was accused of glorifying the 'source and fountain-head of all Prussian jack-bootery', G.D., *Nietzsche or Carlyle?* (18.3.1915) vol.XVI, no.1175, p.535. H. J. C. Grierson's book *Carlyle and Hitler* appeared in London in 1933. And in Germany, as Mander writes, 'Did not Hitler ask for the passage in *Frederick the Great*, in which the accession of the Empress Catherine saves Prussia from destruction in the Seven Years' War, to be read to him in his last hours in the *Führerbunker*?' [MANDER, p.108].

[81] See KAPLAN, pp. 387, 389-390.

[82] Francis Lloyd & William Newton, *Prussia's Representative Man* (London, 1875).

[83] Ralph Waldo Emerson, *English Traits and Representative Men*, [1850] in *Works*, vol.4 (London, 1884). See also Roger Paulin, 'Kleist in Großbritannien', *Kleist-Jahrbuch 1992*, p.185.

[84] I am again indebted to HOWARD, pp.100-116, for her exacting analysis of *Prussia's Representative Man*.

[85] A reception alternating with aestheticizing or existential readings – see note 67.

[86] See REEVE, p.167.

[87] The Kleist-Gesellschaft was founded in 1920, the *Kleist-Jahrbuch* in 1922.

[88] The *Manifest der deutschen Intellektuellen* of 1914 proclaimed Germany a *Kulturnation* fighting for the legacy of a Goethe, a Beethoven, a Kant. Unlike *Le manifeste des intellectuels en faveur de Dreyfus* organized by Emile Zola in 1898, the German version, drawn up by Ulrich von Wilamowitz-Moellendorff, with its original ninety-three and finally four-thousand signatories, signally failed to demonstrate their moral prestige. As Stuart Wallace has shown [*War and the Image of Germany*, 1988], British academics did little better.

[89] Gerhard Fricke in *Zeitschrift für Deutschkunde 1934*, pp.222-238 [see OELLERS, p.xlv], though Fricke, 'aus unserer nationalsozialistischen Überzeugung heraus', thought Kleist the more relevant 'Dichter-Führer'.

[90] *Black Record* (1940); see MANDER, p.252.

[91] R. D. Gray, *The German Tradition in Literature* (Cambridge, 1965; <*cited as*: GRAY>), p.351 – here coupled with *Penthesilea*. Gray analyses the indubitable 'preoccupation with polarity and synthesis in the German tradition', the opposites also 'representing among other things good and evil' [p.5]. But more than that, 'there really is madness of discourse. Kleist's story *Michael Kohlhaas* is a case in point [...] as though the combination of opposite qualities in him were in some way evidence of a superhuman stature' [p.7]; similarly, 'it is difficult to believe that this fantastic ending [to *Die Marquise von O...*] was not, in Kleist's distorted mind, a reflection of the complementary opposites' [p.8]. Consequently, 'it is an oppressive thing to hear, for instance, that one of the most popular authors among sixth-formers in German schools today is Kleist' [p.15]. Mander's chapter on 'Vansittartism' is appropriately entitled 'Black and White'.

[92] GRAY, p.76.

[93] See REEVE, pp.167-8.

[94] See Richard Taylor, *Richard Wagner, His Life, Art and Thought* (London, 1979), p.91.

[95] *Tannhäuser*, Overture and Grand March; see Anne Dzamba Sessa, *Richard Wagner and the English* (Cranbury, New Jersey, 1979) <*cited as:* SESSA>.

[96] Of his own music he conducted only *Tannhäuser*, Overture, *Lohengrin*, Prelude, Procession to the Minster, Wedding March, Bridal Chorus – see SESSA, pp.18, 23, 25.

[97] 5.7.1855 to Liszt; SESSA, p.24.

[98] 'The Teutonic element in the house', noted the *Musical Times*, 'had a marvellous effect in teaching the audience that *Lohengrin* was not to be judged by the ordinary standard [...] a very decided "hush" convinced the astonished Opera habitués that the vocalists must be considered as secondary to the work' – see SESSA, pp.24, 30.

[99] Its least successful aspect was the attempt to recoup his financial losses after Bayreuth opened in 1876.

[100] See Joseph Bennett, *Letters from Bayreuth* (London, 1877), p.77, cited in SESSA, p.33. The allusion is to *Götterdämmerung*, which he thought did not exploit the splendid opportunities supplied by its situations – a criticism shared by George Bernard Shaw and developed in *The Perfect Wagnerite* (1889).

[101] As related by Hubert Parry – see SESSA, pp.25-36. The Darwinian notion of evolutionary breakthrough applied to Kleist in *Prussia's Representative Man* (1875) is perhaps anticipated by Dannreuther's comment [in *Richard Wagner: His Tendencies and Theories* (London, 1873), p.71] that the *Ring* 'is no more a reformed opera than man is a reformed monkey'.

[102] The *Ring* under Angelo Neumann, *Meistersinger* and *Tristan* under Hans Richter.

[103] Francis Hueffer, *Half a Century of Music in England, 1837-1887* (Philadelphia, 1889), pp.79, 80; quoted in SESSA, p.37.

[104] HARROLD, p.9 – a doctrine, it must be said, which Carlyle's active anti-Semitism seems to have associated with the stereotype of the materialistic Jew [KAPLAN, pp.526-7]; for a critique of continuing attempts to identify anti-Semitism in Wagner's *works*, see TANNER, pp. 27-30 and under 'anti-Semitism' in index.

[105] 'Hört, ihr Leut' und laßt euch sagen:/ die Glock' hat elfe geschlagen,/ bewahr euch vor Gespenstern und Spuk,/ daß kein böser Geist eur' Seel' berück'!/ Lobet Gott den Herrn !'

[106] *Sartor Resartus*, end of Chapter X; see MANDER, pp.98-9.

[107] Schopenhauer, Wagner observed in a letter to Liszt in 1854, had been 'recently rediscovered – to Germany's shame – by an English critic' – the same John Oxenford whose 'Iconoclasm in German Philosophy' appeared in 1853, and who had rendered a similar service to Kleist a decade earlier: see note 72. For Wagner's letter of 16(?).12.1854 see *Selected Letters of Richard Wagner*, translated and edited by S.Spencer and B.Millington (London: Dent, 1987) pp.323-4. Oxenford's essay appeared in the *Westminster and Foreign Quarterly Review*, April 1853.

[108] Letter to Henry Buxton Forman, 12.11.1873. Wagner's operatic reforms – no gas-lights! – would doubtless have counted for little.

[109] See J. S. Ennis, *A Comparison of Richard Wagner's* Der Ring des Nibelungen *and William Morris's* Sigurd the Volsung (unpublished Ph.D. thesis, Leeds, 1993), pp.19-23.

[110] G. B. Shaw, 'William Morris as I knew him', Introduction to May Morris, *William Morris: Artist, Writer, Socialist* (Oxford, 1936), p.xxxvii.

[111] Cf. Tannhäuser to Venus: 'nicht Lust allein liegt mir am Herzen,/ aus Freuden sehn ich mich nach Schmerzen' (Act I, scene 2) and the *Weltschmerz* of Childe Harold: 'apart he stalked in joyless reverie,/ [...] with pleasure drugged, he almost longed for woe' (Canto I, vi).

[112] Richard Wagner, *Mein Leben*, vol.I (Munich, 1911), p.382. Cf. 'just as Meyerbeer's *Les Huguenots* was designed to glorify Protestantism', *Tannhäuser* purportedly rejected German Catholic agitation for reform against papal absolutism, celibacy in the priesthood, and other religious extremes. Semper 'contended in particular that the Minnesingers and the pilgrimage-obsessed Middle Ages had no place in art and let me know that he despised me for having chosen such material' – *My Life* (Cambridge, 1983), pp.313-4, 770.

[113] Wilde's Dorian Gray sits in his box at this opera, 'listening in rapt pleasure to *Tannhäuser*, and seeing in the prelude to that great work of art a presentation of the tragedy of his own soul.' See SESSA, p.103.

[114] Maurice Baring, *C*, 2 vols (New York, 1924), pp.206, 195. Nevertheless, Christianity ostensibly triumphs over paganism in *Tannhäuser*, whereas in *Lohengrin* the final balance between the two, symbolizing we suppose good and evil, is fairly even. See also SESSA, pp. 87-117, and Raymond Furness, *Wagner and Literature* (Manchester, 1982).

[115] *Don Carlos*, Act III, scene 10.

[116] 'Neben dem ruchlosen Mord aus Impietät und Ehrsucht steht nunmehr Tells notgedrungene That.' – Schiller to Iffland, *Werke*, Nationalausgabe, vol.10, p.458.

[117] Wallenstein muses if he would have acted differently had he known he would lose Max: 'Kann sein, ich hätte mich bedacht – kann sein / Auch nicht' (li.3660f). Kohlhaas, who has lost his wife, gives Luther the same reply (like Wallenstein, crossing to the window as he does so): 'kann sein! ... kann sein, auch nicht!' [KLEIST-*SW*, vol.2, p.47] – see Hartmut Reinhardt,

'Rechtsverwirrung und Verdachtspsychologie, Spuren der Schiller-Rezeption bei Heinrich von Kleist', in *Kleist-Jahrbuch*, 1988-9, pp.198-218.

[118] His father, General Ewald von Kleist, who died in a Russian prison camp in 1954, was charged by his Soviet captors with having 'alienated through mildness and kindness the population of the Soviet Union'; see Corelli Barnett (ed), *Hitler's Generals* (London, 1989).

[119] Act I, scene 3; for Latin/Roman read, of course, Frenchman/Corsican.

[120] Analysing Prussia's twin defeats at Jena and Auerstedt, as Kleist will have done, Wolf Kittler shows that while the one could be attributed to the impetuous Prince Louis Ferdinand taking personal initiative without express authority, the other derived from Graf Kalkreuth's inflexible refusal to intercede without written instructions ('only obeying orders'...) KITTLER, pp.277ff. For the reconciliatory dimension so obviously missing in *Penthesilea* and *Die Hermannschlacht*, see *Kleist-Jahrbuch 1983*, p.201.

[121] G.B. Shaw, *The Perfect Wagnerite* (1889; New York: Dover, 1957), pp.60, 41, 29.

[122] *ibid.* p.64.

[123] Letter to Riemer, 19.7.1807.

[124] 'ein Retter der Götter und Menschen' – in the School of Hesiod poem 'The Shield of Herakles', see *Kleist Jahrbuch* (1991), p.111.

[125] To say that 'Wotan is barely moved by his daughter's pleadings' (Donald Crosby, 'Freedom through Disobedience: *Die Jungfrau von Orleans*, Heinrich von Kleist, and Richard Wagner', in *Friedrich von Schiller and the Drama of Human Existence*, ed. Alexej Ugrinsky, Westport, Connecticut: Greenwood Press, 1988, p.41) is true only of his initial reaction; her insistence that only a worthy hero should awaken her into womanhood ultimately seizes his imagination: 'Leb wohl, du kühnes, herrliches Kind!/ Du meines Herzens heiligster Stolz!...' (*Die Walküre*, III, 3).

[126] 'Nein, Vater Zeus, zufrieden bin ich nicht!' *Amphitryon*, l.2330. Nor, of course, is Jupiter fully 'satisfied', in spite of his public declaration: 'Zeus hat in deinem Hause sich gefallen,/ Amphitryon, und seiner göttlichen/ Zufriedenheit soll dir ein Zeichen werden' (ll.2316-8). More telling is the imposter's richly oracular lament to Alkmene before he reveals his divine identity: 'O Fluch der Seligkeit, die du mir schenktest,/ Müßt ich dir ewig nicht vorhanden sein.' (ll.2307-8)

[127] See REED, p.75.

[128] See variously KLEIST-*SW* vol.2, pp. 526, 518, 612, 525.

[129] Cosima Wagner, *Die Tagebücher* (München/Zürich, 1982), vol.4, pp.1094f. And she continues directly: 'Dann spielt er den Anfang der 9ten! Einem Phantasieren vergleicht er ihn und sagt: Diese erhabene Naivität!' The fraught topic of Wagner's anti-Semitism – here implicitly Beethoven v. Mendelssohn – need not concern us here, but see also *Tagebücher*, vol.1, p.245.

[130] Cosima Wagner, *Tagebücher*, vol.1, p.230, p.35.

[131] *ibid.*, p.513.

[132] Cosima Wagner, *Tagebücher*, vol.3, p.312.

[133] Kleist to Jos. v. Collin, 8.12.1808. Cf. '[Käthchen] ist die Kehrseite der Penthesilea, ihr anderer Pol, ein Wesen, das ebenso mächtig ist durch gänzliche Hingabe, als jene durch Handeln'; and Kleist to Marie von Kleist, Spätherbst 1807.

[134] SESSA, pp.144, 148.

[135] Cosima Wagner, *Tagebücher*, vol.4, p.694, vol.1, p.178.

A Romantic in Ratzeburg: Coleridge's debt to North German *Provinz*[1]

INGO CORNILS

At the age of 26 Samuel Taylor Coleridge spent the first three months of his stay in northern Germany in the small town of Ratzeburg. What did this place have to offer him? How did he develop his German language skills, his knowledge of the culture and people? How did the town, landscape and season, especially in his state of heightened awareness after his 'richest year', act on his imagination?

There is considerable disagreement as to how much Coleridge really gained from his ten-month stay in Germany. L. A. Willoughby thought that the preliminary stay in Ratzeburg was of little importance:

> When in the January of 1799 Coleridge exchanged the flesh-pots and the agreeable society of Ratzeburg for the higher thinking and cheaper living of Göttingen, he was only following the traditions of the time.[2]

Basil Willey contends that the whole trip was largely a waste of time with no real benefit to show for it:

> Coleridge himself learnt little during his ten months' absence which he could not have learnt at home; the foreign travel, the Göttingen lectures, the collecting of materials for a notional life of Lessing, served mainly, one feels, to perpetuate the illusion of work-in-progress, and blind him to the reality of wasted time and dissipated energies.[3]

Even Richard Holmes, Coleridge's most recent biographer, who devotes several pages to the winter of 1798/99 when Coleridge had his first real taste of German hospitality, seems only lukewarm about potential gains.[4] Probably thinking more about Coleridge's time in Göttingen, he proposes that 'the experience subtly changed many of his attitudes, both literary and political, and gave him a strong new sense of his loyalty to his "Mother Isle" '.[5]

This verdict may be seen as a commonplace true for any intercultural sojourner, but one cannot help wondering how distinct the German influence, and in particular the initial exposure was on the young Coleridge. Being a poet of genius, the new environment, the culture shock, the state of heightened awareness of his surroundings and the encounters with foreign people in their native country must have impressed themselves more deeply upon his imagination than on the average British traveller on the continental tour. Germany was certainly in fashion amongst young Britons at the end of the eighteenth century, and it is no surprise that Coleridge should meet many of them in Göttingen. As Lowes pointed out, 'England was discovering Germany, and found that discovery exciting'.[6]

Yet Coleridge sought to discover Germany for himself: he chose to remain in one place, if not 'to put down roots' then at least to stay in this small town and observe for a winter, to make contact with the 'natives', in spite of usually rather formal patterns of social intercourse (his guardedly polite stance during his visit to the 74-year old Klopstock springs to mind), and to find there, far away from his family and friends, another layer of emotional complexity.

Coleridge's aim in coming to Germany was, as far as can be made out from his letters and notebooks, 'to finish his education', and to acquire a working knowledge of German, seen by him as indispensable for his future projects. Less favourable interpretations are that it seemed a good idea to be out of the country when the *Lyrical Ballads* appeared in print[7] or that Coleridge might have wanted to avoid conscription.[8] He and the Wordsworths duly departed for Hamburg on 16 September 1798. On arrival they were overwhelmed by the sights, sounds and smells of the then rather grimy harbour-town, and soon Coleridge and his adoring companion Chester departed on a mission to Ratzeburg, a small resort fifty miles to the north-east of Hamburg, recommended to them by Klopstock's younger brother, to find more agreeable – and affordable – lodgings.

They arrived on Monday 24 September, and Coleridge was immediately 'enchanted with the appearance'.[9] He had secured an introduction to the Amtmann of Ratzeburg, and they got on very well. He and Chester were then introduced to the pastor, a widower with eight children, who lived on the St. Georgsberg which overlooks the lake and Ratzeburg proper.

After exploring some of the walks Coleridge realised that here he could enjoy himself, be in his element, out of Hamburg, in a clean and peaceful house, with a lovely view of the town, groves and lake. In his notebook there is an entry the following day which suggests that his creative imagination had responded to the new environment: 'could not sleep – saw a curious instance of single and double vision.'[10]

Once they had agreed with Pastor Unruh (significantly, Coleridge didn't quite catch his name,[11] a frustrating initial experience shared by many travelling abroad) on the price for board and lodging, his mind was made up. On his return to Hamburg the Wordsworths decided that Ratzeburg at 36 marks for two per week was not for them. The company broke up and went their separate ways for the winter, the Wordsworths to Goslar and productive seclusion, Coleridge (together with Chester) back to Ratzeburg and what we might now describe as a 'three-month total immersion course in German language and culture'.

On October 3, 1798, Coleridge gave the first exuberant account of his situation in a letter to his wife:

> No little fish thrown back again into the water – no Fly unimprisoned from a boy's hand, could more buoyantly enjoy its element, than I this clear & peaceful house, situated in this wholesome Air! with this lovely view of the Town, woods and lake of Ratzeburg from the window, at which I write.[12]

Establishing this safe base from which to explore his new environment was the precondition for a successful immersion, and, for a man of his restless nature, a gain in itself. Living as a paying house-guest in the vicarage, Coleridge followed Thomas Poole's advice: 'Speak nothing but German. Live with Germans. Read in German. Think in German.' This he did, during morning studies, afternoon walks and evening entertainments, very actively, showing a significant degree of initiative and perseverance: For six weeks he followed the pastor – and his children! – around, increasing his vocabulary, but also listening very closely to idiomatic expressions, turns-of-phrase and tone, thus gaining something he later called 'a more home-like acquaintance with the language, than I could have acquired from works of polite literature, or even from polite society'.[13]

By all accounts Coleridge was never short of company: his enquiring mind (as opposed to what he called Wordsworth's unseeking manner[14]) and his scholarly appearance with his impressive greatcoat made him the talk of the town[15] and a favourite with the local gentry and nobility, a fact he clearly relished: 'To be an Englishman is in Germany to be an Angel – they almost worship you.'[16] He soon started to explore his surroundings, dining and smoking[17] almost every evening with his polite and decidedly pro-English hosts,[18] participating in card games and dances, even though he tries hard to play down how much fun he has when reporting to his wife:

> We have deep snow and a hard frost, and I am learning to skate – There are Balls and Concerts every week – & I am pressed by all the ladies to dance. – But if I could, I am not in the dancing Mood.[19]

Apart from outdoor activities such as walking and, once the lake had frozen over, skating,[20] he went on an excursion to the 'old fantastic Town' of Lübeck, whose spires were visible beyond the north end of the lake, and on to Travemünde, the 'Holsteinische Schweiz' and Kiel. There is only a short entry in his notebook referring to the trip but he was certainly impressed by the churches in Lübeck,[21] as he must have been by the magnificent cathedral (the Ratzeburger Dom), which dominates the view from the vicarage but curiously is never mentioned in his writings.[22]

However, we can catch a glimpse of Coleridge's spiritual life and state of mind in Ratzeburg. After all, he lived in a pastor's house, partaking of the spiritual as well as practical life of the Germans, and presumably went to church with his host family. He was invited to celebrate Christmas with them, where he witnessed the very German way of allowing one's emotions to pour out. Coleridge expressed himself 'very much affected' by the intensity of the evening, and was particularly moved by the pastor who stifled 'the sob that was rising inside him'[23] when surrounded by his children.

Eleven years later, the memory of the evening was still so clear in his mind that he included his observations, thinly disguised as one of 'Satyrane's Letters', as a 'literary amusement' in *The Friend*:

> There is a Christmas custom here which pleased and interested me. – The children make little presents to their Parents, and to each other; and the Parents to the Children. For three or four months before Christmas the Girls are all busy, and the Boys save up their pocket-money, to make or purchase these presents. What the present is to be is cautiously kept secret, and the Girls have a world of contrivances to conceal it – such as working when they are out on visits and the others are not with them; getting up in the morning before day-light, &c. Then on the evening before Christmas day one of the Parlours is lighted up by the Children, into which the Parents must not go: a great yew bough[24] is fastened on the Table at a little distance from the wall, a multitude of little Tapers are fastened in the bough, but not so as to burn it till they are nearly burnt out, and coloured paper, &c. hangs and flutters from the twigs. – Under this Bough the Children lay out in great order the presents they mean for their Parents, still concealing in their pockets what they intend for each other. Then the Parents are introduced – and each presents his little Gift – and then bring out the rest one by one from their pockets, and present them with kisses and embraces.[25]

Coleridge's instinctive emotional identification with custom and mood was certainly an understandable reaction, if one considers that, by this time, he was feeling the separation from his own children and home. Indeed we can observe the typical pattern of a person spending a period abroad for the first time in Coleridge's psychological and emotional state of mind: once the exuberance of discovering his new environment had died down, the weather had worsened and the letters from home took longer to arrive, he became increasingly melancholy and lonely, in spite of the best efforts of his hosts. He conveys this sense of gloominess to his wife: 'the lake looks turbid, and the purple of the woods has degenerated into a shabby Dirt-colour' and he suffers from sleeplessness which allows him to observe: 'At Ratzeburgh the Watchman blows a Tune on a horn, every half-hour thro' the Night.'[26]

Meanwhile, the acquisition of the German language continued; as early as one month into the trip he tells his wife of his 'progress in the language', and in November he proudly informs his friend Thomas Poole:

> Dorothy says – 'William works hard, but not very much at the German.' – This is strange – I work at nothing else, from morning to night – / – It is very difficult to combine & arrange the German Sentences – and I make miserable Havoc with the Genders – but yet my progress is more rapid than I could myself have believed.[27]

It is worth pausing here to consider how Coleridge set about learning German, as it represents the second aspect of potential gain from his stay in Ratzeburg. He had been studying German in England since 1796,[28] though, as Lowes points out, it is doubtful whether he had acquired a reading knowledge sufficient to enable him to draw his inspiration for *Osorio* from Schiller's *Der Geisterseher* in the original.[29] The only option to make progress in the language was to go to Germany. Once there he adopted what Willoughby dryly calls 'the most approved direct method',[30] i.e. the building up of a passive vocabulary, though this was only one of many approaches of a rather unsystematic activity. Coleridge observed all utterances of the Germans with a keen ear, but he soon found that the language was spoken with great speed and a very confusing indistinction when the natives were communicating with each other.

Whilst this observation sufficed for Coleridge to later stipulate 'the necessity of revelation or pre-knowledge for a full apprehension of the truth',[31] it certainly did not make his first steps easier. Nor was learning to read handwritten German any easier, as Coleridge found out to his embarrassment on his first trip to Ratzeburg:

> Here a ludicrous circumstance occured – I had never asked Klopstock the Name of the Gentleman, but only took the letter – When I arrived at Ratzeburgh, I consulted the direction – but lo! it was in German characters – which, (the written) I cannot even now read. However there was one word which I made out, & which from it's situation I took for the name – this was Wohlgebohrne. – So I began to enquire where Mr Wohlgebohrne lived – No body knew such a Person – I was a little frightened and shewed my letter – A Grin! – The address was to the Amtmann Braunes – An Amtmann is a sort of perpetual mayor – at once the Mayor & the Justice of the Peace; – and Wohlgebohrne or 'Well born' is one of the common titles of Civility, & means no more than our Esqr.[32]

Immediately upon his return to Hamburg, he began his vocabulary lists, initially noting down odd words and expressions which took his interest because they were close to the English but had a different meaning (as in 'sterben' vs 'to starve') or which he could explain to himself using his knowledge of Latin and Greek. He explored the facility of the German language to create compounds, thus extending his knowledge more rapidly (*Fenster -rahm**,[33] *-scheiben, -laden*) or (*Schlüssel -loch, -bund*). Yet Coleridge must have felt dissatisfied with such an unstructured approach, for he soon abandoned the simple listing of words. The following sections in his notebooks classify expressions of sensation, of sight and motion, etc. Holmes writes:

> These categories suggest the way he approached language poetically, less a taxonomy of objects, but rather a creative power in itself, "re-inventing" the world in terms of human perceptions, rather like the Epic Poem which he was continually urging upon Wordsworth.[34]

While one could argue that this comment is rather over-enthusiastic considering the meagre evidence (the sections barely cover five pages), it is interesting that in ordering his new vocabulary in this way he quickly acquired many of the key words for an inventory of the romantic and gothic world (such as *Kobolt, Nachtgeist, Bestürzung, Traum, Erscheinung, Verwirrung, Mondscheinschwärmer, Schauder und Entsetzen, Blitz und Donner, Lufterscheinung, Zwielicht*).[35] Most of these words stem from Bürger's adaptation of *Macbeth*, but we can also assume that Coleridge was still involved – subconsciously, perhaps – in the composition of *Christabel* (Part 1 written in 1797, Part 2 in 1800 after his return from Germany) with its evocation of 'midnight wood' (li.29), 'moonlight' (li.60), and 'madness' (li.412), which would explain his interest.

He certainly profited from these labours in his translation of Schiller's *Wallenstein* for the publisher Longman in the first half of 1800,[36] for example when finding evocative equivalents to match Thekla's dark-romantic premonitions (*Die Piccolomini*, Dritter Aufzug; Neunter Auftritt: 'böse Ahnung', 'finstrer Geist', 'holder Zauber', 'Abgrund'). In spite of his protestations that he repeatedly finds himself unable to render an adequate translation of Schiller's lines, and in spite of the fact that he takes the liberty to omit lines (which he freely admits), he succeeds in re-creating the mood and flow of this particular passage (*The Piccolomini*, Act II, Scene 7) through his newly acquired linguistic prowess:

> I thank thee for the hint.
> It turns my *sad presentiment* to certainty.
> And it is so! – Not one friend have we here,
> Not one true heart! we're nothing but ourselves!
> O she said rightly – no auspicious signs
> beam on this covenant of our affections.
> This is no theatre, where hope abides,
> The dull thick noise of war alone stirs here.
> And love himself, as he were arm'd in steel,
> Steps forth, and girds him for the strife of death.
> There's a *dark spirit* walking in our house,
> and swiftly will the Destiny close on us.
> It drove me hither from my calm asylum,
> it mocks my Soul with *charming witchery*,
> it lures me forward in a seraph's shape,
> I see it near, I see it nearer floating,
> It draws, it pulls me with a god-like power –
> And lo! the *abyss* – and thither am I moving –
> I have no power within me not to move![37]

At the time, though, he must have felt listing words to be a futile exercise, or maybe he simply got bored with the exercise of writing it all down once he made faster progress, for the project was soon abandoned. Kathleen Coburn wrily comments that 'the system was about as practical as the plan for the "Opus

Maximum", and is indeed reminiscent, or rather a faint foreshadowing, of schemes of that sort to come', and that, consciously or not, the sections 'have the feel and flavour of some of his favourite seventeenth century naturalist or physicist theologians presenting the case for a designed universe'.[38]

Evidently, the system did not serve Coleridge well, because his method of acquiring his data, as Coburn points out, 'was essentially social, not theoretical'.[39] After all, it was through company and conversation that he learned to speak German, very inaccurately maybe, but nevertheless fluently enough.[40]

Another method he used was the reading in German of works he already knew well in English. Apart from reading Bürger's adaptation of *Macbeth*, he wrote down poems and transcribed newspaper articles that interested him. The picture we get is of a writer who actively seeks improvement in the language for his specific purposes. Clearly he had little interest in learning to write in German. Coburn expresses it kindly when she sums up his achievements as a linguist (in our modern sense) in this area:

> The list is inaccurate at times to the point of imcomprehensibility [...] He does not seem to have realized the importance of learning the correct article with each noun – or he did not care about it. [...] Coleridge's interest is clearly in word meanings, not in accidence or syntax. [...] The umlauts present a problem.[41]

But there are positive things to be said. To begin with, it took a lot of determination to study German. Engell reminds us of the difficulty of the task:

> How many of us, after the age of twenty-five, study a difficult language well enough so that we can read and translate its denser prose with considerable ease, a language only one or two acquaintances have even begun to master?[42]

He certainly did the right thing by parting from the Wordsworths, for he must have realized that so long as they kept together they would speak English, with little chance of learning the German language. This left his travelling-companion Chester, but we know little more about him than the occasional 'Chester is well' or 'Chester's love and duty to his mother &c &c &c' from the letters. We can only assume that Chester remained speechless in adoration and dutifully studied German agriculture (possibly helping Coleridge to accumulate material for his long description of the German Bauern for his patron Josiah Wedgwood, sent in February 1799) and did not represent a serious obstacle for Coleridge to speak German with the Germans.

In contrast to the Wordsworths, who never managed to come to grips with it, Coleridge soon found communicating with Germans surprisingly easy. The pastor is 'unpretentious', the children 'chatter away' with him, and 'the little one of all corrects my pronunciation with a pretty pert lisp and self-sufficient tone, while the others laugh with no little joyance.'[43] A happy household then, we can imagine, leaving him a lot of time for reading (the children not being his responsibility), so that after three months he can report to Poole with great pride:

> I now read German as English – that is, without mental translation as I read. I likewise understand all that is said to me, and a good deal of what they say to each other. On very trivial and on metaphysical subjects I can talk tolerably – so, so! – but in that conversation, which is between both, I bungle most ridiculously. I owe it to my industry that I can read old german, and even the old low German, better than most of even the educated natives. It has greatly enlarged my knowledge of the English language.[44]

Here we find another typical experience of the intercultural traveller, the realization that, when abroad, one learns just as much or even more about one's own culture. Holmes writes:

> The study of German language immensely increased his critical attention to English, and his subtle theories of the imagination arose in part from this early intensive period of translating between the two languages.[45][45]

This process is of course one of the most exciting aspects of language learning: very much like being confronted with a puzzle or a narrative account with supernatural elements, one is forced to put the assumptions and approximations for the expression into a mental holding tank and finally come to a conclusion, maybe with the realisation that there does not exist a correspondence in the experience of two people, which again has profound effects on one's understanding of the culture one studies. What can be said is that all his activities, observations and experiences prepared him for his later studies and, as Holmes puts it, that Coleridge found 'something teutonic in his own soul'.[46] This affinity enabled him to study Kant, Lessing, and Schiller, to translate German thought, literature and ideas into English, thus 'smuggling valuables across a closed border',[47] in short, to become a true philologist.

We must now turn to the third aspect of potential gain from Coleridge's stay in Ratzeburg. If it is true that Coleridge was initially more anxious to master German philosophy and learning than seeing the country, the sheer physical beauty of his surroundings soon had its effect on his imagination.[48] We can see a clear development in his appreciation of Ratzeburg over many years, from his first notes and letters to the final and sublime account in *The Friend* and the *Biographia Literaria*. There are two examples of this, but while the one, his imaginative response to the beauty of skating, is frequently cited, it is his pleasure in and identification with his temporary home itself that is often overlooked but equally deserves consideration.

We first come across it in his notebooks: On October 10, 1798 he writes:

> Saw the Town of Ratzeburgh completely beautiful – 20 minutes past 5 – sky the western with light sandy clouds – the East blue – blue over Ratzeburg – / A red light in complete harmony, with the red Town, the fading Woods, & the reeds on the skirts of the Lake, and of the Isthmus, yellow-red, a few boats on the lake with single persons paddling them.[49]

Here, in this short entry, we have the original epiphany with the two key words already in place: complete harmony. If, as most of his biographers assert, Coleridge was in a troubled state of mind when coming to Germany, here we see him at peace, able to perceive and enjoy a moment of balance. He certainly realised the potential for expansion of the image, and its soothing qualities might have moved him to convey the image to his wife four days later. The fact that he calls himself a 'wretched describer' supports the assumption that he has to struggle to hold on to the image whilst enlarging and sharpening it. On 14 January 1798, and three weeks before he left Ratzeburg, he sent to his wife the following description:

> The water to the South of Ratzeburgh is called the little Lake, & the other the large Lake, tho' they are but one piece of water. – This little Lake is very beautiful – the Shores just often enough green & bare to give the proper effect to the magnificent Groves, which mostly fringe them. The views vary almost every ten steps, such & so beautiful are the turnings & windings of the Shore – they unite beauty and magnitude, & can be best expressed by feminine Grandeur! – At the north of the great Lake, and peering over, you see the seven church-towers of Lubec, which is twelve or 14 miles from Ratzeburgh – yet you see them as distinctly as if they were not 3 miles from you. The worse thing is that Ratzeburgh is built entirely of bricks & tiles – & and is therefore all red – a clump of brick dust red – it gives you a strong idea of perfect neatness; but it is not beautiful...
>
> The Sun both rises & sets over the little Lake by us / & both rising and setting presents most lovely spectacles – In October Ratzeburg used at Sunset to appear completely beautiful – A deep red light spread over all, in complete harmony with the red town, the brown red woods, & the yellow red Reeds on the skirts of the Lake & on the Slip of Land. A few boats paddled by single persons used generally to be floating up & down in the rich Light. But when first the ice fell on the Lake, & the whole Lake was frozen, one huge piece of thick transparent Glass, O my God! what sublime scenery I have beheld.[50] – Of a morning I have seen the little (lake) covered with Mist; when the Sun peeped over the Hill, the Mist broke in the middle; and at last stood as the waters of the red Sea are said to have done when the Israelites passed – & between these two walls of Mist the Sunlight burnt upon the Ice in a straight road of golden Fire, all across the lake – intolerably bright, & the walls of the Mist partaking of the light in a multitude of colours. – About a month ago, the vehemence of the wind had shattered the Ice – part of it, quite smattered, was driven toshore & had frozen anew; this was of a deep blue & represented an agitated sea – the water, that ran up between the great islands of Ice, shone of a yellow green (it was at sunset) and all the scattered islands of smooth ice were blood; intensely bright Blood: on some of the largest Islands the Fishermen were pulling out their immense nets thro' the Holes made in the Ice for this purpose, & the Fishermen, the net-poles, & the huge nets made a part of the Glory! O my God! how I wished you to be with me!

While the original notebook entry, almost vision-like, concentrates perception and feeling to a single moment, the description in this letter is a sprawling panorama, but with certain ripples, counter-currents (the colour of the bricks 'is not beautiful'), and unsteady, as it takes us from autumn to winter. Yet it demonstrates his capacity for developing an image of Ratzeburg that would endure, curiously in contrast to his difficulties in responding to a much grander scenery in the Lake District, a year later.

It may have been a desire to re-create his positive mood which prompted him to return to the image in *The Friend* (No18, 21 Dec 1809). In this pastiche of four letters written to Poole and Mrs. Coleridge, the image comes into focus, to all intents and purposes complete, for it is used again – unchanged – eight years later in the *Biographia Literaria* (1817).[51]

Recapturing the moment, restructuring it in a way reminiscent of a painting by Caspar David Friedrich, distilling the essence of the scenery whilst giving it a supernatural sublimity, juxtaposing what is there to see for all and what he perceived in his momentary vision of beauty, he writes:

> The lake of Ratzeburg runs from south to north, about nine miles in length, and varying in breadth from three miles to half a mile. About a mile from the southernmost point it is divided into two, of course very unequal, parts by an island, which being connected by a bridge and a narrow slip of land with the one shore, and by another bridge of <u>immense</u> length with the other shore, form a complete isthmus. On this island the town of Ratzeburg is built. The pastor's house or vicarage, together with the Amptman's, Amptschreiber's, and the church, stands near the summit of a hill, which slopes down to the slip of land and the little bridge, from which, through a <u>superb</u> military gate, you step into the island-town of Ratzeburg. This again is itself a little hill, by ascending and descending which, you arrive at the long bridge, and so to the other shore. The water to the south of the town is called the Little Lake, which however almost engrosses the <u>beauties</u> of the whole: the shores being just often enough green and bare to give the proper effect to the <u>magnificent</u> groves which occupy the greater part of the circumference. From the turnings, windings, and indentations of the shore, the views vary almost every ten steps, and the whole has a sort of <u>majestic</u> beauty, a <u>feminine grandeur</u>. At the north of the Great Lake, and peeping over it, I see the seven church towers of Lubec, at the distance of twelve or thirteen miles, yet as distinctly as if they were not three. The only defect in the view is, that Ratzeburg is built entirely of red bricks, and all the houses roofed with red tiles. To the eye, therefore, it presents a clump of brick-dust red.
>
> Yet this evening, Oct. 10th. twenty minutes past five, I saw the town <u>perfectly beautiful</u>, and the whole softened down into <u>complete keeping</u>, if I may borrow a term from the painters. The sky over Ratzeburg and all the east, was a <u>pure evening blue</u>, while over the west it was covered with light sandy clouds. Hence a <u>deep red light</u> spread over the whole prospect, in <u>undisturbed harmony</u> with the red town, the brown-red woods, and the yellow-red reeds on the skirts of the lake. Two or three boats, with single persons paddling them, floated up and down in the rich light, which not only was itself in harmony with all, but brought all into <u>harmony</u>.[52] [emphases: IC]

This then, we could say, is Coleridge's way to express his gratitude to Ratzeburg. No longer a 'wretched describer', he manages to find the right adjectives, to hold all the elements of the picture together until they transcend into a vision of harmony; acknowledging also that certain mental reservations must be overcome – can be overcome – in order to allow the harmony to exist.[53] All his impressions, his encounters with people who may have pointed out certain elements of the picture, all his efforts to seek understanding have been melted into one; blended with a recreation of the state of mind he was in at the time, his thinking and his feeling, to create an image so clear in its message: 'here I was happy'.

Ratzeburg, Coleridge's first three months in a foreign country, certainly sharpened his faculties, and allowed him to understand the Germans through interaction, whilst balancing the initial culture shock with the exhilaration of a new freedom, in terms of domestic responsibilities, of behaviour, and of observation. The three months constitute a significant part of Coleridge's experience, to be drawn upon again and again in his later life, and enabled him to view the world from a very different standpoint. Coleridge's stay in Ratzeburg has been much underrated, but he clearly benefitted in many ways from his sojourn, so much so that, in spite of the apparently trivial events, it became a contributing factor in his attitude towards Germany.

Whilst the initial realisation of the importance of genius and imagination may have come to the Germans from the English, Coleridge's 'short sojourn in Germany' was, as Willoughby pointed out, 'epoch-making for his intellectual development', because it allowed him a wider perspective, to look at poetry and language, science and philosophy with 'the understanding of the conditions which had brought it forth'.[54] He invested even this experience with 'a message from the other world'.[55]

His was certainly not the 'Grand Tour', but an invaluable if fragmented experience – what he gained was the proverbial broadened horizon, the memories of happiness and insights into a foreign mentality which stayed with him all his life, the penetration of language, literature, and ideas, the understanding of his own moods and emotions, and the experience of communicating with another culture, which were later to help him in Malta and Italy.

But more than that: because they mattered so much to him, the months in Ratzeburg have become part of his writing, and thus have been read by thousands of his fellow countrymen. These writings influenced the British perception of German life (the description of a German Christmas is a case in point), and have helped shape British attitudes towards German culture. And through his study of the language he was enabled to penetrate older and contemporary German literature as well as the latest German romantic philosophy, works which he then publicised in England, admonishing his readers to 'judge of them in some measure with the feelings of Germans',[56] thus again becoming a mediator between the two cultures. Friedrich Schlegel must have had someone like Coleridge in mind when he wrote:

> Vermitteln und Vermitteltwerden ist das ganze höhere Leben des Menschen, und jeder Künstler ist Mittler für alle übrigen.[57]

Notes and References

[1] Many scholars have been encouraged by Lowes' suggestion that Coleridge's time in Germany would 'repay investigation' – see John Livingston Lowes, *The Road to Xanadu* (London, 1927, repr. 1955; <*cited as*: LOWES>), p.497n. Naturally they tend to concentrate on the development of Coleridge's ideas in Göttingen, rather than on the preceding, comparatively mundane and uneventful quarter-year in Ratzeburg. However, as a teacher professionally engaged in preparing young Britons for a period in Germany, I feel that a closer look at precisely this early encounter with Germany is warranted. I am not trying to unearth any new items overlooked by previous Coleridge scholars, but to offer a new angle from which to interpret this period and its effect on his later work.

[2] L.A. Willoughby, 'Coleridge as a Philologist', *Modern Language Review* XXXI (1936) <*cited as*: WILLOUGHBY>, p.176.

[3] Basil Willey, *Samuel Taylor Coleridge* (London, 1972), p.74. He does seem to contradict himself, though, for in the same paragraph he concedes: 'Still, it certainly was important to him to learn German, and this he did, probably with much greater speed and effectiveness in Germany than he could have done anywhere else.'

[4] Richard Holmes, *Coleridge: Early Visions* (London ,1989; *cited as*: HOLMES>), Chap.9.

[5] HOLMES, p.205.

[6] LOWES, p.221.

[7] HOLMES, p.199.

[8] See Marilyn Butler, *Romantics, Rebels and Reactionaries* (Oxford, 1981), p.86.

[9] Earl Leslie Grigg, *Collected Letters of Samuel Taylor Coleridge*, vol.1: *1785-1800* (Oxford, 1956; <*cited as*: LETTERS>), p.448.

[10] Kathleen Coburn (ed.), *The Notebooks of Samuel Taylor Coleridge*, vol.1, *1794-1804 (Text),* (London, 1957; <*cited as*: COBURN (Text)>), item 343.

[11] In his notebook he recorded: 'Agreed with a Pastor for boarding and lodging for myself and Chester.' (COBURN (Text), item 344).

[12] LETTERS, p.420. Not much has changed in Ratzeburg: The town, still a resort if less fashionable, impresses with its quiet serenity, and continues its dreamlike existence in spite of unification and the opening of the border only ten miles to the east. It should be noted that Coleridge did not live in Ratzeburg proper, but on a hill, the St. Georgsberg, to the west of the lake and the island. One ascends a steep cobbled street up the hill, with the vicarage (the Pastorat, a large traditional farmhouse, replaced in 1968) to the left and the old church (St. Georg auf dem Berge, one of the oldest brick buildings in northern Germany) to the right. The view from the vicarage, providing a breathtaking panorama spanning from the Ratzeburger See, the island with the town and the Cathedral, and the Küchensee (the 'little lake'), is not the same

today because of the trees planted since Coleridge's days, but we get a fair impression from a standpoint east of the church, in the cemetery.

[13] J. Shawcross (ed), *"Biographia Literaria" by Samuel Taylor Coleridge*, vol. I (Oxford, 1907; <*cited as*: SHAWCROSS>), p.138.

[14] LETTERS, p.459.

[15] See Lawrence Hanson, *The Life of Samuel Taylor Coleridge: The Early Years* (London, 1938), p.327: 'Coleridge, it is evident, had not failed to spread – and not improbably overstate – his prowess in Ratzeburg society.'

[16] LETTERS, p.435. If his account in a letter to his wife of October 20th, 1798, is anything to go by, he occasionally surprised his hosts with German versions of his poems: 'There is a very beautiful little Woman, less I think than you – a Countess Kilmansig [Kilmannsegg] – her father is our Lord Howe's cousin. ... I have quite won her heart by a German poem which I wrote ... It has excited no small wonder here for its purity and harmony (LETTERS, p.429).

[17] The German practice of smoking at all times of the day certainly baffled Coleridge. On several occasions he remarks on the social custom and on the beneficial effect it has on his well-being: 'Indeed, a pipe at Breakfast is a great addition to the comforts of Life: I shall smoke at no other time in England. Here I smoke four times a day – 1 at breakfast, 1 half an hour before dinner, 1 in the afternoon at Tea, and one just before bedtime.' (LETTERS, p.462). The pastor supplies him with a veritable bonmot when he first expresses his surprise at him smoking first thing in the morning: "O – Herr Gott! quoth he – it is delightful – it invigorates the frame, & it cleans out the moutt so !" (LETTERS, p.463).

[18] On 8 November 1798 he writes to his wife: "I have now dined at all the Gentlemen's & Noblemen's Houses within two or three miles of Ratzeburgh." (LETTERS, p.439). On November 17 he writes to William Wordsworth: 'If the manners at Goslar resemble those at Ratzeburgh, it is almost necessary to be able to bear smoke. ... Here, when my friends come to see me, the candle nearly goes out, the air is so thick.' (LETTERS, p. 441).

[19] LETTERS, p.449. To Thomas Poole (4 January 1799) he writes: 'I am pestered every ball to dance, which very modestly I refuse', – only to launch into a description of the sensual attraction of the dance he so obviously enjoys attending: 'They dance a most infamous dance called the Waltzen – There are perhaps 20 couple – the Man and his Partner embrace each other, arms round waists, & knees almost touching, & then whirl round and round, the whole 20 couple, 40 times round at least, to lascivious music.' (LETTERS, p.458).

[20] An experience immortalized in many letters. Richard Holmes demonstrates in *Early Visions* (p.212) how Coleridge's description of the 'melancholy undulating sound from the Skate' and the 'tinkle' in the air inspired Wordsworth's passage on Cumberland skating in *The Prelude*, 1805, Bk 1, lines 467-72.

[21] 'I would, had it been possible, have loitered a week in those churches; & found incessant amusement. Every picture, every legend cut out in gilded wood-work, was a history of the manners & feelings of the ages, in which such works were admired and executed.' (LETTERS, p.461).

[22] Lothar Roessler, a local historian, wrily observes that to Coleridge the foreigner the sheer endless variety of wines served at a dinner party in Kulpin (about 3 miles from Ratzeburg) was of much greater import than the magnificence of the architecture of the cathedral (built between 1165 and 1220). See *Lauenburgische Heimat*, Heft 43, Dec. 1963, p.43.

[23] LETTERS, p.485. Walking around the cemetery of St Georg, one can see the gravestone of Pastor Unruh's wife. She had died three years earlier, in 1795, aged 32. Small wonder, then, that the pastor was overwhelmed by his emotions under the Christmas tree!

[24] The christmas tree was a new introduction to the German custom at this time!

[25] 'Christmas within Doors, in the North of Germany', in *The Friend*, No.19, Dec. 28, 1809. see *The Collected Works of Samuel Taylor Coleridge, The Friend*, Vol.II, ed. by Barbara E. Rooke (Princeton 1969), p.256.

[26] LETTERS, p.435/438. There is little evidence that Coleridge used Laudanum during his time in Ratzeburg. Apart from a stye in early December, for which he took 'physic', he seems to have been relatively healthy. see Alethea Hayter, *Opium and the Romantic Imagination* (London, 1969), p.191.

[27] LETTERS, p.445.

[28] F.W. Stokoe, *German Influence in the English Romantic Period* (Cambridge, 1926; *cited as*: STOKOE>), p.91.

[29] LOWES, p.221/222.

[30] WILLOUGHBY, p.176.

[31] WILLOUGHBY, p.176, fn4.

[32] LETTERS, p.448.

[33] It should be *Fensterrahmen*.

[34] HOLMES, p.218n.

[35] COBURN (Text), item 354.

[36] Although a financial disaster at the time, and a task that Coleridge found made him unfit 'for anything but sleeping or immediate society', its impact has long been recognised: 'Coleridge contributed chiefly to the understanding of German literature in England by his translation, in many respects excellent, of Schiller's *Piccolomini* and *Wallensteins Tod*.' (STOKOE, p.143).

[37] *Friedrich Schiller, Wallenstein*, translated by Samuel Taylor Coleridge (Longman, 1800), p.95 (emphases: IC).

[38] Kathleen Coburn (ed.), *The Notebooks of Samuel Taylor Coleridge*, Vol.1, *1794-1804, (Notes),* (London, 1957; *cited as*: COBURN (Notes)>), on item 354.

[39] *ibid.*

[40] Richard Holmes cites Clement Carlyon, one of Coleridge's English friends at Göttingen: 'There was something inexpressibly comic in the manner in which he dashed on, with fluent diction but the very worst German accent imaginable.' (HOLMES, p.236).

[41] COBURN (Notes), on item 354.

[42] James Engell, 'Coleridge and German Idealism: First Postulates, First Causes', in Richard Gravil and Molly Lefebure (eds.), *The Coleridge Connection* (London, 1990), p.155.

[43] LETTERS, p.429.

[44] LETTERS, p.454.

[45] HOLMES, p.218.

[46] HOLMES, p.221.

[47] HOLMES, p.232n. For an introduction to Coleridge's lifelong involvement with German literature see Rosemary Ashton, *The German Idea* (Cambridge, 1980, repr. 1994) chap.1. For his interest in German idealism, see James Engell, 'Coleridge and German Idealism: First Postulates, First Causes', cited above, note 42.

[48] There is a certain indication for this in the *Biographia Literaria.* Coleridge writes with hindsight that 'a more thorough revolution in my philosophical principles, and a deeper insight

into my heart, were still wanting' (SHAWCROSS, p.137), that the trip had great importance to his intellectual activity and, 'of course, to my moral happiness'. Clearly this means that Coleridge now regards his experience as more than just a vehicle for learning the language, but as a vital aspect of his maturing as a poet.

[49] COBURN (Text), item 357.

[50] see *The Friend*, No.19, 28 Dec. 1809, for a revised version of the preceding lines, entitled 'Christmas out of Doors'.

[51] Admittedly, the 'Satyrane's Letters' only found their way into the *Biographia Literaria* because the second volume was thought by his publisher to be too short. But, as Engell and Bate point out in their introduction to the BL (p.lxi): 'The 'Letters' were by no means an unfortunate choice. They certainly fitted in with the autobiographical character of the book, especially the first few chapters. Though their intellectual significance is limited, they are attractive in an anecdotal way, especially to the modern reader, who takes Coleridge's greatness for granted and who is naturally interested in the experiences of such a man on a trip that proved an important turning-point in his life.'

[52] James Engell and W. Jackson Bate (eds), *The Collected Works of Samuel Taylor Coleridge, Biographia Literaria: or Biographical Sketches of my Literary Life and Opinions*, vol. II (Princeton, 1983), p 192-3.

[53] One of the first moments of realisation for the intercultural sojourner that he is indeed in a foreign place, and often the cause of culture shock, is the difference in architectural practice. While to Coleridge's aesthetic norms the red bricks and the red tiles are 'not beautiful', to me who grew up in this part of Germany these colours are an integral part of what constitutes 'Heimat' and belonging, and are therefore very beautiful indeed. It speaks for Coleridge that he is able to make that conceptual breakthrough to perceive that this can be so. The roofs of the buildings and the cathedral still retain their bright red, but might have mellowed a bit over the years. In fact, what Coleridge saw was a new town: the Danes had laid siege to Ratzeburg, which was a stronghold of the Welfen in the 17th century, and nearly destroyed it without being able to take it. Rebuilding (using the offending type of brick and tiles) had begun in 1695, but was still in progress in 1790.

[54] WILLOUGHBY, p.180.

[55] WILLOUGHBY, p.201.

[56] Preface to *Wallenstein*, (London, 1800).

[57] Friedrich Schlegel, 'Athenäum Fragment, No.44, 1798-1800', *Kritische Ausgabe*, Bd.II, p.260.

William Poel's *Wallenstein*-Moment

JOYCE CRICK

Selbst Gebildetes ist Stoff nur dem bildenden Geist.
(*Votivtafeln*, Nr.19)

Texts are less fixed than the printed page suggests. They are subject to multiple transformations by readers; more radically by translators; in the case of drama most radically of all by directors and actors – from print to embodiment. And all in times and in places. Sometimes with drama, the current flows in the opposite direction: from the malleable script to the fixities of the edition, which recognises fluidity only in terms of recorded variants. This was the route taken by *Hamlet*, for example, from the stage of the Globe through the hit-or-miss contemporary records of the Quartos to the magisterial posthumous Folio; thence through the history of Shakespearean scholarship and round again to the reproductions of the Folio and the Quartos – but all the time side by side, though not always in parallel – with performances, interpretations, re-writes for the stage.

When Schiller was drawing to the end of the long composition of *Wallenstein*, it was the stage which claimed it first. Goethe in Weimar and Iffland in Berlin both directed the three dramas in a form whose structure Schiller had not yet finalised and whose metrics he had not yet revised. *Wallensteins Tod* was disproportionately short; *Die Piccolomini* excessively long, though it did bear that title meaningfully, ending as it did with Max and Octavio's farewell. (In his definitive printed version, of course, Schiller made this the end of Act II of a longer *Wallensteins Tod*, establishing a better balance between the two main dramas, but at the expense of the unity of *Die Piccolomini*.) It was this unrevised version, with its own distinctive variants, which travelled to England ahead of Cotta's printing to receive further transformation in Coleridge's translation and (provisional) fixity under Longman's imprint.[1] But in the endless chain of transformations, this too was changed, at first to match Schiller's fixture, by Henry G. Bohn for his Standard Library edition of 1846. He added James (not 'Janus', as Bohn first printed it) Churchill's translation of *Wallensteins Lager*, which Coleridge had not translated, and made the necessary cuts and additions by G. F. Richardson and himself to Coleridge's text so that this patchwork rendered Schiller's printed version.[2] But that in turn has been subsequently translated by fresh hands, most notably by Frank Lamport for Penguin (Harmondsworth 1979), which was in its turn used as the basic script (not without its own substantial transformations) of Tim Albery's production in the winter of 1993/94 for the Royal Shakespeare Company at the Pit theatre in the Barbican.[3]

This article is a study of one such set of multiple transformations: from a text itself not finalised through a translation by no means transparent, but with its own poetic and historical colorations, to one production which was distinctive to the point of idiosyncracy.

It was undertaken by the theatre reformer William Poel (1852-1934), who staged the plays on two occasions. The first, the British première, was put on, according to the programme[4] as 'Schillers's tragedy, the "Death of Wallenstein" and Scenes from "The Piccolomini" ' on 22 June 1900, a hundred years after its first publication, with Lillah McCarthy as Countess Tertzky and Percy Anstey as Wallenstein, in the Lecture theatre of the University of London, Burlington Gardens.[5] Poel staged them for a second time, much later, on 11 August 1911, with a different cast, including Frank Cellier as Wallenstein and Poel himself as Wrangel, at the New Theatre, Oxford (now the Apollo theatre), as a contribution to the University Extension Delegacy's Summer Meeting. For purposes of registration with the Lord Chamberlain he gave his adaptation the title "Life in the Camp",[6] even though he did not use the *Lager*. These locations alone suggest that the performances might perhaps be appropriately understood within a much wider context of reform, not only theatrical, but social and educational as well.

We have quite substantial remains of them – and 'remains' is the appropriate word for such records of living performance: programmes with full programme notes by Poel; reviews from *The Times* of 25.6.1900 for the London performance; from the *Oxford Chronicle* of 18.8.1911 and the *Oxford Times* of 26.8.1911 for the Oxford performance – and, importantly, from someone who had himself edited an edition of the *Wallenstein*[7] plays, Professor Karl Breul of Cambridge, an account of the Summer Meeting and the performance for the *Magdeburger Zeitung*.[8] Above all, there is the producer's working prompt-book, as used for the 1900 performance and modified for 1911. Poel used Bell's 1895 paperback editions[9] of Coleridge's translations as emended by Bohn for his Standard Library. Their pages are pasted into a sturdy account book and are marked up with cuts, re-arrangements and condensations, cues, notes for movement, grouping, exits and entrances, intervals etc. The prompt-book also has an additional sheet pasted in with a rough sketch of the stage arrangements for Oxford – a simple permanent set on two levels, the upper stage smaller, with the possibility of curtaining it off. Cuts, textual alterations and stress-marks on key words made on the printed text are in pencil, together with a few staging notes. The staging notes are mainly on the cropped account-book leaves, in black ink (dating from 1900) and in red (as revised for 1911).[10] The directions are not entirely transparent; some are contradictory, and there are some discrepancies between the prompt-book and the programmes, and between the prompt-book and the accounts of the performances. But taken together, the sources all suggest a strong interpretation on Poel's part, one which appears to have grown stronger with time. For he did not leave *Wallenstein*. In 1934, the last year of his life, aged 82, he re-drafted a version, more a collage for voices than a drama, and had it printed privately, hoping to direct it for the Coleridge centenary. But he died before he could execute it. The cover-title he gave it, *Schiller on War*,[11] provides the key to his interpretation.

I shall try to show that Poel's reading of *Wallenstein* was coloured in a number of ways, and that his specifically dramaturgical decisions in adapting the dramas for a one night stand are all of a piece with this reading. First, it is coloured theatrically, in that he read Schiller with a Shakespearean's eyes. Secondly, culturally, for to Poel the stage was a great instrument of education – this is congenial Schillerian ground, of course. And thirdly, as a convinced pacifist, he read these plays, if not as anti-war dramas – he was too aware of the imaginative complexity of drama for that – then certainly as explorations of the effects and impact of 'the vortex of militarism',[12] as he called it. The three moments of his concern with Wallenstein all took place under the shadow of war. The first time, it was the Boer War – Mafeking had just been relieved when the Ministry of Works gave permission for him to use University premises for his first *Wallenstein*. 1911, the year of Agadir, came at the end of the decade that cast such a threatening countenance upon our continent, as *Death in Venice* reminds us. The urgency of international tensions were such that they left their mark on the Oxford Extra-Mural Summer Meeting in more ways than a pacifist's *Wallenstein*, and certainly provide its political context. 1934 is a date which speaks for itself. He intended a platform performance (possibly, he wondered, with Charles Laughton as Wallenstein),[13] similar to those he had recently done of *Coriolanus* (1931) and Fletcher's *Bonduca* (1929). He had also put together a set of dramatic readings from Cicero, Macaulay, Shakespeare and George Chapman's *Caesar and Pompey* under the title *Julius Caesar the Dictator* (1930). *Bonduca* he described as 'a play illustrating the psychology of war',[14] the Caesar readings as ' "reasons // Why and wherefore Caesar was dangerous . . ." ',[15] Coriolanus he saw as a young man destroyed by his mother, '. . . who has taught him to look upon war as the sole aim and end of his existence . . . No! Volumnia is not the tragic queen of the play; she has educated her "boy" to his ruin, and is responsible for his death.'[16] True, 1934 was the Coleridge centenary year, but the last projected *Wallenstein* was also part of a Series on War. It was intended, his wife recalled, 'on behalf of the Peace Movement, "showing", as he said, "a glimpse of the futile misery of war." '[17]

But I am beginning at the end. Who was he? Poel's is a famous name in theatrical history. He was the pioneer, idealistic, obsessive, quixotic, of a revived 'Elizabethan' mode of performance of Shakespeare's plays in the early years of the present century. He was a well-connected, scholarly autodidact. His father was Professor of Engineering at University College London, a gifted musician, moving in pre-Raphaelite circles.[18] He began as an actor and moved into production by way of recitals and theatre management. For a short time he managed Emma Cons' respectable reformed Music Hall, the Old Vic. At first he gave solo recitals and rehearsed amateur reading circles, starting with *The Merchant of Venice* with the Shakespeare Reading Society in the English Department at UCL.[19] He operated on a shoe string, experimentally on the fringes of 'real' theatre, with mixed casts of professional beginners and talented amateurs, but with the support of other theatre reformers such as Shaw, Granville-Barker (who played Richard II for Poel in 1899) and C.E. Montague,[20] and importantly, of Shakespeare scholars such as E.K. Chambers, F.J. Furnivall, and the influential literary great and the good, such as Edmund Gosse – to the extent that in 1894 he was able to found the Elizabethan Stage Society and launch a series of performances of plays by Shakespeare and his contemporaries, well-researched and rehearsed – but for rarely more than single performances and those rarely in real theatres.

He waged war on the prevailing commercial theatre and above all on the monumental 'historicist' mode of producing Shakespeare – the Lyceum style of Henry Irving and later of Beerbohm Tree – which claimed period accuracy down to the last Roman toga or Illyrian cross-garter, Great Hall in Hampton Court or rampart in Elsinore, but only succeeded in inflating the stage spectacle and slowing down the action. The equivalent in Germany, of course, was the famous Meiningen style. Indeed, the Meininger made a successful visit to London in the summer of 1881, impressing Poel with their *Julius Caesar*.[21] They also brought *Wallensteins Lager* as part of their repertory, though it is uncertain whether Poel saw it.[22] What is certain, however, is that there was much in it he would not have approved of. For his answer to the kind of historicism which repainted the *Lager* backcloth with snow when the Duke discovered that the action had taken place in winter (Osborne, p.160), was to affirm a different kind of historical authenticity: a replay of the conditions and style of performance that prevailed in Shakespeare's own theatre. Or at least what the scholarship of his time – and his own confident readings – could authenticate. There are of course historical relativities at work here which his single-minded reformist idealism was simply not aware of, though a dry remark of William Archer's on the occasion of the Elizabethan Stage Society's first *Twelfth Night* in 1895 should give us pause: 'Staged (more or less) after the manner of the sixteenth century and acted after the manner of the Nineteenth Century Amateur'.[23]

Poel's other enemy was the false fixity of the posthumous printed edition, the First Folio of 1623 and its successors, with their divisions into acts and scenes, imposed, he claimed, by bookish editors with a neo-classical model in mind; with their locations and stage-directions carefully deduced from the text, all spurious hindrances, he argued, to the original movement of the action. The Quartos were preferable to the Folio as acting texts just because they were closer to the plays as originally performed. On the Elizabethan public stage, the action was rapid and continuous, fluently intertwining double plots, rarely interrupted, even for an interval; scenery and stated location, even stated time of day, were minimal, for the poetic language itself was richly expository of just this information.[24] Stage décor was anathema to Poel. Speech was paramount. The spectators were physically close to the action. Spectacle resided in splendour of dress, not in the scenery. Poel insisted on Elizabethan dress throughout. In 1881, the very year of the Meiningers' visit, cutting through two centuries of theatrical tradition, he put on his first extended experiment, a performance of the 1st Quarto *Hamlet*, on a plain curtained platform, played continuously. The contrast between the splendours of ducal Drury Lane and the austerity of St.George's Hall, Langham Place, could not have been greater. His ideal was to abandon the proscenium with drop-curtain, and revive the apron stage. With this in mind, he developed a fluid and economic production style suited to platform performance, and insisted on rapid and pointed elocution. He had a painter's eye for stage grouping, and only spent money on costumes. Necessity made him ingenious in finding performing spaces: the grand staircase of Imperial College for Euripides' *Alcestis* (1911), the Conservatory at Regent's Park for Kalidasa's *Sakuntala* (1899, music by Arnold Dolmetsch, interval choruses in the original Sanskrit).

For he also extended the repertory. He revived the lost Elizabethans – and they included Marlowe's *Edward II* and *Doctor Faustus* at this time. His one great public success was *Everyman* (1901), but he left it to Ben Greet in America and Reinhardt in Europe to exploit it. Reinhardt (Speaight, p.165) was among the first audiences at the Charterhouse. It is in this early extension of the repertory in the Shakespearean manner that we may place Poel's first *Wallenstein*.

Now, Schiller himself was quite consciously drawing on both classical and Shakespearean models in writing the dramas,[25] and it is the – loosely – Shakespearean aspects that Poel takes up and develops. To start with, the text used (Coleridge as adapted by Bohn to Schiller's printed version) already pointed him in a Shakespearean direction. I have written at length elsewhere[26] about the nature of Coleridge's translation-language in these plays, so it is enough now to say that there is a strong Shakespearean input into their diction, and, cumulatively, into the more individualised – i.e. Shakespearean rather than neo-classical – mode of characterisation (Countess Tertzky is more shrewish, Gordon more fuddy-duddy, Wallenstein more noble, even tenderer, than in Schiller). In addition, Coleridge's 'Preface of the Translator' to *The Death of Wallenstein* makes the comparison with Shakespeare, though with the histories, not the tragedies as their point of reference.[27]

Poel extends this linguistic shakespeareanising radically to structure. He does not centre the interest on the single hero, Wallenstein, but distributes it also to Max and Thekla. Working for the open stage, he boldly overrides act and scene divisions. He did divide into three Acts for Oxford, but rather as a concession to the contemporary playgoer.[28] He always insisted that the Elizabethan stage operated with at most one interval, after the climax of the drama, so he gave his 1900 production only one, though the deliberate effect then was to treat *The Piccolomini* largely as a prelude to *The Death of Wallenstein.* As for Schiller's neo-classical unit of the 'Auftritt', Poel obliterates it entirely, making way to continuous action in a continuous location, which is identified by stage-space not by change of scenery – exactly as Poel understood Elizabethan drama to function. 'Kein Zwischenvorhang', noted Breul [p.7]. Poel used schoolboys, borrowed from Christ's Hospital, to move minimal stage furniture and props: a settle for interiors, a table for generals to sign papers. In Oxford, he was able to divide his stage space by three strong steps across the width of the stage, giving him two playing areas,[29] not unlike the Elizabethan inner stage and apron in function. This not only enabled him to indicate change of place economically, but to obtain very rapid movement from scene to scene: as one scene was ending on one level, the next was beginning on the other. One recurring instruction in the prompt-book indicates how great a store Poel set by fluency of action: the *offstage* line-up of actors *about* to enter, with their point of entry, is noted throughout – LL and UL, LR and UR. (Whether this actually produced the desired result of speed in his first run, however, may be doubtful: the review in *The Times* of 25.6.1900 complained, at condescending length, of tedium.)

Two instances will indicate what I mean. First a simple one. Poel begins his Act III for Oxford with the beginning of Schiller's *Wallensteins Tod* Act IV: with Butler's arrival at the Burgomaster's house in Eger, confirming the news to Gordon of Wallenstein's defection. Whereupon Schiller slows the action as Gordon meditates on the great fall and recalls the strange incident of the boy Wallenstein's fall from the window and rapid rise to 'Graf und Fürst und Herzog und Diktator'. This is followed by the third 'Auftritt', where Wallenstein enters, sounding out the Burgomaster of Eger. The pace accelerates as the fourth and fifth 'Auftritte' bring in Terzky with the apparently good news of a Swedish victory, followed promptly by Illo with the bad news that it was in fact the defeat of Max and his Pappenheimers. Poel's procedure with the pacing of this material is characteristic: Butler and Gordon enter Upper Right; he cuts their exchange ruthlessly to about thirty lines to produce a skeletal action; essential information between the two is exchanged; there is space for reaction, but not for rumination or narrative; Gordon's account of Wallenstein the strange boy and reflections on his rise and fall are lost. With Butler's last lines, 'No more. He comes', promptly, immediately, but in a different location, Lower Right, in come Wallenstein and the Burgomaster. Their scene too is heavily cut, lacking Wallenstein's strange tale of the two moons, and makes rapid way for Tertzky and then Illo. My point for the moment – though, as we shall see, it has further implications – is that operating with two acting spaces encourages the effect of fluency. Nowadays we take this for granted. But Poel was the pioneer.

Poel's 1911 treatment of the sequence of 'Auftritte' in Act I of *The Death of Wallenstein* is also illuminating (Prompt-book pp.152-78). As Schiller orchestrates them, they start slowly with the destiny-laden astrological scene, and together constitute an accelerando movement, intermittently halted by Wallenstein's rallentando hesitations, towards his irrevocable commitment to the Swedes. In the second scene, Tertzky brings the bad news of Sesin's capture; in the third Illo and Tertzky continue to urge Wallenstein to act, producing the generals' signatures to strengthen their case, while Wallenstein still prevaricates. With Wrangel at the door, they leave Wallenstein to his great suspensive monologue: 'Wär's möglich . . .' (scene iv); there follows Wallenstein's exploratory meeting with Wrangel (scene v); on Wrangel's departure, the pace increases as Illo and Tertzky reenter to find out how it has gone (scene vi); as Wallenstein still temporises, in comes the Countess (scene vii) with her extended tirades of calculated scorn which finally push him into a decision. Now, as Poel treats this sequence, cutting – and his cuts are even more ruthless here – and arranging his actors' moves, his main concern appears to be to keep the line of action, i.e. the continued pressure on Wallenstein, building up without interruption – without, that is, Schiller's crucial retardations. The movement is headlong. It entails the drastic steps of reducing the astrological scene with Seni to its last lines just to launch the action; more, of reducing Wallenstein's great monologue to a mere seventeen lines, thus moving virtually straight on from Illo and Terzky's impatient persuasions to the meeting with Wrangel, which, though heavily cut, replaces the monologue as the pivot. Poel played this role himself in Oxford – very vividly, according to *The Oxford Chronicle*'s reviewer.[30]

Poel also reduces the scope of the Countess's rhetoric considerably: she simply completes the action, but without any delaying verbal ado. As for the movements, Poel choreographs them in such a way that Illo and Terzky usher in Wrangel and then 'retire centre' (Prompt-book pp.160, 168) i.e. they remain on stage throughout the scene with Wrangel, to the audience a subliminal presence, silently embodying the pressure on Wallenstein to act, ready to come forward with their eager questioning the moment Wrangel leaves. All this time, the Countess is instructed to wait Right Lower in the wings, ready to sweep in rapidly from a different level and a different location. The will to fluent and continuous action seems very successful here, but it also has the effect of transforming the rhythm and tempo of the sequence, and of considerably cutting Wallenstein down to size. As the astrological theme is played down, cumulatively including the omissions of the three moons and the dreaming boy, we lose sight of Wallenstein as Man of Destiny. With the truncation of the monologue poised on the brink of deed, Wallenstein as Man of Action is also reduced. Changes in production style have their effect on interpretation, and in this case the effect is appropriate to Poel's concern with the 'vortex of militarism' – the self-propelling, all-consuming momentum of the action, rather than with the Great Man as Agent.

One last point before I leave the Shakespearean mode. Schiller is very good at resounding curtain lines. But resounding curtain lines require a curtain, which Poel's Elizabethan zeal rejected. At Oxford he appears not to have used the proscenium curtain, but to have made effective use of curtains between his two stage levels. He began with an open empty stage, the traditional 'trois coups' and the military signals of drum and bugle, opening, incidentally, not with the arrivals of the generals, but with Questenberg (Schiller's *Piccolomini* I, iii), horrified at the seditious talk he has already heard, exclaiming to Octavio as they walk on: 'What have I not been forc'd to hear, Octavio!' (Prompt-book p.54). But the endings on occasion seem to have been fudged. Octavio's line: 'Is it then true? I have a son no longer?', for example. This the last line of his long and painful farewell to Max; it ends Act II of *Wallensteins Tod*; indeed, it once actually ended – most appropriately – the original *Piccolomini*. It is a significant punctuation point. But Poel overrides it in the interest of rapid scene change on an open stage. For 1900, he cut their stage embrace and marked his own direction: 'Exit Max and Octavio. Boys remove furniture R. Then enter Thekla and Countess.' He modified it for the Oxford performance only insofar as he had the curtains dividing the two stage levels part for the women to enter and play on the Upper Stage. Again, this produces rapid continuity, and even the illusion of simultanaeity.[31]

But whether the model is Shakespearean or classical, the primary problem for any director in cutting down three dramas to one is just that: meaningful cutting. These plays are big, with a complex historical 'Vorgeschichte' requiring exposition, doubly unfamiliar to an English audience, a host of minor characters, mass scenes, and a substantial interwoven subplot. What to remove? What to retain? How to dispose the emphasis when the passages, scenes and figures which *are* retained carry all the more interpretive weight on account of what has been excised? Is it a drama of ambition? Of Fate? A tragedy? Of the great Flaw? Of the Great Fall? An historical drama? How to read the central enigma of Wallenstein himself?

Some of Poel's provisional answers are beginning to emerge.

Poel's choices in what he keeps and what he rejects are sometimes both radical and puzzling, and do not seem to be merely dramaturgical. Some have to do with resources: the mass banqueting scenes and generals' oath are cut, which results in loss of spectacle and power; contrariwise, the Countess's role, though truncated, is given full value: in 1900 he had his best actress, Lillah McCarthy, playing her. Some seem simply to have to do with the rough-and-ready accidents of performance. The 1900 programme indicates a much reduced cast list for *The Piccolomini* (but restored for 1911): no Duchess (and so no account of her humiliation at court). This, in conjunction with the strategic decision to reduce the generals to Terzky, Illo and Butler (and so no concerted defiance of Questenberg) would seem a great gap in exposition; no Seni (and so, presumably, no servants' scene); no Wrangel (and so no pivotal decision seen to be made); no Burgomaster. The prompt-book is much fuller in text: the generals remain reduced in number, but the Duchess, Wrangel and the Burgomaster are present; so is Seni, though the role is much cut. The cast list for 1900 in the prompt-book actually includes the names of the players (proposed? rehearsed? dropped?) for these missing roles,[32] so one is left concluding that decisions to reduce were made on the hoof at rehearsal. Weak performances? Under-rehearsed? Too long? Poel's 'Remarks' in the programme rationalise the reduced *Piccolomini* as exposition of material unfamiliar to an English audience: 'a selection of scenes from *The Piccolomini* has been added by way of introduction.' The weight of the performance lay on the *Death of Wallenstein*.

But other choices are interpretive, and here Poel's 1900 'Remarks', reprinted in the much fuller programme notes for the 1911 performance, do indicate how he read the dramas and may help to account for some of his reshaping, particularly in foregrounding Max and Thekla. They draw attention to Schiller's 'conceptions of the idealising functions of the dramatic art . . . Thus everything in these plays is idealised . . . and above all, the character of Wallenstein himself.' All the figures, even the minor ones, are 'raised in the moral scale'.

> More potently than the humours of the camp, the sweet story of Max and Thekla, which survives treason and death itself, is designed to exemplify the principle on which Schiller dwells in the concluding lines of his Prologue. According to his conception of the poetic drama, its function is to bid the sombre figure of Truth assume, were it only for a while, the serener aspect of Art.

And he goes on to print most of Schiller's Prologue of 1799 (which, incidentally, resonates very powerfully in 1900, and even in 1999: 'Darkly the century moveth towards its end etc . . .'). This is recognisably standard Schiller, whose utopia of art Poel shared, simply and without the unease of 1999. Apart from one item, that is: the idealising of Wallenstein himself. Poel's statement simplifies what has always been a problem in *Wallenstein*-interpretation, not least for Schiller himself. It scarcely accords with Schiller's early judgement 'Er hat nichts Edles', and it delegates to Wallenstein's character what Schiller, explaining retrospectively, applied rather to the flight of his thought.[33] Poel might be impicitly contrasting the poetic figure with the historical Wallenstein; his view might owe something to Coleridge's filter: the translated Wallenstein is more unambiguously noble than Schiller's. But whether as cause or effect, this reading might help to account for the overall reduction, already noted, of Wallenstein's role, especially as manipulator and power-monger: one monologue is reduced, the other, Wallenstein in armour, entirely removed; we do not see him backed by his generals defying Questenberg (Breul particularly regretted this – p.7); more subtly, his manipulative attempt to persuade Max to stay, part bullying, part appealing, is drastically cut. The mystery and the charisma too are mitigated by the reduction of Seni's role, the removal of the strange tales of moon and fall, and of Gordon's reflections on Wallenstein's rise.

The will of the Great Leader, then, is played down in Poel's text, though his actor still found something there to build on: in reviewing Frank Cellier's performance, *The Oxford Times* wrote of his 'Napoleonic glamour', and 'a kind of inner force and magnetism'. For the theatre treats text as pretext for embodiment, and the faded marks remaining on Poel's pages may be a more enigmatic testament to what really went on on the stage of the New Theatre than that of the witnesses who were there in the audience. Similarly, if we are to judge from Poel's truncated text alone, Fate too, as written in the stars, does not seem to be the driving force in these dramas. But though Poel may have removed Fate as a voice, his distinctive production style enabled him to keep it as an unspeaking physical presence. The *Oxford Chronicle*'s reviewer drew particular attention to:

> that picture of Wallenstein and his generals and family in the lower room at the close of the second act (in this version) agitated and terror-struck by the bad news of revolt coming from one regiment after another, while a servant stood leaning against the wall at the top of the steps looking on through it all silently and half contemptuously. The last was almost like a representation of the immovable Destiny of whom Wallenstein spoke so often.[34]

The 1911 programme notes also indicate a much more defined interpretation of Wallenstein's character and a more fine-tuned meshing of experimental dramaturgy with ethical (one of Poel's favourite words) interpretation. By then, Poel had ceased to see Wallenstein as 'idealised'; the soldier's 'moral bluntness of vision'[35] had become a much more important aspect of the figure. As in 1900, this programme too reprints a substantial part (51 lines) of the Prologue, exploring the function of art:

> . . . while at our feet the struggle is unfolded
> Of giant natures for a giant prize.
> When thus men battle for the loftiest
> Of human aims, for Empire and for Freedom
> Art may herself upon her shadowy stage
> Attempt – nay must attempt – a bolder flight.
> Or stand abashed by the great scene of life.[36]

Poel's 1911 revival was, I suggest, far more than his first essay, his attempt at a bolder flight, to meet the challenge posed by the great scene of life, so that his own shadowy stage should not stand abashed. It might be worth asking how the battle for Empire and for Freedom might be understood in 1911? And why a fringe director should think it so important to perform these plays of all plays at the Summer Meeting of the Oxford Extra-Mural Delegacy?

This is the place for an excursus into what the great scene of life looked like that summer. I am not an historian. I can only repeat the received wisdom that the long Edwardian summer of myth was over. (Though 1911 was in fact the hottest summer in living memory – on the day of the performance Greenwich registered 100 degrees[37] – and Breul [p.6] noted that Poel's audience would have been larger had many of the Summer School not preferred to go punting.) The years which with hindsight we now identify as leading up to the First World War mark a period of great social unrest at home and political tension abroad. Radical political and social and educational reforms were at issue. The Trades Unions were working for an 8-hour day and for a national minimum wage. The franchise had been massively extended in the Third Reform Bill of 1884, but it was still not universal: women did not have the vote, and neither did all men: there was still a minimal property qualification. Educational reform had long been on the agenda at all levels, from elementary to adult, and with the extension of suffrage it had been, ironically and realistically, but scarcely idealistically, recognised as essential by the governing classes: 'We must educate our masters' was the notorious remark of Robert Lowe of his reforms of elementary education in 1862. Abroad, the relationship with expanding Germany was highly charged and highly ambivalent. It was also a time of literary and artistic renewal. Modernism was knocking at the door: '. . . in or about December, 1910,' Virginia Woolf declared, 'human character changed.'[38] European Naturalism, as domesticated by Shaw and Granville-Barker, had become accepted socially-critical fare: indeed, the up-to-date reviewer of *The Oxford Chronicle* considered that Sudermann's *Magda* (*Heimat*, 1893), which had been a great vehicle for Mrs Patrick Campbell, might be more to current taste than Schiller's 'sentimentalism'. In such a context, Poel's unsceptical search for a new old authenticity might seem remote, even regressive. But that would be to miss his roundabout point.

In search of reviews, I found the newspapers of the month of August, 1911, providing a vivid snapshot of Poel's *Wallenstein*-moment.[39] Politically, the Liberals had been returned again in 1910, still with a much reduced majority, but this 10th August – the eve of our performance – saw the bare passage of their Parliament Bill, reforming the recalcitrant House of Lords and resolving the constitutional crisis. Domestically, this is above all the month of widespread industrial strikes: the London and Liverpool docks were out; so were the Sunderland shipyards and the railways (I wonder how people *got* to the Summer Meeting!); so were the engineering workers and the women of the Bermondsey jam factories, enrolling for the new Federation of Women Workers. Winston Churchill as Home Secretary refused an inquiry and, as he had the previous year in Tonypandy, sent in the army. There was rioting at the military presence in Liverpool, where the employers turned the dock strike into a lock-out. Great hardship and great violence were widespread. As for foreign affairs, negotiations over conflicts of interest in Turkey between England and Germany over the

Baghdad Railway are reported. So is the backwash for Great Britain – as France's ally – of the Franco-German dispute over Agadir, which provoked a violent outburst against perfidious Albion in the German press. As an absurdist diversion, the Kaiser, wearing the uniform of a British Admiral, unveiled a memorial to his uncle Edward VII at the English Church in Bad Homburg. (*The Times*' German coverage, by the way, is consistently very full.[40]) Nearer home, in Oxford, on the evening of our performance, there was a rally in support for Votes for Women held at the Martyrs' Memorial.

In the run-up to all this, Poel offered his play to the Oxford Extra-Mural Delegacy for their Summer Meeting. He had a long-standing connection with it, and with its counterpart in Cambridge, providing a drama most years from 1895 onwards. In 1901 he had brought his *Everyman* to Oxford, performing it in the Quadrangle of University College; in 1903, *Edward II*. The Summer Meeting was a very big affair, with upwards of a thousand adult students from outside the universities, women, school-teachers, women, workers, women, an increasing number of foreign students, who all came for a month's intensive high-level education, with lectures and tutorials from very distinguished teachers on multiple aspects of a single chosen topic each year. It was held in alternate years in the two university towns. This year – a brilliant, urgent choice – the topic was 'Germany'. Total immersion – apart from the pleasures of punting – in German history, German literature, German theology, German institutions, German industry, German economics, German foreign policy. The local newspaper covered it in detail, with a regular 'Who's Who' of the lecturers, and a printed booklet of the lectures. The opening speech was given by Viscount Haldane, Asquith's Secretary for War, the Göttingen-educated one who was suspected of being 'pro-German', as the phrase went: its burden was a highly informed 'greater knowledge of Germany means better understanding of Germany, and hence international conciliation', which set the tone for the entire programme.[41] (He also advised his audience to read Heine.) Breul, who had his own interest in adult education,[42] was enormously impressed, and suggested to his Magdeburg readers that German universities should set up something similar [p.4]: Germany too was in need of that informed understanding of the other which brings recognition.

Poel, then, was bringing a German drama of the ravages of war to a Meeting concerned with understanding a belligerent Germany. But this time the Delegacy seemed less enthusiastic about Poel's participation, especially in the person of its Secretary and indefatigable organiser, the historian, later the Tory MP for York, Sir John Marriott. Unfortunately, only the Delegacy's very unforthcoming side of the correspondence seems to have survived.[43] But the list of patrons on the programme indicates that Poel was able to find some influential establishment and non-establishment support.[44] My guess – and it is only a guess – is that in this disturbed summer of all summers, Marriott feared that Poel would be an uncomfortably radical presence in a Summer School made up of temporary students, many with radical sympathies themselves.

I do not have to guess at a fundamental difference in the way the two men understood education. To judge from his autobiography, Marriott's driving motive in the tremendous work he did for Adult Education was the realistic pragmatism of the governors.[45] Quoting Sir Richard Jebb, he wrote, 'the object of University Extension could not be more succinctly stated: "to teach our democracy to think".' His own indefatigable teaching and travelling from centre to centre he regarded, in inverted commas, as ' "missionary journeys" ' out of the ' "need for colonization" ' [p. 100]. He was able to quote Robert Lowe with approval and without irony [p. 116] – about granting the vote to women: their education, he was satisfied to note, had preceded their franchise!

Poel's view of Adult Education, on the other hand, was closer to making the ideal of *Bildung*, of self-cultivation, widely available beyond the confines of the high bourgeoisie. This may, of course, have been a social illusion of the high-minded high bourgeoisie, but it was a noble vision despite its contradictions[46] and very close to Schiller's. His theatre had a powerful ethical impulse. Within the confines of theatrical illusion, Thekla could well declare of her father's beleaguered castle: 'This is no theatre, a place of hope', but that could only serve to underline how much, to Schiller and to Poel, it was just that. As Poel put it, 'as the actual manifestation of man's spiritual energies, [tragedy] defeats any tendency towards pessimism.'[47] 'Theatres for the People' was a vision he shared with his friend Jocza Savits in Munich [see note 24] and with Emma Cons in the Waterloo Road. Schiller was important to him here. He illustrated the complex imaginative and pedagogic function of the theatre with the anecdote of the Weimar public's reverent reception of Schiller after the première of *Wilhelm Tell*.[48] Referring to his wish to perform *Wallenstein* in the year of his death, his wife drew attention in her *Personal Notes* to his ultimate aims:

> . . . the purpose he had in view, namely, to induce people to value what he thought to be beautiful and of real worth and to bring it into the lives of those whose daily routine was dull and hard [pp.18-19].

> . . . he never regarded the drama as a mere decoration of life but realised the effect on men's mental growth and balance [p.23].

And this, which 'was a favourite quotation of my late husband' [p.24]:

> The assertion so commonly made that the public degrades Art, is not well founded. It is the Artist who brings the public to the level of his own conceptions; in every age in which Art has gone to decay, it has fallen through its professors. The people need feeling alone; and feeling they possess. They take their station before the curtain with an invoiced longing, with a multifarious capacity. They bring with them an aptitude for what is highest, they derive the greatest pleasure from what is judicious and true; and if, with these powers of appreciation they begin to be satisfied with inferior

> productions, yet if they have tasted what is excellent for them, they will, in the end, insist on having it supplied to them [p.23].[49]

That, I think, is the best reason for bringing Schiller's play to the Extra-Mural Summer Meeting in that disturbed summer. His theatre need not stand abashed.

This lengthy account of the wider context of Poel's 1911 performance has thrown some light, I hope, on his interpretation of the play, on his retentions and deletions and what they might mean. He expands his programme notes for 1911 by a 'Story of the Play' and, importantly, by a reprint of the article already quoted which he had written for *The Arbitrator*, the journal of the International Arbitration League. The League was founded in 1870 as the Workmans' Peace Association to campaign for neutrality in the Franco-Prussian War; later, funded by Andrew Carnegie, it worked for an Anglo-American Arbitration Treaty, but by 1911 had lost any significant membership.[50] Here too, Poel found himself on the fringe. But the article and the journal it appeared in indicate his understanding of the dramas: as with Fletcher's *Bonduca* many years later, this is a drama of 'the psychology of war', of the irresponsibility, moral bluntness and arrogance of the Soldier. His article transforms Questenberg and Isolani (*Picc* I,ii 136-150 *variatim*) into the absolute types of the Civilian and the Soldier (something learned from *Everyman*, perhaps?). It also gives him the opportunity to quote at greater length than he does in his truncated adaptation those speeches by Octavio and Max on the emptiness of the soldier's life, the ravages of war and the joys of peace (*Picc* I,iv). (However, he does not take the opportunity to rescue Octavio's defence of the old narrow ordinances; it would be too conservative a sentiment for him to be able to quote with approval.) It is entirely in keeping with this concept that his Wallenstein, now no longer conceived as 'idealised', but as morally blunted, should be powerless to control 'the vortex of militarism'; even more so that he should give such prominence to Max and Thekla, as the pure victims who are destroyed by it.

The article also helps to make sense of one otherwise very arbitrary-seeming aspect of Poel's adaptation: for all the need to cut and reduce, he keeps a very large number of the minor roles, even seemingly dispensible ones. Lady Neubrunn, for example, the Swedish Captain, and the Pappenheimers (only five of them, not ten, with a corporal, not Coleridge's curious 'Anspessade'). But if Max and Thekla were to be so strongly foregrounded, then the Swedish Captain had to be retained for his account of Max's desperate and heroic death, which Poel kept almost entire; and Lady Neubrunn had to remain to accompany Thekla on her sacrificial flight. There seems little reason for keeping Major Geraldine, or even the Burgomaster – though the Shakespearean chronicle-model, with its wide range of characters, may be at the back of it. But retaining the Pappenheimers[51] makes sense, I think, in the light of Poel's remark that 'the soldier is as much a minor as the child with regard to his responsibilities to his fellow men'.[52]

Speaight [p.220] calls this a 'curious view', but it certainly applies to the reckless self-interest of the generals. In contrast, Schiller – and after him Poel – represents the soldiers of the line as mature and responsible adults coming to their own considered – and loyal – decision. This is in any reading an important variant on the sub-theme of 'Mündigkeit' in the drama.[53] But it may also have been important to Poel to establish this possibility of mature action on the part of the lower orders – especially in the middle of widespread strikes – precisely in order to highlight the anti-social irresponsibility of the General-as-Abstract-Soldier. This is speculation, of course. Poel might just have taken the opportunity to give his spear-carriers something more to do. But it does make sense. The only worrying thing is Breul's comment on them: 'nicht eindrucksvoll sondern geradezu komisch.' [p.8].

Poel's *Wallenstein*, then, does not seem to be a tragedy of the great fall or the fatal flaw – the reduction of the figure of Wallenstein himself argues against that. Both Breul [p.7] and the reviewer of *The Oxford Chronicle* confirm this: 'we almost lose the sense of a great overpowering figure; the outlines become blurred . . .' – though the latter ascribes this to that idealising of the figure which, I have suggested, has more to do with Poel's simple concept than with Schiller's more complex conception. (And in any case, *The Oxford Times* might disagree). It is, as Poel restructures it, a drama in which the action becomes its own self-driven motor, turning its figures into victims or brutes. Though it is not a drama of destiny as conveyed by the great metaphor of the stars – the removal of the astrological scenes and the minimising of Seni's role disqualifies it for that – the idea of an ironical fate does return in the sheer helplessness of the apparent agents and becomes incarnated in the figure of the louring servant on the stairs.

Pursuing these performances has been rather like dropping a stone into a pond. I found them rippling outwards, from a text which had been Englished, partly at least, into the Shakespearean diction which dominated nineteenth-century poetic drama to a radical adaptation of its structure to approximate to the Elizabethan fluid form, and that as part of a reform of theatrical style common to both the English and the German stage at the turn of the century. Schiller's – unreconstructed – idealism fed into this reform. Not so much in the 'blurring' of the Wallenstein figure as in the ethical motivation of Poel's theatre, the place of hope which was his contribution to the larger social and educational reforms of the time. It may seem fortuitous that the immediate social and political situation had reached a critical point just in August 1911: the constitutional crisis was still fresh, the industrial crisis acute, the international tensions with Germany a growing threat. But they made *Wallenstein* more timely than *Magda*. Poel seized his moment.

And I would like to think that he took time off from dismantling his stage that evening to attend the meeting at the Martyrs' Memorial.

Notes and References

[1] See Walter Grossmann, 'The Gillman-Harvard Manuscript of Schiller's *Wallensteins Tod*', in *Harvard Library Bulletin*, 11 (1957), 319-45.

[2] *The Works of Frederick Schiller*, Bohn's Standard Library, 4 vols. (London, Bohn, 1846-49), II *Historical and Dramatic*, (1846), pp.139-448. For the textual history of Coleridge's translation, see B.Q. Morgan, 'What happened to Coleridge's *Wallenstein*', in *MLJ*, 43 (1959), 195-201 (pp.195-99).

[3] See Frank Lamport, '*Wallenstein* on the English stage', in *GLL* 48, 2 (1995), pp.124-47 <*cited as*: LAMPORT>. I am greatly indebted to Frank Lamport for much of the information incorporated in this article. We found ourselves working on the same material, he for the Royal Shakespeare Company's production of *Wallenstein* in the winter of 1993-4, which used his translation (Harmondsworth: Penguin, 1979), I for the editorial notes to Coleridge's translation for Vol. XVI of the *Collected Coleridge* (Princeton and London: Princeton University Press). We collaborated on the preliminary research, exchanging information and ideas in the most constructive and agreeable way, and I, for one, am very grateful for it.

[4] Programme for the 1900 performance. In Box 7 of the Poel Collection at the Theatre Museum, Covent Garden. <Hereafter referred to as **PC**, **TM**>. My warmest thanks are due to the help and interest shown by the staff of the Museum in these researches.

[5] Now the – unrecognisably altered – Film Theatre of the British Museum's Museum of Mankind.

[6] The certificate, dated 22.8.1911, is in **PC**, Box 6, **TM**.

[7] Schiller, *Wallenstein*, ed. by Karl Breul 2 vols (Cambridge: Cambridge University Press, 1894, 1896).

[8] ''Schillers *Wallenstein* in Oxford', Sonder-Abdruck aus dem Montagsblatt, Wissenschaftliche Beilage der *Magdeburger Zeitung* 34 (1911), 3-11.

[9] Schiller, *Wallenstein's Camp and the Piccolomini* with a memoir, trans. by J. Churchill and S. T. Coleridge, Bell's Modern Translations, (London: George Bell, 1895); *The Death of Wallenstein*, trans.by S. T. Coleridge, Bell's Modern Translations, (London: George Bell, 1894). Bell purchased Bohn's Libraries in 1864. See F. A. Mumby and Ian Norrie, *Publishing and Bookselling* rev. ed. (London: Cape, 1974) p.226. Poel's Prompt-book is in **PC** Box S1181 – 1983, labelled *Death of Wallenstein*, **TM**. The box also contains three full (actor's?) copies of the Bell paperback of *Wallenstein's Camp and the Piccolomini* (1895), variously marked up in pencil; a group of loose pages of the same edition; one partial copy of the Bell paperback of *The Death of Wallenstein* (1895) and two loose pages and two loose covers of the same edition, as well as the material recorded below in Note 11.

[10] See Prompt-book, p.55.

[11] *WAR: as shown by Scenes from Schiller's "Piccolomini" and "The Death of Wallenstein"* (Translated by S. T. Coleridge). The scenes are abridged and arranged by William Poel, (Putney: A. W. Patching and Co., 1934). Copies in BL and in **PC** (*Death of Wallenstein* Box), **TM**. The latter also contains a variant typescript of the same version, perhaps intended as the basis of performance.

[12] William Poel, 'Life in the Camp. (Schiller's "Wallenstein.")', *The Arbitrator*, 387 (August 1911), 99-100 (p.99). Reprinted in programme for the 1911 performance. Programme in Box 6 **PC**, **TM**.

[13] Robert Speaight, *William Poel and the Elizabethan Revival*, (London, Melbourne and Toronto: Heinemann, 1954), pp.270-71 <*cited as*: SPEAIGHT>.

[14] Note on programme cover, **PC** Boxes 2 and 6, **TM**.

[15] Motto on programme cover, **PC** Boxes 1 and 6, **TM**.

[16] Programme note, **PC** Boxes 2 and 6, **TM**.

[17] Ella Constance Pole [sic], *Personal Notes*, p.16. Typescript Memoir, probably intended to preface Allan Gomme, *William Poel (1852-1934). A Bibliography of his Writings on Shakespeare and the theatre, with Extracts* (1939). Typescript. **PC** Box 4 **TM**.

[18] SPEAIGHT, pp.15-16.

[19] *UCL Gazette* (28.2.1887) p.104. **PC** Box 6, **TM**.

[20] C.E. Montague's essay, 'The art of William Poel' is one of the most informative and appreciative sources for Poel's production style. Unfortunately, he does not give an account of *Wallenstein*. See *Dramatic Values* (London: Methuen, 1911), pp.225-46.

[21] SPEAIGHT, p.103.

[22] For the Meiningers' visit to England, see John Osborne, *The Meiningen Court Theatre 1866-1900* (Cambridge: Cambridge University Press, 1988), pp.79ff. Of their reception he comments: 'the grand historicist style [was] recognised as English and familiar' (p.81).

[23] SPEAIGHT, p.78.

[24] 'Gesprochene Dekoration' was the term given to it by Jocza Savits, Poel's theatrical ally at the Münchener Hoftheater, whose *Shakespearebühne* (1889-1904) was conducted on lines very close to Poel's. See Jocza Savits, *Shakespeare und die Bühne des Dramas* (Bonn: Cohn, 1917; <*cited as*: SAVITS>), p.377 and *passim*. Later in the same year as his first *Wallenstein*, Poel visited Munich and was greatly impressed by Savits' revival of his 'Shakespearean' *Lear* of 8.9.1900. See William Poel, 'A lost art', *The New Age* (16.9.1909), 378-9; and 'An Actor Author' (1915) in *Monthly Letters*, selected and arranged by A.M.T. (London: Werner Laurie, 1929), pp.91-4. Hans Durian, *Jocza Savits und die Münchener Shakespearebühne*, *Die Schaubühne: Quellen und Forschungen zur Theatergeschichte*, 19 (Emsdetten: Lechte, 1937) itemises the dates on which Savits revived his *Lear* (p.59). For their further friendship, see SAVITS pp.14-19 and SPEAIGHT pp.218-19.

[25] For the critical impact both Shakespeare and Sophocles had at a key point in the composition, see Schiller's letter to Körner of 7.4.1797, *Schillers Briefe 1796-1798*, ed. by Norbert Oellers and Frithjof Stock, Nationalausgabe (Weimar: Hermann Böhlaus Nachfolger, 1977) XXIX, p.60 <Hereafter referred to as *NA*>.

[26] Joyce Crick, 'Some Editorial and Stylistic Observations on Coleridge's Translation of Schiller's *Wallenstein*', *PEGS*, 54 (1984), pp.37-75.

[27] Schiller, *The Death of Wallenstein. A Tragedy in five Acts*, trans. by S.T. Coleridge (London: Longman and Rees, 1800), p.[ii].

[28] For 1900, Poel considered two possibilities for the interval, both marked in the promptbook and later deleted: the first at the end of *The Piccolomini* V,iii with Max's conflict at having been made privy to Octavio's plans ('Knock for Interval' marked in black ink and deleted in pencil, p.151); the second well into *The Death of Wallenstein* II,iii as Illo and Terzky reflect on Wrangel's sudden departure. Here Poel makes a resounding finale of Terzky's: 'This is my comfort. – Max remains our hostage' and Illo's reply: 'And he shall never stir from here alive.' ('End of Act I' marked in pencil; 'Knock for Interval' in black ink; both deleted in red ink, p.187.) It is not known which, in the event, Poel used. According to the revisions for 1911 – 'act-drop' is inserted in red ink at '. . . alive.' and a strong line drawn – the latter does indeed

appear to be the end of the Oxford Act I. Act II began with Octavio's adjutant (*The Death of Wallenstein* II,iv) and continued to Max's departure (III,xxiii); Poel's Act III consists of Schiller's Acts IV and V.

[29] See review in *The Oxford Chronicle* of 18.8.1911 and the rough stage plan attached to the prompt-book.

[30] The prompt-book cast-list for 1900 includes the name of the actor to play Wrangel, one H.C. Rose. There are no signs on the text that the role may have been deleted, but the figure, remarkably, does not appear in the programme. It is, for the plot, a curious cut to make, though not impossible: Macready had dispensed with the figure, making the action turn on the flourish of the signed document (for details of the adaptation of the *Wallenstein*-dramas made by the actor-manager W. C. Macready some time in the 1840s, see LAMPORT, pp.126-31). But the character, strongly cast, appears to have been a highlight of the 1911 performance: '. . . the energy of attack, the almost rioting invention in details, the real joy of creation which he [Poel] brought to it, made it tell immediately, and made everybody else seem colourless and cold and precise.'

[31] See also Poel's 1911 treatment of Max's resounding curtain line at the end of Schiller's *Piccolomini* V,iii, which Schiller even turned into a closing Shakespearean rhyming couplet, echoed by Coleridge's half-rhyme: 'And ere the daylight dawns, it must be known / Which I must lose – my father or my friend.' This is one of the possible interval-lines for the 1900 performance (see Note 28), but for 1911 Poel simply weaves it into the overall movement, blurring it by the direction (in red ink): 'Exit L. During his exit Servant re-enters RL and follows Max' (Prompt-book, p.151), and having two boys enter RL to replace chair on settle and move small table on chair forward R. This mere shift of furniture is sufficient for the action to move straight on to what was the opening of the next drama, the last remains of the astrological scene.

[32] The part of the Duchess was allotted to Miss Alexandrina Ramsay, that of Seni to L. Howerd, while H. C. Rose was down to double Wrangel and the Burgomaster.

[33] See Schiller's letter to Humboldt of 21.4.1796: 'Er hat nichts Edles . . . ich hoffe aber nichtsdestoweniger auf rein realistischem Wege einen dramatisch großen Character in ihm aufzustellen.' *Schillers Briefe 1795-1796* ed. by Norbert Oellers, *NA* XXVIII (1969), p.204. See also his letter to Böttiger of 1.3.1799: 'Der historische Wallenstein war nicht groß, der poetische *sollte* es nie seyn . . . Was an ihm groß erscheinen, aber nur *scheinen* konnte, war das Rohe und Ungeheure, also grade das, was ihn zum tragischen Helden schlecht qualifizierte. Dieses mußte ich ihm nehmen und durch den *Ideenschwung*, den ich ihm dafür gab, hoffe ich ihnen entschädigt zu haben.' *Schillers Briefe 1798-1800* ed. by Lieselotte Blumenthal, *NA* XXX (1961), pp.33-4.

[34] The prompt-book gives no indication of this impressive piece of staging.

[35] *The Arbitrator*, p.99, reprinted in the 1911 programme.

[36] It is unclear what translation Poel used. Apart from eight lines, Schiller's *Prolog* written for the first Weimar performance was not published in the Bohn edition of 1846, nor in its successor, the Bell paperback used by Poel. Neither Coleridge (1800) nor Moir (1827) translated it when they did the dramas into English, nor does it appear in the selections of poems translated by Bulwer Lytton (1844) or Edgar Bowring (1851). It *was* translated by Lord Francis Leveson Gower (1830) and by C. J. Hempel (1879), but Poel's is neither of these. Perhaps it is his own. The rendering of 'Herrschaft' by 'Empire' points towards him.

[37] According to *The Manchester Guardian* of 12.8.1911.

[38] 'Mr Bennett and Mrs Brown' (1924), in *The Captain's Deathbed* (London: Hogarth, 1950), p.91.

[39] Mainly *The Times*, *The Manchester Guardian* and *The Oxford Chronicle*.

[40] However, the obituaries for August 1911 do not appear to carry one for Gustav von Aschenbach.

[41] Reported in full in *The Times* of 4.8.1911. *The Arbitrator* carried a shortened version in its September issue, 388, pp.107-09.

[42] Breul prepared an 'Introductory Essay' for a course of study on Schiller for the *National Home Reading Union Magazine* 8 (1896).

[43] Preserved in the University Archives. See particularly Marriott's letters of 17 March and 1 June 1911 (LAMPORT, p.132).

[44] The literary among them included Coleridge's grandson, Ernest Hartley Coleridge, whose edition of his grandfather's *Complete Poetical Works* was published the following year; Mr and Mrs Bernard Shaw; Professors J.W. Mackail and Gilbert Murray; Sir Herbert Beerbohm Tree and Mr Somerset Maugham.

[45] See Sir John Marriott, *Memoirs of fourscore Years* (London and Glasgow: Blackie, 1946) pp.99, 133-34, 139-40.

[46] Some of the cross-currents can be read, crudely, from the addresses of the 1900 cast. Most of the actors, amateur and professional, have good addresses: in West Kensington, Regent's Park or Hampstead. The Corporal and his Pappenheimers come from Dalston and the Mile End Road.

[47] William Poel, 'A great tragedian [Salvini]' (1916), *Monthly Letters*, p.1.

[48] 'It is a tribute of reverential gratitude to a man who has helped them to solve something of the mystery of existence and to walk life's path with a firmer step and nobler purpose' (*ibid.* pp.1-2).

[49] The formulations of Mrs Pole's quotation are those of the anonymous [query Adam Lodge?] translation 'On the Use of the Chorus in Tragedy' in *The Works of Frederick Schiller*, 4 vols, Bohn's Standard Library (London: Bohn, 1846-9), III *Historical Dramas etc.* (1847), p.439. But she could equally well have used a later edition. Bell and Routledge both published a number. See Note 9.

[50] For this information my thanks are due to Dr Martin Ceadel, through the good offices of Frank Lamport.

[51] Both Macready and Albery dispensed with them. See LAMPORT, pp.130, 145.

[52] *The Arbitrator* p.99; 1911 Programme Note.

[53] Wallenstein's paternalistic address to the Pappenheimers as 'children' is in fact part of a larger cut (Prompt-book p.230), but in this reading the irony would have been on him.

'Our Wretched German Cousins': A.R. Orage and Germany

DIANE MILBURN

Alfred Richard Orage (1873-1934) is something of a forgotten figure in literary circles. He is remembered chiefly as the radical editor of the influential weekly journal the *New Age*, which between 1907 and 1922 not only boasted amongst its contributors such major figures from English literary life as G.K. Chesterton, H.G. Wells and Bernard Shaw, but also offered younger writers, such as Katherine Mansfield and Ezra Pound, the opportunity to have their work published. Many of these writers had strong connections with Germany. In the 1890s, as the music critic of *The Star*, Corno di Bassetto, Bernard Shaw was acknowledged as the perfect Wagnerite, promoting the German composer to English audiences when Wagnerism was at its height. Furthermore, his play *Man and Superman* gave rise to suggestions that the dramatist had been influenced by the most recent developments in German thought, although he was swift to deny to both English and German audiences that he was merely repeating Schopenhauer and Nietzsche parrot-fashion.[1] Of the younger generation of writers encouraged by Orage, Katherine Mansfield's short stories about her experiences in Bavaria that later formed the anthology *In a German Pension*, appeared first in the *New Age*. Other writers, such as Edwin Muir, who subsequently played an important role in Anglo-German literary relations through his collaboration with his wife Willa on translations of Kafka,[2] showed an early interest in German literature whilst writing for the *New Age*. The interest in Germany was sustained throughout the First World War and continued into the 1920s, with both Muir and the young Herbert Read (recently returned from fighting in the trenches) exploring the work of Oswald Spengler, Hans Vaihinger and Hermann Graf Keyserling, then only just appearing in Germany. The *New Age* was also swift to grasp the importance of the work of Freud and Jung, with Orage again taking a keen personal interest in the subject, hailing psychoanalysis as 'the hopeful science of the dawning era'.[3] In addition, Ashley Dukes, who later translated Georg Kaiser and Ernst Toller into English, owed his interest in German dramatists to his period as drama critic at the *New Age*. At Orage's instigation,[4] he introduced modern German dramatists to readers of the *New Age*. In the course of 1910, for instance, he discussed plays by August Strindberg, Hugo von Hofmannsthal, Gerhart Hauptmann, Hermann Sudermann, Frank Wedekind, Ludwig Thoma and Arthur Schnitzler – whom he singled out for particular praise.

As editor Orage was an important intermediary in the reception of German literature and ideas in England. This is perhaps surprising, given that Orage was part of a generation that grew up at a time when political events were causing a dramatic revision of the British perception of Germany. The Franco-Prussian War (1870), with the crushing defeat of the French at the Battle of Sedan and the annexation of Alsace Lorraine, followed by the founding of the German Empire (1871), did not appear as the work of the peaceable German cousins, the musicians and philosophers of early nineteenth century literature, but the work of a new breed of aggressive German militarists. Although this deterioration in the *Deutschlandbild* took place gradually, it accelerated after 1900, culminating in the rabid propaganda tracts of the First World War.[5] Despite this Germanophobic background, Orage betrays a constant interest in German life and literature throughout his editorship. Whilst it was never a pacifist periodical, the *New Age* avoided some of the xenophobic excesses of contemporary publications in the war of words against Germany, and Orage was instrumental in presenting to his English readership an understanding of Wilhelmine Germany.

Reducing 'Leeds to Nietzscheism'.

Orage's interest in Germany began long before he was a London editor. It can be traced back to his early years as a schoolmaster in Leeds. In 1903 Orage and Holbrook Jackson (1874-1948) launched an ambitious scheme whose avowed aim was 'to reduce Leeds to Nietzscheism'.[6] This took the form of founding the Leeds Arts Club where the latest developments in literature, philosophy, music and painting were to be discussed. In this respect the interests of the Arts Club anticipated some of the cultural questions debated on the pages of the *New Age* when Orage became editor. The Club was ambitious on two counts. In the first place, it was a platform for the avant-garde, based not in London, where English cultural life was traditionally centred, but in the provinces. In the second place, speakers were often dealing with subjects little discussed outside the metropolis. Nevertheless, the Club was well supported, mainly by teachers, but also by journalists, clergymen, architects and some university lecturers. Guest speakers were invited to attract larger audiences. Such luminaries included Edward Carpenter, W.B. Yeats, Bernard Shaw and G.K. Chesterton, who in the autumn of 1904 spoke on 'Man – The Great Man – The Superman'. Programmes of talks given at the Club reveal something of a predilection for Germanic subjects. Lectures were given on Richard Wagner, Hugo Wolf, Heine's poetry, German Romanticism and, of course, Nietzsche. In addition, the Club encouraged members to learn European languages, promoted Esperanto and organised lectures on Ibsen, Strindberg and Turgenev. The concerns of this provincial society were far from parochial. By comparison, syllabuses of study at Leeds University confined themselves to earlier periods. The course on modern thought in the Philosophy Department, for example, ended with Kant, whilst the German Department under Professor Schüddekopf concentrated on Middle High German, Lessing, Herder, Klopstock, Wieland, Goethe and Schiller. Not until 1910 did Gerhart

Hauptmann's *Die versunkene Glocke* (1896) creep onto the syllabus as a concession to modernity. Meanwhile at the Arts Club Orage was lecturing almost monthly on Nietzsche,[7] occasionally offering an impromptu talk on the German philosopher as well. Clifford Bax recalled a meeting in 1906 when:

> The lecturer had sent a last-minute message to say that he was too ill to come. The Chairman was in a fix. Orage then got up from his seat in the hall and offered to give a lecture on "Three Great Philosophers". They were, I think, Plato, Schopenhauer and Nietzsche: and I shall always remember the brilliant manner in which he gave the discourse which completely saved the awkward situation.[8]

Schopenhauer's *Die Welt als Wille und Vorstellung* had first appeared in English between 1883 and 1886, when Richard Burdon Haldane (later Viscount Haldane of Cloan) and John Kemp collaborated on a translation. The first English translation of Nietzsche's *Also sprach Zarathustra* had not been published until 1896 and at the time of Orage's lectures no complete edition of Nietzsche's works was available. As Tom Steele observes, Orage's lectures in Leeds mark 'the first sustained attempt at a popular introduction to Nietzsche'.[9]

Orage, who was employed as a schoolmaster at Ellerby Lane Boys in one of the worst slum areas of Leeds, lived in the more comfortable suburb of Chapel Allerton.[10] In 1900 he borrowed a copy of Thomas Common's translation of *Also sprach Zarathustra* from Holbrook Jackson, whom he had first met, appropriately enough, in a Leeds book shop.[11] He read it in a single night, then walked from his home in Chapel Allerton to Jackson's house in Headingley, fired with enthusiasm for his new intellectual master.[12] In the course of the next seven years he was to make a detailed study of the philosopher. Moreover, there is evidence to suggest that he was not wholly dependent on the English translations. Orage knew both French and German and, according to Jackson, whilst in Leeds Orage translated Nietzsche's poems into prose for Jackson to render into poetry.[13] As an adolescent he had been a voracious reader of Carlyle and Arnold – both important intermediaries for the reception of German literature and thought in England. Arnold, for instance, had written on Heinrich Heine; A.J. Penty, who knew Orage in Leeds, remembered the latter's interest in the German writer at this stage.[14] However, it would be a misrepresentation to suggest that Orage was solely interested in German culture. Throughout his life his interests spanned a wide range of fields. In Leeds he divided his time between the Independent Labour Party, Plato, Theosophy and the eastern mysticism contained in the *Mahabharata* and the *Bhagavadgita*. It was possibly the concept of eternal recurrence found in *Also sprach Zarathustra*, with its evocations of eastern notions of spiritual transcendence and reincarnation, that initially attracted Orage to Nietzsche. Commenting on the interests of Orage and the Leeds Arts Club Holbrook Jackson acknowledged:

> Orage went over the top and so did the group. We all developed supermania. He wanted a Nietzsche circle in which Plato and Blavatzky [sic], Fabianism and

> Hinduism, Shaw and Wells and Edward Carpenter should be blended, with Nietzsche as the catalytic [sic].[15]

It was certainly a potent mixture. Perhaps it was too potent, for in 1906 Orage came to the conclusion that 'Dionysos and Leeds would not mix'[16] and, armed with what were reputed to be the only three English translations of Nietzsche in Leeds,[17] borrowed indefinitely from the Arts Club,[18] moved to London with Jackson. Here he helped H.G. Wells, Eric Gill and William Rothenstein form the Fabian Arts Group which was based on the Leeds model. He returned regularly to the Leeds Arts Club, which continued to flourish under Michael Sadler, Frank Rutter and Jacob Kramer, and occasionally published reports on the Club's activities in the *New Age*. He wrote two volumes on Nietzsche – *Friedrich Nietzsche: The Dionysian Spirit of the Age* (1906) and *Nietzsche in Outline and Aphorism* (1907) – both of which were well received in the press. However, it was as editor of the *New Age* that he would be best remembered.

Bernard Shaw and Germany: 'I can neither claim knowledge of the German language nor plead ignorance of it.'

During the period that A.R. Orage edited the *New Age* from May 1907 until September 1922 the list of contributors to this weekly periodical reads like a directory of figures from English literary life. More remarkable still was Orage's ability to secure articles from his established contributors without payment, so high was their esteem for him. Writers from whom he coaxed contributions, paid and unpaid, included: Arnold Bennett, H.G. Wells, G.K. Chesterton, Hilaire Belloc, William Archer, Bernard Shaw, Hubert Bland, Edith Nesbit, Holbrook Jackson, Oscar Levy, A.M. Ludovici, J.M. Kennedy, T.E. Hulme, Havelock Ellis, Edward Carpenter, A.J. Penty, Herbert Read, Paul Selver, John Middleton Murray, Katherine Mansfield and Ezra Pound. Of these, several already had links with Germany: prior to 1900 Havelock Ellis had written a penetrating series of essays on Nietzsche in the *Savoy*. The scholar, Oscar Levy, was editing a complete version of the German philosopher's work, with Ludovici and Kennedy, amongst others, as translators. Kennedy's first contribution to the *New Age*, for instance, was a review of the German edition of *Ecce Homo* in October 1908, although his interests were not confined to literature. From 1911 he reported on foreign affairs for the *New Age*, signing himself S. Verdad (from the Spanish 'es verdad', meaning 'it is true'). The £1000 necessary to enable Jackson and Orage to buy the *New Age* was put up by Bernard Shaw, a personal friend of Jackson,[19] and Lewis Wallace, a banker known to Orage through Theosophist circles. Although Shaw might have hoped to be investing in a journal which would propagate his views, it soon became clear that editorial policy was to keep the review independent and to give contributors *carte blanche* to disagree with one another. Nevertheless, the link with Shaw was important because of his own connections with both German music and philosophy. The question of Shaw's knowledge of German is debatable. In an article for *Die Neue Rundschau* in 1911 he claims that he has 'every intention of learning German one day; it is something everyone should do', but as he is 'not yet fifty five, there is no hurry'.[20] Admittedly he was being somewhat economical with the truth. Although, as his biographer Michael Holroyd points out, he read the first volume of Marx's *Das Kapital* in French (no English version was available in the British Museum in 1883), his German 'not being up to deciphering an original text',[21] by the 1890's he had accompanied May Morris to German classes and gained some knowledge of the language. Shaw probably gave the most accurate description of his acquaintance with German when he asserted

> I can neither claim knowledge of the German language nor plead ignorance of it. I am like most literary persons: I have spent several holidays in Germany (mostly in Bayreuth), and have just managed to ask my way, and get what I wanted in the shops and railway stations, without the aid of an interpreter. The proverbial bits of Goethe and Wagner and Nietzsche are familiar to me; and when a German writes to me I can generally make out what he wants provided he uses the Latin and not the Gothic script. And that is all.[22]

The implication that 'most literary persons' of Shaw's generation had either knowledge of the German language or contact with German culture is significant for an understanding of the outlook of contributors to the *New Age*. It was this generation of writers that was to play such a large part in what has recently been called the 'great war of words'[23] against Germany in 1914.

The Germans: 'reasonable, fallible creatures – much as we are.'

Given the multiplicity of contributors to the *New Age*,[24] many of them expressing conflicting opinions, it may perhaps appear doubtful whether any single attitude towards Germany can be traced. However, if we consider the themes that recur in the periodical, we may come closer to understanding the perception of Germany of Orage and his circle. In its approach to German politics, literature, art, music and philosophy it betrays none of the Germanophobic outpourings that were the norm during the First World War. Although never the sole work of one man in the way that *Die Fackel* of Karl Kraus or *Die Aktion* of Franz Pfemfert were, it did perhaps share some of the radicalism of contemporary publications in Vienna and Berlin, even if it did not espouse the pacifism of these journals. Indeed, only in Germany would Orage have been 'a pioneer of pacifism in the world'.[25] Pacifists in England 'outrage the proprieties of language when they refer to war as murder'.[26]

Generally, contributors to the *New Age* favoured some form of armament. As early as 1907 G.K. Chesterton's brother Cecil argues that 'one need not be a Jingo to recognise that so long as nations exist they must be prepared to resist by force if necessary the wanton aggression of other nations'.[27] Orage also advocates a defence system, but before 1914 he never perceives Germany as a threat. He claims that 'There neither is, was, nor will be any real German peril to England; but an artificial one is always there to be created'.[28] He fears not German invasion, but the 'triumphant capitalist'.[29] The *New Age* circle was far from chauvinistic. The less well-known contributors also attacked the bellicosity of their contemporaries. Throughout the war Orage allowed the conscientious objector and co-founder of the No Conscription Fellowship, C.H. Norman, to voice his opposition to the hostilities in the periodical. Perhaps the most outspoken critic of wartime attitudes was Beatrice Hastings (1879-1943), who contributed regularly to the journal using a variety of pseudonyms,[30] and exerting considerable influence over Orage, with whom she lived between 1907 and 1914 in a relationship, which was by all accounts stormy. Early in 1914 she moved to Paris, initially to send a series of reports on life in the French capital back to the periodical. Caught up in the city at the outbreak of war and seeking permission to travel back to England, she produced probably her most effective pieces of journalism, describing French attitudes towards the Germans and her own ambivalent feelings. In August 1914, for instance, she admitted to feeling alienated by French jingoism, confessing 'I feel so out of things, with no possibility of suddenly hating my German friends'.[31] Even in 1918 she had still

> never said anything very bad of Germans, even when their airmen came bombarding Paris; honestly, I couldn't, knowing only nice ones in England, whose worst fault was a confidence in our ideals of liberty which verged on the scandalous.[32]

After briefly joining in the jingoistic outpourings of his countrymen by suggesting that the Allies face an 'untamed, snapping, barking brute' as they confront the 'nakedness of the Teuton',[33] Orage is quick to concede that Germany's aim to be ranked as a world power is 'legitimate and necessary to her', even if her methods are 'tragically mistaken'. He reminds readers that the Germans are acting like 'reasonable, fallible creatures – much as we are'.[34] During the height of the hostilities he opposes vilification of Germany on the grounds that 'Germans are men even if they are possessed by a collective madness; and we are to assure them that when their fit is over we shall treat them again as men rather than as madmen'. He believes that the 'people of Germany' are 'much the same as ourselves'. Indeed, 'our wretched German cousins' have become 'temporarily bestial and insane' only 'under the provocation of popular fear and Prussian ambition'.[35]

Anti-German sentiment in England: it is the duty of civilians to be 'polite to foreigners.'

One of the saddest aspects of the war was the persecution by certain fanatics of people living in Britain whose only crime was to have German surnames or German ancestry. Employers came under pressure to dismiss employees with such enemy connections, and in May 1915 the London Stock Exchange excluded brokers of German birth.[36] The situation became ridiculous when, in a burst of patriotic zeal, German shepherd dogs were renamed Alsatians and on at least one occasion a dachshund was stoned in the street.[37] Amongst Britons who were descended from Germans, opinion was divided on how to tackle the problem. The British royal family surname, Battenberg, was hastily changed to Mountbatten. W.T. Sonnenschein, the Vice Principal of Brasenose College, Oxford, thought it wiser to revert to his paternal grandmother's name of Stallybrass, although his uncle, E.A. Sonnenschein, Professor of Latin at Birmingham, kept the name, whilst his son preferred Somerset as a surname.[38] The Professor of German at Leeds University, Albert William Schüddekopf, a graduate of Göttingen University and a naturalised British citizen, was hounded until the University, bowing to outside pressure, granted him indefinite leave in November 1915 and in June 1916 Michael Sadler, the Vice Chancellor, advised him to resign. He died in a Harrogate nursing home three months later, apparently killed by the 'mental anguish of seeing the two countries he loved best at war with each other, and by the shoddy treatment he received from the community in which he lived'.[39]

The *New Age* was swift to come to the defence of Germans persecuted in England. On 20 August 1914, for example, Orage condemns pen-knife attacks on Germans in the East End of London and calls on his fellow countrymen to remember that it is the duty of civilians to be 'polite to foreigners' even in time of war.[40] However, it soon transpired that racial abuse was much closer to home than this when one of Orage's regular contributors, Oscar Levy, became a victim. As a German living in England, and having edited the first complete English edition of the works of Nietzsche[41] – who, as we shall see, was a prime target for vilification – Levy was especially susceptible to attack, eventually finding it necessary to flee his adoptive country to the sanctuary of Switzerland for the duration of the war. The irony of the situation was not lost on Levy who recalled in a letter to the *New Age* that twenty years earlier he had left his native Germany, where he practised medicine, because he was boycotted for being a Jew, only to find himself persecuted again for being a German in England.[42] Once exiled, Levy continued to send articles to the *New Age* dealing mainly with literary subjects.

Orage's tolerant attitude towards the Germans is shared by Ezra Pound and Janko Lavrin. Pound, who began his career in journalism at the *New Age*, contributed some highly perceptive pieces on Germany, even though his experience of the country was limited and his impressions far from favourable.[43] In 1920 he confesses that he is 'as ready as the next man to see the Kaiser hung, drawn and quartered', but recognises the transience of 'national loves and hates'. He contends that 'You can be ready to torture the man who has tortured you or your brother or your friend in a German prison, but you cannot be made to extend that hate to some other man of a different district, of different features, and maintain that hate indefinitely'.[44] Janko Lavrin, the Professor of Slavonic languages at Nottingham University who contributed regularly to Orage's journal, also favours reconciliation on the grounds that 'it would be ridiculous to condemn as merely "barbaric" a race which has given the world Goethe, Kant, Bach, Beethoven, Mozart, Wagner, and a score of other great men, of whose works not only Germans themselves but the whole of humanity would be proud'. Germany is 'something of a parvenu', respecting 'learned titles', and is impressed not by original thoughts but 'by the quantity of learned authorities' used to back up an argument. Lavrin suggests that 'in things intellectual, as in things culinary', the German has 'more sense for quantity than for quality'. The Germans mistook 'knowledge and learning' for 'culture itself' but, once the war is over, they may concentrate on real culture.[45]

Prussia at war: 'with *kultur* in one hand and a bomb in the other.'

Only J.M. Kennedy (1886-1918), one of the English translators of Nietzsche and a possible government spy,[46] challenges the faith in Germany expressed by Orage and some of his contributors. As early as 1910 Kennedy argues that his own experience of Germany within the last few years has proved to him that 'nothing would be more popular throughout the [German] Empire than a war with England'.[47] He disapproves of modern Germány, preferring instead the early nineteenth century *De l'Allemagne* of Madame de Staël. Germany was 'a land where the inhabitants were lost in the clouds of abstract idealistic, romantic thought, a land whence no "practical" proposal ever emanated.' The German was 'an amiable sort of clumsy animal' whom the English, a 'thoroughly practical people', could not take seriously.[48] He is convinced that the modern German spirit is so 'thoroughly anti-cultural, anti-poetic, anti-philosophic' that it is inconceivable that it will ever again produce writers of the calibre of Heine or Goethe. According to Kennedy, Wilhelmine Germany is 'too materialistic, too Imperialistic, too modern'.[49] He prefers the Austrians, Bavarians and Southern Germans – 'a peaceful people'.[50]

The belief that the southern German states were less interested in military, territorial or material issues proved just as dubious as the view that Austria was any more pacific than Prussia. On 15 August 1914 King Ludwig III of Bavaria laid claim to the whole of Alsace as a Bavarian war aim to revitalise the economy of southern Germany, in addition to demanding that Belgium disappear and that the mouth of the Rhine become German. Not to be outdone, Wilhelm III of Württemberg and the Grand Duke Friedrich of Baden demanded compensation for the lives and material which the war was costing them.[51]

Nevertheless, it is Prussia, rather than Germany or Austria, which is criticised in the *New Age*. Orage is sure that 'Prussia alone is responsible for the war'. The Allies must therefore defend Europe and the world against the domination of the Prussians who go about 'with *kultur* in one hand and a bomb in the other'.[52] At the same time he was prepared to attack the bellicosity of G.K.Chesterton in his *New Witness*. Prussia, Chesterton roars, is 'like prussic acid; its poisonous essence is a fact, not a theory; and all other theories are labels printed on a bottle'.[53] Orage retaliates with a caution that 'it is useless to merely vilify the Prussians' or 'to declare that they must be exterminated like rats before peace can reign'.[54]

Since Prussia is perceived as the true enemy, Orage is dismayed to find England transformed by the war into a state run on Prussian lines. The real war criminals he identifies not as the Germans but 'our capitalist and governing classes', who, 'as the price for destroying Prussianism abroad, are insisting upon establishing Prussianism at home'.[55] The negotiations at Versailles only prove to him that 'the jackboot we have taken off the German people is now on the other leg'.[56] Four years earlier both Orage and Kennedy had accused Lloyd George of threatening England with Prussianism when he came out in favour of conscription. Kennedy brands him 'the Welsh champion of Prussianism in the Cabinet' for lending support to that 'essential feature of the Prussian system'.[57] Orage favours 'voluntaryism' [sic] rather than conscription, or compulsion as it was invariably called by contributors to the *New Age*. He seeks only 'the conscription of wealth' to pay for the war.[58]

The masterminds of German policy: 'Nitch and Tritch'.

Opinion was divided amongst contributors as to which thinkers had influenced German policy. In 1914 English writers engaged in writing propaganda tracts against Germany looked to traditions in German thought to explain away modern German strategy. However, they did not necessarily base their assumptions on the work of academic specialists, but instead drew their conclusions from the popular form into which the original philosophy had been filtered. In 1912 General Friedrich von Bernhardi's *Deutschland und der nächste Krieg* had stirred up anti-German sentiment by arguing that Germany must prepare to defeat England in a war that could no longer be avoided. Bernhardi, a member of the German General Staff, had written his treatise under the direct influence of the Morocco crisis, in October 1911. Published early in 1912 it ran through no less than six impressions in a year,[59] followed by an English translation in 1914. Bernhardi voiced the opinions of many of his contemporaries and his tract met with great approval in Germany, although German propagandists in 1914 would deny that Bernhardi had ever had any impact on policy making.[60] In addition, the title page of Bernhardi's treatise bore a quotation from Nietzsche's *Also sprach Zarathustra*:

> Der Krieg und der Mut haben mehr große Dinge getan als die Nächstenliebe. Nicht euer Mitleiden, sondern eure Tapferkeit rettete bisher die Verunglückten. Was ist gut? fragt ihr. Tapfer sein ist gut.[61]

Although this was the only reference made to Nietzsche by Bernhardi, there were extensive quotations from the Prussian historian Heinrich von Treitschke, whose works were first translated into English at the beginning of the war and confirmed English suspicions that he was typical of German greed for power.[62] The potent combination of a sabre-rattling German professor, a mad German philosopher of dubious 'morality' and a member of the German General Staff who endorsed them both was seized upon by writers of anti-German tracts. All the brutal and destructive aspects of this new, aggressive Germany were alleged to take their inspiration from the triumvirate of Bernhardi, Treitschke and Nietzsche. Thomas Mann, who was far from innocent when it came to distorting Nietzsche for his own propagandist ends in his *Betrachtungen eines Unpolitischen*, joined fellow German writers in a vigorous denunciation of this grouping on the grounds that it was a ridiculous association since Treitschke and Nietzsche hated one another, Treitschke had long since ceased to be an influential thinker, and Bernhardi was never influential in the first place.[63] Nevertheless, the trio remained uppermost in popular English perceptions of Germany.

In the opening stages of the war of words against Germany, Nietzsche and Treitschke found themselves transformed into 'two sinister demons, called Nitch and Tritch'.[64] The campaign against the philosopher and the history professor was so fierce that even when the military hostilites ended 'it was a disappointment to the British public to learn that Nitch and Tritch could not after all be hanged, as they had been dead a good many years'.[65] There were, of course, slight variations on the spelling and pronunciation. One pamphlet advised pronouncing 'Neets-shay' and 'Tritsh-kay',[66] whilst others spoke of 'the execrable "Neech"' and 'the German monster Nietzsky',[67] and one enterprisirig London bookseller advertised 'the Euro-Nietzschean War. Read the Devil in order to fight him the better'.[68] Evidently this sales tactic met with some success for the *New Age* relates a tale of 'two regular Tommies' who went to a Charing Cross Road bookshop in order to purchase a work by "this Nich or Nych"'. When shown a book of extracts from Nietzsche they 'examined it together in blank astonishment for a while and then handed it back, saying they couldn't see anything by the Kayzer [sic] in it'.[69]

J.M. Kennedy could not blame General Friedrich von Bernhardi, the author of *Deutschland und der nächste Krieg*, for the war. In 1912 Kennedy regretted that more Englishmen had not taken notice of 'authoritative Germans' such as Bernhardi, who had been 'writing and speaking about the inevitable struggle with England'. He admires the German general for stressing the 'evil effects of pacifism on the average State' and for asserting that it is the 'sacred right' of a nation to 'explain itself by force of arms'.[70]

In his examination of the same general question, the Spanish writer Ramiro de Maeztu (1874-1936) was unable to apportion responsibility for the war to any thinker in particular, tracing instead the cause to a flaw in the German national character. He denies that Treitschke's historical writings were as influential as J.A. Cramb supposed in *Germany and England* (1914). This book, based on lectures delivered eighteen months earlier and subtitled 'A reply to Bernhardi', had been instrumental in making Bernhardi known to the English public. Indeed, according to Cecil Chesterton, it constituted 'a whole-hearted welcome to Bernhardi, an enthusiastic endorsement of Bernhardi, an embracing of Bernhardi's big boots'.[71] Cramb (1861-1913) had studied in Bonn in the 1890s, heard Treitschke lecture in Berlin, and subsequently taught Modern History at Queen's College London,[72] although he remained on the periphery of academic life.[73] De Maeztu argues that Nietzsche's sole influence on the Germans was 'teaching them how to write beautifully'. Bernhardi, he claims, was 'only one of hundreds of officers who have used their pen to extol the importance of their trade'. According to de Maeztu, it was not a militarist philosophy which made the German people 'the passive tool of a military caste', but 'the radical pacifism of the German people, its incredible docility, and above all, the mania for abstractions of its intellectual classes, which has withdrawn them from any kind of political action'.[74]

Orage was far from agreeing with his colleagues. He absolved neither Bernhardi nor the professor of Prussian history, Heinrich von Treitschke, from war guilt, contending that 'the utterances of General von Bernhardi and Dr. von Treitschke are very far from being the exaggerated opinions of specialists; the whimsical beliefs of eccentric people whose views may be disregarded'. He alleges that, contrary to popular opinion, Bernhardi was inspired not by Nietzsche but by Houston Stewart Chamberlain. The 'Treitschke-Bernhardi school includes every German professor, every German journalist, every pamphleteer, every poet, every dramatist, every scholar'.[75] Writing under the pseudonym G.D., Orage accords some of the blame to Carlyle. He reasons that Carlyle wrote a biography glorifying Frederick II, the 'fountain head of Prussian jack-bootery', which is respected in all German universities. The only Englishman to merit the admiration of Treitschke was Carlyle, thus proving to Orage that Carlyle 'had undoubtedly more to do with the cause of the present war than Nietzsche'.[76]

German Culture: from the 'period before the Fall' to the post-war era.

Orage encouraged his contributors to take an interest in German literature, art, music and thought before, during and after the First World War. In 1910, for example, he published the short stories of the then unknown Katherine Mansfield. She knew German,[77] had read Heine and Nietzsche and was a relative of Countess von Arnim, the renowned author of *Elizabeth and her German Garden.*[78] She was therefore another of Orage's contributors with first hand knowledge of German language and culture. Nevertheless, the tone of the stories that now form *In a German Pension* was not particularly Germanophile. Based on her experiences as a guest in a Bavarian boarding house, Mansfield's depiction of the Germans is not always sympathetic. The mood of *Germans at Meat*, for example, is especially hostile towards a type of German encountered in the pension. Anglo-German antagonism comes to the fore at the dinner table when Kathleen, the English narrator of the story, falls into disagreement with Herr Rat. Arguing that the English have every reason to worry about being invaded because they 'have got no army at all – a few little boys with their veins full of nicotine poisoning', Herr Rat 'fixed his cold blue eyes upon Kathleen with an expression that suggested a thousand premeditated invasions'. Herr Hoffmann from Berlin increases the tension when he adds 'Don't be afraid. We don't want England. If we did we would have had her long ago. We really don't want you'.[79] Such a negative depiction did not meet with wholehearted approval from *New Age* readers. It is curious that the complete anthology did not appear in German translation until as late as 1983, although certain individual stories that were less hostile towards Germany had been published earlier in German translation.[80] Katherine Mansfield quickly grew dissatisfied with these short stories and in 1914 refused £500 to republish *In a German Pension* on the grounds that she did not wish 'to be increasing the odium against Germany'.[81] She came to consider the youthful bitterness and cynicism of her work to be untrue and unworthy of her talents. Interestingly, in 1911 Orage published a story that did not appear in the anthology, namely *The Breidenbach Family in England*. In almost a complete reversal of *Germans at Meat*, Katherine Mansfield here attempts a sympathetic depiction of Germans, making its omission from *In a German Pension* all the more striking. In this story her concern is with 'Herr Doctor Breidenbach' [sic], his wife, Emelie, and daughter, Maria, adapting to English life after leaving Munich. They take a walk in the countryside near their lodgings, 'the stout Herr Doctor with stick and scarf, his wife in a navy print and a smart hat and a stick, and Maria in white muslin and stick' and all the while 'rural England giggled audibly from behind its window curtains'. Even against this pastoral background Anglo-German hostility threatens. The conversation between the Breidenbachs inevitably turns on the likelihood of war when they notice a farm labourer staring at them. Although Breidenbach discounts such a possibility, his wife is convinced by the 'enmity' of the labourer's gaze that the English as a nation 'are dying for war'.[82]

Curiosity about Germany and its culture was not diminished by the war. In the post-war period some of Orage's more established contributors, such as Huntley Carter (d.1942), discussed the latest developments in German literature. The *New Age* accorded considerable attention to the German theatre both before and after the First World War, with Carter contributing a large number of articles on the subject based on his own observations as he travelled throughout Europe. From spring 1911 onwards he depicts Germany as a centre for theatrical innovation, although he disapproves of 'hypermodern perversities and atrocities' such as Wedekind's *Frühlings Erwachen* and Shaw's *Mrs Warren's Profession*.[83] During a visit to Germany in 1920 he is still favourably impressed by the German theatre, admiring both its productions of Shakespeare and of modern writers such as Walter Hasenclever. When he turns his attention to art he finds much to praise: amongst the German post-war innovators are Kurt Schwitters, Bruno Taut, Eric Mendelsohn, Wassily Kandinsky, Paul Klee and Georg Grosz.

Contemporary German writers always fascinated Paul Selver who, in his articles for Orage's prized literary column 'Readers and Writers' (known irreverently as 'Bleeders and Blighters' by at least one waggish contributor),[84] never tried to disguise his 'wholly romantic' attitude to Germany.[85] Between 1913 and 1915 he discussed Hermann Bahr, Arno Holz, Karl Bleibtreu, Georg Hermann, Schnitzler's stories and Thomas Mann's *Buddenbrooks*. He reacted sharply against the deluge of anti-German propaganda that accompanied the outbreak of war and confessed that he was 'heartily sick of the yelp, yelp, yelp about Huns'.[86] At the same time he relished the absurd translations that the hostilities prompted. Thus, as the Germans try to expunge all enemy words from their vocabulary, he notes that they must change 'Notre Dame' to 'Unsere liebe Frau', whilst a dinner jacket, hitherto called a 'Smoking' in German, must be 'variously metamorphosed into *Rauchjackett*, *Abendsakko*, *Frackjacke*, *Halbfrack*, *kleiner Frack* !'[87]

Selver's interest in German literature is shared by Orage. The latter praises Lichtenberg's aphorisms, commends Schopenhauer whom he regards as 'more English than German', hails Chamisso's *Peter Schlemihl: The Shadowless Man* likewise Lessing's *Laokoon* as 'a fine example of German criticism in the period before the Fall', and he suggests that readers 'skip Hegel' in favour of Kant.[88]

Orage and Nietzsche: 'A little Nietzsche is a dangerous thing.'

Arguably the most striking aspect of the *New Age* is the predominance of Nietzsche. It has been estimated that between 1907 and 1913 Orage published no fewer than eighty items relating to the German philosopher, who held enormous appeal for early twentieth century intellectuals.[89] The influence of Nietzsche on Orage can be traced from the latter's early attempts at giving lectures on the philosopher to his decision to leave for London. There, as editor of the *New Age*, he continued to champion Nietzsche, arguing that the German philosopher 'will always appeal to the Latin more than the Teutonic temperament',[90] and remonstrating with the first publishers of Nietzsche in English for having priced the philosopher out of the reach of ordinary people.[91]

Despite this early enthusiasm for promoting Nietzsche, Orage was quicker than most to seize upon the philosopher's shortcomings. As early as 11 March 1909 Orage distinguishes between Nietzsche the political philosopher and Nietzsche the poet, contending that 'Nietzsche as a poet learned more than Nietzsche as a thinker could ever express. His doctrine, besides, is vulgarly Imperialist. Nietzsche was the German Eagle!'[92] He went on to describe Nietzsche as 'The Lyrical Bismarck', as 'Bismarck's intellectual executor,

Bismarck's justification', and identified 'the essentially Prussian, and Imperial-Prussian, character of his speculations'.[93]

Orage was very much alone in his views and was not always in agreement with Oscar Levy, A.M. Ludovici and J.M. Kennedy, the self-styled Nietzscheans. However, despite his reservations, Orage was swift to defend the philosopher against any suggestion of having inspired German military policy in 1914. Although Nietzsche anticipated a conflict on the scale of the First World War, it was 'for a remote future'.[94] Orage believes that the question as to whether Nietzsche influenced German wartime strategy must be 'left open; for there is as much evidence for the one view as for the other'. He finds that Nietzsche's work is full of ambiguities because Nietzsche, 'not being a man of action', was never 'compelled to make up his mind upon any point': he 'could afford (or he allowed himself) to express contradictory judgements upon almost every problem that occurred to him'. Indeed, there is 'too much praise of force in Nietzsche to permit us to doubt that if the unity of Europe had been achieved by force he would have repudiated it'. Thus, in 1917, a 'Lyrical Bismarck' still 'best defines Nietzsche in relation to Germany'.[95] In 1919 Orage predicts that Nietzsche will be superseded, probably by psychoanalysis and Indian philosophy. Whilst some 'fragments' may be worth preserving, the 'Nietzsche of the future may be contained in a very small volume', comprising mainly aphorisms. He doubts if the German will be read in his entirety again and sees little appeal to the post-war generation on the grounds that 'Germany refused to attend to Nietzsche after 1870 when he spoke to them as one alive; they are less likely to listen to a voice from the dead after 1918'.[96]

Perhaps Orage's most valuable contribution to Anglo-German literary relations was his indefatigable promotion of Nietzsche to an English audience. This lies not only in his wholehearted admiration for the philosopher, expressed both at the Leeds Arts Club and in his books on Nietzsche, but also in his defence of Nietzsche against the more outrageous claims of wartime propagandists and in his criticism of Nietzsche and the Nietzscheans. In view of the pitfalls into which both the devotee and the opponent of Nietzsche may tumble, as highlighted by Orage, it might be fitting to conclude with his own epigram on the subject:

> *Drink deep or taste not the Nietzschean spring:*
> *A little Nietzsche is a dangerous thing.*[97]

Notes and References

[1] See Bernard Shaw, 'Was ich der deutschen Kultur verdanke', in *Die Neue Rundschau*, 22 (Berlin, 1911), p.335. However, Shaw did inform his Austrian translator, Siegfried Trebitsch, on 26 December 1902: 'I want the Germans to know me as a philosopher, as an English (or Irish) Nietzsche (only ten times cleverer).' See Patrick Bridgwater, 'English Writers and

Nietzsche', in *Nietzsche: Imagery and Thought*, edited by Malcolm Pasley (London, 1978; <*cited as*: BRIDGWATER>), p.225.

[2] See Elgin W. Mellown, 'The Development of Criticism: Edwin Muir and Franz Kafka', *Comparative Literature*, 16 (1964), pp.311-20.

[3] 19 June 1919; *New Age* <*cited as*: *NA*> vol.XXV, 8, p.134.

[4] Ashley Dukes, *The Scene is Changed* (London, 1942), p.32. For a more detailed discussion of Dukes' work see Diane Milburn, *The Deutschlandbild of A.R. Orage and the New Age circle* (Frankfurt/Main, Berlin, Bern etc., 1996), pp.62-70.

[5] Günther Blaicher, *Das Deutschlandbild in der englischen Literatur* (Darmstadt, 1992), pp.157-8.

[6] Holbrook Jackson, quoted in BRIDGWATER, p.225.

[7] For the Spring session of 1904, for example, Orage offered a series of three lectures on Nietzsche's 'Beyond Man' or superman. The session ran between January and March. See Tom Steele, *Alfred Orage and the Leeds Arts Club 1893-1923* (Aldershot, 1990; <*cited as*: STEELE-1990>), pp.71-2.

[8] Clifford Bax, *New English Weekly. A. R. Orage Memorial Number* <*cited as*: *NEW*>, VI, 5 (15 November 1934), p.117.

[9] Tom Steele, 'From Gentleman to Superman: Orage and Aristocratic Socialism', in *The Imagined Past. History and Nostalgia*, edited by Christopher Shaw and Malcolm Chase (Manchester, 1989), p.114.

[10] See STEELE-1990, pp.25-6.

[11] Holbrook Jackson, *Bernard Shaw* (London, 1907), 'Prefatory Letter', p.9.

[12] Holbrook Jackson, *NEW*, vol.VI, 5 (15 November 1934; <*cited as*: JACKSON *NEW*>), p.114.

[13] Holbrook Jackson, 'Personal Recollections', *The Windmill* (1948), p.47. Two notebooks of Orage's translations of Nietzsche's aphorisms survive. Dated 1902 they run to twenty-four and nineteen pages respectively. See STEELE-1990, p.49.

[14] A.J. Penty, *NEW*, vol.VI, 5 (15 November 1934), p.113.

[15] See JACKSON *NEW*, p.114.

[16] Quoted by Tom Steele, 'The Leeds Arts Club: A Provincial Avant-Garde?', in *Literature and History*, 14, 1 (1988), p.98.

[17] Mary Gawthorpe, *Up the Hill to Holloway* (Maine, 1962; <cited as: GAWTHORPE>), p.201. By 1906 only four volumes were available in English translation: *Thus spake Zarathustra* (1896), *The Case of Wagner. Nietzsche contra Wagner, The Antichrist* (1896), *A Genealogy of Morals. Poems* (1899) and *The Dawn of Day* (1903).

[18] It is likely that Orage, who was responsible for 'the unusual collection of books' at the Arts Club, had supervised the purchase of the three volumes of Nietzsche in English translation. See GAWTHORPE, p.191.

[19] Philippe Mairet, *A. R. Orage: A Memoir* (London, 1936; <*cited as*: MAIRET>), p.37.

[20] 'Ich habe die feste Absicht, eines Tages Deutsch zu lernen, das sollte jeder Mensch, aber ich bin noch nicht fünfundfünfzig und so hat es keine Eile'. See *Die Neue Rundschau*, 22 (Berlin, 1911), p.336.

[21] Michael Holroyd, *Bernard Shaw, Vol. I, 1856-98. The Search for Love* (London, 1988), p.130.

[22] Bernard Shaw, *Translations and Tomfooleries* (London, 1926) , p.5.

[23] Peter Buitenhuis, *The Great War of Words. Literature as Propaganda 1914-18 and After* (London, 1989).

[24] It has been estimated that between 1907 and 1922 approximately seven hundred writers contributed to the *New Age*. See Wallace Martin, *The New Age under Orage: Chapters in English Cultural History* (Manchester, 1967), p.295.

[25] 16 March 1916; *NA* vol.XVIII, 20, p.461.

[26] 20 April 1916; *NA* vol.XVIII, 25, p.581.

[27] 2 May 1907; *NA* vol.I, 1, p.2.

[28] 13 January 1910; *NA* vol.VI, 11, p.243.

[29] 14 November 1912; *NA* vol.XII, 2, p.27.

[30] Beatrice Hastings, *The old 'New Age'. Orage – and others* (London, 1936), p.43.

[31] 13 August 1914; *NA* vol.XV, 15, p.350.

[32] 17 January 1918; *NA* vol.XXII, 12, p.227.

[33] 20 August 1914; *NA* vol.XV, 16, p.362.

[34] 9 March 1916; *NA* vol.XVIII, 19, pp.438-9.

[35] 3 May 1917; *NA* vol.XXI, 1, pp.1-2.

[36] Stuart Wallace, *War and the Image of Germany. British Academics 1914-1918* (Edinburgh, 1988; <*cited as*: WALLACE>), p.162.

[37] Paul Fussell, *The Great War and Modern Memory* (New York and London, 1975), p.176.

[38] See WALLACE, p.161.

[39] *Ibid*., p.163.

[40] *NA* vol.XV,16,p.379.

[41] For an account of how Levy was accused of having 'brought this poison to England', see Oscar Levy, 'Nietzsche im Krieg', in *Nietzsche und die deutsche Literature. Texte zur Nietzsche Rezeption 1873-1963*, edited by Bruno Hillebrand, 2 vols (Tübingen, 1978), I, p.193.

[42] 5 November 1914; *NA* vol.XVI, 1, p.23.

[43] Humphrey Carpenter, *A Serious Character: The Life of Ezra Pound* (London, 1988), pp.160-9.

[44] 8 January 1920; *NA* vol.XXVI, 10, pp.153-4.

[45] 15 April 1920; *NA* vol.XXVI, 24, pp.383-4.

[46] Kennedy was something of a mystery figure and opinion was divided amongst those to knew him as to whether he was involved in espionage or not. See MAIRET, p.61 and Paul Selver, *Orage and the New Age Circle* (London, 1959; <*cited as*: SELVER>), p.20.

[47] 12 May 1910; *NA* vol.VII, 2, p.27.

[48] 13 April 1911; *NA* vol.VIII, 24, p.555.

[49] 28 September 1911; *NA* vol.IX, 27, p.510.

[50] 1 October 1914; *NA* vol.XV, 22, pp.515-16.

[51] Fritz Fischer, *Griff nach der Weltmacht* (Düsseldorf, 1961), p.217.

[52] 28 February 1918; *NA* vol.XXII, 18, pp.341-4.

[53] 23 August 1917; *New Witness* X, 251, p.387.

[54] 1 November 1917; *NA* vol.XXII, 1, p.4.

55 17 May 1917; *NA* vol.XXI, 3, p.51.

56 15 May 1919; *NA* vol.XXV, 3, pp.33-4.

57 30 September 1915; *NA* vol.XVII, 22, pp.519-20.

58 4 May 1916; *NA* vol.XIX, 1, p.5.

59 T.J. Reed, *Thomas Mann. The Uses of Tradition* (Oxford, 1974), p.215.

60 See Fritz Fischer, *Krieg der Illusionen* (Düsseldorf, 1969), pp.344-7.

61 Nietzsche, *Werke*, edited by Karl Schlechta, 3 volumes (Munich, 1956), II, p.312.

62 Gertrud von Petzhold, 'Nietzsche in englisch-amerikanischer Beurteilung bis zum Ausgang des Weltkrieges', *Anglia*, 53 (1929), p.148.

63 Letter from Thomas Mann to Ernst Bertram, quoted by R. Hinton Thomas, *Nietzsche in German Politics and Society 1890-1918* (Manchester, 1983; <*cited as*: HINTON THOMAS>), p.128.

64 Recalled by E. R. Dodds, *The Ancient Concept of Progress and Other Essays on Greek Literature and Belief* (Oxford, 1973), p.104.

65 *Ibid*., p.105.

66 Canon E. McLure, *Germany's War Inspirers: Nietzsche and Treitschke* (London, 1914). Quoted by James Joll, 'The English, Friedrich Nietzsche and the First World War', in *Deutschland in der Weltpolitik des 19. und 20. Jahrhunderts*, edited by Imanuel Geiss and Bernd Jürgen Wendt (Düsseldorf, 1973), p.287.

67 Patrick Bridgwater, *Nietzsche in Anglosaxony* (Leicester, 1972), p.203.

68 See HINTON THOMAS, p.128.

69 10 September 1914; *NA* vol.XV, 19, p.455.

70 4 April 1912; *NA* vol.X, 23, p.533.

71 Cecil Chesterton, *The Prussian Hath said in his Heart* (London, 1914), p.85.

72 M.E. Humble, 'The Breakdown of a Concensus: British Writers and Anglo-German Relations 1900-1920', in *Journal of European Studies* (March 1977), p.45.

73 See WALLACE, p.68.

74 4 March 1915; *NA* vol.XVI, 18, p.481.

75 15 October 1915; *NA* vol.XV, 24, p.573.

76 18 March 1915; *NA* vol.XVI, 20, pp.534-6.

77 German appears to have been one of her best languages at school, even if her grasp was not wholly grammatical. See Claire Tomalin, *Katherine Mansfield: A Secret Life* (London, 1987), pp.21-3 and Jeffrey Meyers, *Katherine Mansfield: A Biography* (London, 1978), pp.13-16.

78 John Carswell, pp.54-6.

79 3 March 1910; *NA* vol.VI, 18, p.419.

80 B. J. Kirkpatrick, *A Bibliography of Katherine Mansfield* (Oxford, 1989), pp.198-204.

81 John Middleton Murray, 'The Literary Review', *New York Evening Post* (17 February 1923), p.41. Quoted by Ruth Elvish Mantz, *Critical Bibliography of Katherine Mansfield* (New York, 1968), p.30.

82 3 March 1910; *NA* vol.VI, 18, p.419.

83 27 July 1911; *NA* vol.IX, 13, pp.293-4.

[84] The term was coined by C. E. Bechhofer (1894-1949). See SELVER, p.50.

[85] *Ibid.*, p.55.

[86] 8 October 1914; *NA* vol.XV, 23, p.555.

[87] 1 April 1915; *NA* vol.XVI, 22, p.589.

[88] See *NA* vol.XIII, 6, p.145, *NA* vol.XVI, 26, p.695, *NA* vol.XVII, 20, p.477 and *NA* vol.XVII, 4, p.85.

[89] John Carey, *The Intellectuals and the Masses: Pride and Prejudice among the Literary Intelligentsia, 1880-1939* (London, 1992), p.4.

[90] 17 October 1907; *NA* vol.I, 25, p.398.

[91] 20 June 1908; *NA* vol.III, 8, p.153.

[92] *NA* vol.IV, 20, p.399.

[93] 27 January 1910; *NA* vol.VI, 13, p.304.

[94] 27 August 1914; *NA* vol.XV, 17, p.396.

[95] 14 June 1917; *NA* vol.XX, 7, p.158.

[96] 18 December 1919; *NA* vol.XXVI, 7, pp.109-10.

[97] 20 August 1914; *NA* vol.XV, 17, p.396.

Mephisto in Modern English Guise

RICHARD BYRN

Meine Dichtergluth war sehr gering, *So lang ich dem Guten entgegenging,* *Dagegen brannte sie lichterloh,* *Wenn ich vor drohendem Übel floh.* Goethe, *Werke* I,2, *Sprichwörtlich*	*Poetic fire sank low in me,* *When it was good I sought to see;* *But up it flamed, up to the sky,* *When it was evil I sought to fly.* W.H. Auden[1]

A quotation from Goethe provides the starting-point for this paper and Goethe remains the presiding spirit, but it has to be acknowledged from the outset that there is one major constraint when considering the inspiration for modern English *Faust* versions, namely, the likelihood of alternative sources, particularly English ones. As regards the outcome of the play's action – its most important aspect – Goethe allowed Faust to be saved in the end, whereas in the old *Chapbook* versions and in Marlowe's 'Tragical History' Faust was damned. The difference is crucial. Modern creative artists have difficulty with the theological concept of Salvation, as also with the concepts of Eternal Life and Heaven. Thus, with Christian Hope demythologised, and since this present life is undoubtedly for so many a 'Hell on Earth', the temper of our times evidently finds it easier to prevent Faust from coming to the experience of Salvation or even to some form of authentic human happiness, choosing rather to observe him degenerate or, at best, to enter the oblivion of death in a despairing state of unfulfilment – that is, of course, in so far as 20th century writers take the Faust myth with its notion of a pact with the Devil seriously at all. For the strong odour of sulphur it is necessary to go back to Marlowe.

But why focus on Mephisto rather than on Faust himself? Faust, one might argue, since he is human and is so recognisably a representative of 'homo academicus', would be the obvious subject for academic enquiry – the sort of subject which Faust's pupil Wagner (or any other subsequent incarnation of scholarly endeavour) must surely handle very competently. Mephisto, by contrast, although his behaviour may be human, is, by definition, not human but a supernatural manipulator of men's weaknesses – an emanation of that baneful negative principle in human affairs which sets out to deceive and destroy. Why spend time on him? The answer lies in the brief, aphoristic fragment from Goethe's 'große Konfession' quoted at the start of this paper. Here Goethe 'was speaking for all artists' – as Auden observed. Goethe's telling perception of the power of Evil to inspire creativity explains why Mephisto, rather than Faust, is the focus of this paper. That baneful principle which Mephisto embodies invariably arouses a frisson of excitement – exercising a mesmerising, barely resistible attraction, undoubtedly of greater appeal than the strivings and pinings of an earnest, presumptuous, self-absorbed scholar.[2] It is a central concern of this paper to observe the enduring power of the metaphor of Hell in the evocation of Evil. It is, thus, Mephisto who beckons more strongly than Faust or Wagner. Mephisto is, in a commonplace of critical response, 'wicked, but interesting'.

One wonders if Faust's other would-be pupil (in Goethe's version) even remotely understood what was happening when he left Faust's study reverently, having just received Mephistopheles' autograph: *Eritis sicut Deus, scientes bonum et malum* [*Studierzimmer*, 2048]. Goethe's irony, here as elsewhere, is very evident. Whether or not *homo academicus* (as distinct from *homo pedagogicus*) will ever admit to knowing with confidence a clear distinction between Good and Evil, he, like *poeta*, continues to be fascinated by Evil – and to be inspired by it. And if Faust is born again afresh in every generation (or even if 'every man must write his own *Faust*'[3]), then Mephisto will always be one step ahead, lying in wait, smoothing his way and, as likely as not, speaking English – nowadays, indeed, he is more likely than not to be speaking English. Nowadays, too, he could quite possibly take on female guise.

Accordingly, this essay concentrates on five modern English incarnations of Mephisto, with publication-dates ranging between 1979 and 1992. The first two are direct descendants of the Chapbook-Marlowe-Goethe story-line – though they are wholly different from each other in every respect: D.J. Enright, *A Faust Book* (1979); Robert Nye, *Faust [...]* (1980). The other three are more distantly related: Terry Pratchett, ~~***Faust***~~ *Eric* (1990); Emma Tennant, *Faustine* (1992); and Fay Weldon, *Growing Rich* (1992).

In order to make comparisons easier, we may begin by recalling how Goethe imagined Mephisto. In general terms – through all the ironies of shifting, partial definition – Goethe's Mephisto is most readily remembered as 'a rogue': *der Schalk* [339, 4885], *der Schelm* [2515]. Despite his powerfulness and despite the play's many ironic, oblique references to the 'Teufel' as if to Mephisto,[4] he is not 'the Devil Himself' but a servant of the Devil – while at the same time, ironically, he is also a servant of Almighty God, since it is God who sends forth Mephisto to goad men out of their cosy-slippered comfort into creative action:

> DER HERR: Des Menschen Tätigkeit kann allzuleicht erschlaffen,
> Er liebt sich bald die unbedingte Ruh;
> Drum geb ich gern ihm den Gesellen zu,
> Der reizt und wirkt und muß als Teufel schaffen. [340-3]

Mephisto claims that he pre-dates Creation, thus making him coeval with God, even a part of God: *'Ich bin ein Teil des Teils, der Anfangs Alles war'* [1349]. But, of course, his 'part of God' is God's downside, the obverse of Light: *'Ein Teil der Finsternis, die sich das Licht gebar'* [1350]. When Faust asked him his name – be it *'Fliegengott, Verderber, Lügner'* [1334] – Mephisto's reply includes the statements: *'Ich bin der Geist, der stets verneint!'* [1338] and – of special significance for Goethe's concept of the limits on Evil's power – *'ein Teil von jener Kraft, die stets das Böse will, und stets das Gute schafft'* [1335f]. Thus, in general terms, Goethe's Mephisto is a secondary, negative power, and his negativity – with whatever reluctance on his part – always has a creative outcome. Goethe's version is indeed unique in the limitations it places on Mephisto: the challenge-cum-wager with God is found in no other version, and Mephisto's pact with Faust is not the straightforward deal found elsewhere but a carefully calculated wager: Goethe gives the Devil no guarantee of success, either with man or with man's Creator.

In physical appearance Goethe's Mephisto also varies widely according to the requirements of the occasion: Black Poodle [*Vor dem Tor*], Wandering Scholar [*Studierzimmer*], Master of Rats and Mice, Flies, Frogs, Bugs and Lice [*Studierzimmer*], ready-witted drinking companion [*Auerbachs Keller*], Court Jester [*II, Act 1*]; he even appears, to the witch's eyes, as *'Junker Satan'* [*Hexenküche*]. In Frau Marthe's presence he is a honey-tongued story-teller and liar; in the seduction of Gretchen he is a silver-tongued procurer, and in his response to Faust's despair at Gretchen's disgrace he speaks with the consummate cynicism which so shocked young Goethe: *'Sie ist die erste nicht!'* [*Trüber Tag. Feld*]. Above all, Mephisto is an unparalleled master of verbal wit.

What, now, becomes of him in modern English guise?

Mephisto thwarted with irony: D.J. Enright, *A Faust Book.*[5]

Of the five Mephistos here considered, Enright's is the one which most closely resembles Goethe's. Enright, indeed, greatly admired Goethe. As a 25-year-old he published *A Commentary on Goethe's 'Faust'* (Part I only – it has to be said)[6]. Enright's later poems, essays and book-reviews often treat ideas or works of Goethe's.[7] Then, in his late 50's, Enright went on to publish a *Faust Book* of his own. This *Faust Book* has also been paid the compliment of appraisal in the critical literature by a distinguished Germanist – Leonard Forster. Uniquely well qualified to appreciate the *Book's* pervasive ironies, Forster's commentary falls short of enthusiasm but does convey clear respect for Enright's poetic conceptions and rhetorical skills.[8]

In form, Enright's version of the Faust story is a cycle of 73 short scenes, most of them crafted as unrhymed (by and large) but skilfully rhythmical poems. They tell a story which develops in subject-matter from the opening *'Dr Faust discourses on training and heredity'* through to the concluding *'Faust and Mephistopheles make their adieus'*. There are no large-scale set pieces. Amongst its characters it introduces two modern females to share Faust's bed: one of them is a go-go dancer with a name which could have come straight out of Goscinny: *Meretrix* (pronounced 'Merry Tricks'); the other is the Wittenberg University Rektor's wife (she is bored by her husband's constant ratiocination and lack of sparkle in bed). Just as anything resembling a major soliloquy is eschewed so, conversational exchanges in these poems are also rarely held between more than two people at a time. Laconic wit sets the tone. Five of the scenes are written partly in prose, and four of them wholly in prose. – Not the least of the composition's pervasive ironies can be sensed in Enright's choice of scenes to set wholly in prose: they include *In the tavern*, *In the Senior Common Room*, and *Faust's farewell to his friends* – this latter is related by a perplexed friend.

The cycle's overall structure bears one superficial similarity to Goethe's *Tragödie* in that it is divided into two Parts. But the similarity extends only to the fact that Faust meets and fathers a son by Helen of Troy in Part Two. Other than this, Part Two contains little trace of 'die große Welt'. It includes two scenes which, in Goethe's version, belong in Part One: *Faust is set upon by Gretchen's brother* and *Gretchen at the sewing machine*. Forster found this latter scene to be the most moving in the cycle, and he expresses surprise that the Germans he has discussed it with do not share his admiration.[9]

Irony pervades Enright's *Faust Book* almost throughout – but we stress the 'almost'. It is the knowing irony of a story-teller who knows that his listener/reader knows a lot about the Faust story, maybe even thinks he knows what's coming next – only to be surprised. At the same time it is also the weary irony of a poet who knows that, nowadays, single-parenthood is hardly an issue, seduction no special thrill. Indeed, with the arrival of sexual equality, the woman is as likely to be the predator as the man – taking her cue, no doubt, from the second of those words of modern womanly wisdom for an ambitious woman bored by home surroundings recorded in Weldon's *Growing Rich*: 'You can work your way out, you can sleep your way out, you can sell your soul to the Devil'. Nowadays, indeed, with sexual innocence easily lost to the ready prescription of pill and condom, we need expect no 'Gretchen tragedy', and certainly none in this particular *Faust Book*. Ironically echoing Shakespeare, Enright has Faust name Gretchen in his will:

> 'My second-best bed I bequeath to Fräulein Gretchen,
> of address unknown'
> (She lived far off, with a man who wanted children).

If eloquence and mastery of verbal wit are the main characteristics of Goethe's Mephisto, then Enright's Mephisto is certainly his double. What Enright's Faust mostly wants from Mephisto during their early acquaintance is an explanation for the 'big' questions: 'Who was it made the world?' [12], 'Why is it little children suffer, Guiltless beyond dispute?' [16], 'What can fallen angels know of love?' [19]. Mephisto always has an answer – even if it is a prevarication. But even when prevaricating, he is never less than witty, and generally, as one might expect, facetious.

Our first awarenes of Mephisto comes in the opening scene where he enters – here mirroring Goethe's version – as a poodle. This dog-shape provides several opportunities for drollish punning, starting with the fact that 'dog' spelled backwards (after the widdershins fashion of devilry) gives 'god'. Thus Mephisto explains that Lucifer, the Lord of Hell, is known to his minions as the 'Drol Dog.' 'Talking of which,' he finishes, 'every god has its day – What would you like to do with yours?' [3]. Later, when Helen and Faustus' son is born, Mephisto 'offered to stand dogfather to the babe.' [46].

Apart from this initial canine front, Mephisto appears only in the guise of a human being – and as such he is naturally distrusted by Wagner ('that Levantine') and Gretchen ('that creepy fellow') and by Faust's parents and by the other mere mortals who have to do with him, but he does not appear in quite the protean variations envisaged by Goethe. He is best evoked and remembered, perhaps, simply by the amiable phrase which Faust uses of him: 'my skinny friend'.

Where Enright's Mephisto most clearly differs from Goethe's is in the sense of failure which he emanates. He may have appropriate miraculous powers in physical and spiritual matters, but Enright does not invite the reader to marvel at them. Remarkably enough for one so inclined to facetiousness, there are also several significant moments when Mephisto's eloquence falters, as he refuses to indulge in easy rhetoric: Enright's Mephisto does have limitations. Irony may be, in practice, the only mode suitable for serious discussion of the problem of Evil, but elsewhere Enright does not necessarily indulge in this 'analgesic of the privileged'.[10] In his essay 'What happened to the Devil?',[11] for example, he takes modern churchmen to task for their failure to take Evil seriously – in the interests, as they claim, of ecumenism and removing barriers. It is thus particularly striking for our theme that Enright's Mephisto, too, does not invariably speak with irony. There is a special poignancy in his reluctance to talk about Heaven, for example. When finally obliged to do so in conversation with Faust, he says:

> '[...] – heaven is full.
> That's not to say it's chock-a-block with people.
> Simply, full – that's what you feel.
> The word is fullness.'
> 'For one so renowned for eloquence
> I find you sadly tongue-tied!'
> 'Whereof one cannot bear to speak,
> Thereof one says but little.' [12]

A skilful adaptation of Wittgenstein this may be, but its tone does not strike the reader as ironical – any more than does Wittgenstein's original aphorism. At this moment in the dialogue the reader is struck by the intimation that the antonym of: 'wicked, but interesting' is not 'good, but dull', so much as 'good, but terrifying'.

At the end of the cycle Mephisto remains thwarted. He has done his bit well – indeed, one could even say he has done it honourably. Enright's Faust has lived his 24 years to the full (actually it is only 12 years, but Mephisto argues that, since he had worked for Faust both day and night, 12 years is really worth 24).

Unfortunately for Mephisto, however, his boss intervenes directly at this point. It turns out that Lucifer has lost interest in this particular scholarly friend of Mephisto's:

> 'Someone in Weimar has tacked together
> An artful defence of your friend, I gather. [...]
> I think we yield to the cunning Geheimrat,
> And suffer your fortunate friend to depart. [...]
> We let the Doctor go scot-free,
> To encourage the others ...
> *Experto credite!*' [74]

Thus *Lucifer advises Mephistopheles of the device known as throwing a sprat to catch a school of mackerel.* How many latter-day Fausts, one wonders uneasily, did Enright imagine have been caught since?

So, with all due acknowledgment to Goethe, the would-be victim of Enright's Mephisto is reprieved. 'It's roses roses all the way for Faust...' [74]. The cycle finishes with the two good companions taking leave of each other:

> 'You'll miss me, Faust. I was your muse.
> Who will amuse you now?' [...]
> 'That's true, my friend,' Faust sighed.
> 'You've ruined me for other company.
> I'll pass my days in some far wilderness.'
> Was there no wilderness at hand?
> 'I'll miss you too,' said Mephistopheles.
> 'But then, I'm used to missing ...'
> *(Faust and Mephistopheles make their adieus).*

There is no trace of tragedy here. Mephisto is reduced to an ironical punster.

In the presence of such ubiquitous jocularity a pun of our own obtrudes involuntarily: 'End right? – All's right!'

Monk-ey business: Robert Nye's *FAUST, being the 'Historia Von D. Johann Fausten dem wietbeschreyten* [sic] *Zauberer und Schwartzkünstler', or 'History of Dr John Faust the notorious Magician and Necromancer', as written by his familiar servant and disciple Christopher Wagner, now for the first time Englished from the Low German.*[12]

This lengthy novel will not detain us long. Where Enright's *Faust Book* is a slim, tautly-constructed cycle, Nye's novel is as prolix as its baroque sub-title suggests. Enright may disappoint ultimately because of too much irony, but Nye's *Faust* does not even begin to satisfy: it is arch, pretentious, quasi-learned, childish, scurrilously anti-Protestant, fantastical, scatological, nihilistic, offensively anti-Catholic and, from about half-way onwards, penitentially boring. As the sub-title also suggests, the novel is in fact as much about Christopher Wagner as about Faust. Here, for a flavour of its style, is how Wagner introduces himself:

> I'm Christopher Wagner. Never mind about my parents. They didn't give two fucks about me.
>
> Just the one fuck. Ha ha.
>
> OK. I'm a bastard.
>
> I don't know who my father was. Some waggoner or other. My mother was cook at the Wartburg. The waggoner stuck his spoke in her soup and I'm the comestibles.
>
> The Wartburg. That castle near Eisenach. Like a wart it is, too. A brown papillary excrescence on top of a hill. [9]

– Poor Marlowe! Poor Goethe!

The novel is narrated in three Parts, entitled respectively: 'The Tower', 'The Road to Rome', and 'Holy Week'. It is set at the start of Lent in the year 1540. Faust, now aged 60, has just 40 days left before he must surrender his soul. Helen, beautiful but sanctimonious, persuades Faust – on the strength of a vision from the Blessed Virgin Mary – to go on pilgrimage to Rome where, having confessed to the Pope and done penance, he will be saved. Faust eventually agrees but only because, unbeknown to Helen, Mephistopheles has meantime offered him a reprieve of 24 more years if he will take the opportunity to murder the Pope.

A significant dog features in the novel: large, black and ungovernable. When Faust and Wagner pause en route through Geneva in order to listen to Calvin preaching, the dog – Calvin's pet – transfers its affection and loyalty to Faust. Its nick-name is Satan. (Helen claims that this name is really the corruption of a Cornish Saint's name: Sampson.)

Mephisto features in the novel in the guise of a Franciscan Monk – a Grey Friar. Most of the time he is concealed in the background – a malevolent power whom Faust fears. Part of Faust's pact with him is that Mephistopheles should never appear unless summoned, and then only in the guise of a Grey Friar, and even then only after he has rung a bell a couple of times.

Ever-present, on the other hand, from about one-fifth of the way through the narration, is a simian which we may think of as Mephisto's alter ego – a Capuchin, kept in a cage. This monk-ey, named Akercocke, is also the incarnation of Faust's own spirit, and it was made over to a most unwilling Wagner three days after Wagner was rash enough to ask Faust to bequeath him his 'cunning'. Since Faust interpreted 'his cunning' as 'his spirit', and since Faust's familiar spirit was Mephisto, then this Capuchin monkey is a Grey Friar in disguise.

The malevolent Akercocke gradually takes over the reluctant Wagner. At the end of the novel, on Holy Saturday, Wagner seizes the opportunity to get his own back on Faust by twisting off Faust's head – this is manifestly the revenge of the buggered on the buggerer. Then, as the bells ring out on Easter Sunday, Christopher Wagner finally releases Akercocke from his cage: "Akercocke's nice. Akercocke's really nice" he says.

The novelist's only hint of self-irony comes when Wagner reflects, about two-thirds of the way through: '[I'm] bleary from too much writing about things which no sane man should ever have to write about' [180f].

What, if anything, we may ask, can be taken seriously in this novel? – If anything at all, perhaps it is the moment when Nye has Wagner reflect, towards the end of Part One:

> I'm writing this book because neither Faust nor Helen *can* be right. No damnation. No salvation. People who believe in such stuff say 'It is written', don't they? Meaning there's some Great Book in which we're all characters. Meaning there's some over-all Fate which determines our lives.
>
> Well, there is no such Fate. No Great Book. And 'it' isn't 'written'. I'm writing it ... Just a little book. [94].

These lines no doubt reflect a substratum of spiritual anguish, of struggle with the concept of Salvation and its antonym. But the outcome as a novel is bathetic.

As for Mephisto: he may indeed appear in various shapes and sizes, he does have the magical power to transport Faust and Wagner to the 3rd Wedding of Henry VIII and back, he can procure for either man an international variety of bed-companions, he may even sometimes sound witty, but the net effect is a lurid farrago.

Comic relief: Terry Pratchett's ~~***FAUST***~~ *Eric*.[13]

Suspend disbelief. – But on the other hand, if Marlowe, Goethe *et al.* can project something as improbable as a mortal summoning up a spirit/demon, why shouldn't Discworld's creator do likewise? Certainly, it is impressive to find echoes of *Faust* in children's literature. Prepare, then, to make believe.

The 'Faust' of this story is a 13-year-old going on 14, named Eric Thursley, who suffers from acne and the tiresome adolescent habit of poking his nose into other people's business.[14] He knows nothing about the mythical or historical Faust but, under the impulse of his own imagination and the desire to have three wishes fulfilled, he conjures up a spirit by means of a magic circle and a magic spell.[15]

The 'Mephistopheles' of this story is named Rincewind.[16] Eric assumes that Rincewind is a demon. He himself thinks he is a wizard, but it turns out that he is a human – at least, that is what Astfgl, King of Hell, declares him to be. Astfgl could be wrong, though, since a snap of Rincewind's fingers is enough to transport him and his companions anywhere through Time and Space – which no mere mortal can do (unless s/he be a writer?). Rincewind's main ally is an extraordinary, oblong-shaped box with legs and a mind of its own, known as 'the Luggage'.[17]

There is no 'Gretchen'. (Nor is there any Salvation.) 'Helen of Troy' appears briefly in the form of Elenor of Tsort.

Eric declares his three wishes thus: 'I want mastery of the kingdoms of the world, I want to meet the most beautiful woman who has ever lived, *and* I want to live for ever' [22]. The story's main action[18] follows their experiences as Rincewind sets about fulfilling Eric's wishes, first in one of the Amazonian-type rain-forest Kingdoms of Tezuman, then in the midst of the Classical war between Ephebes and Tsort, finally at the very Dawn of Creation – their fulfilment, however, brings nothing but disillusion.[19]

'Hell' certainly features large. Rincewind's penalty for defying the King of the Demons will be everlasting torture in Hell. This is evoked as containing, amongst other things, eight Circles with traditional torments rendered exquisite by potted plants, music and the refinements of boredom[20], and with a path whose pavings are inscribed with good intentions.[21] In the end, however, our two heroes succeed in escaping – to that extent not only is Eric 'saved', but so too is Rincewind.

How seriously, we may ask in conclusion, does Pratchett present Mephisto and Hell and the issues raised by the matter of mankind's Salvation (– insofar as that is not an absurd question to ask of children's fiction)? Let the following quotation from an early footnote in the novel serve as the author's own tongue-in-cheek answer:

> Interestingly enough, the gods of the Disc have never bothered much about judging the souls of the dead, and so people only go to hell if that's where they believe, in their deepest heart, that they deserve to go. Which they won't do if they don't know about it. This explains why it is important to shoot missionaries on sight [31].

The Devil and his handmaiden: Emma Tennant's *Faustine*.[22]

In Emma Tennant's *Faustine* we meet a female-orientated but anti-Feminist variation on the Faust-theme. It does not mirror as much of the traditional 'Faust' as Weldon's *Growing Rich*, but it does include several significant features of the main story, i.e. a Faust figure, a Mephisto figure, and a pact with the Devil. Also, a little more remotely, it has what can be seen as a Gretchen figure and a Frau Marthe figure. Most strikingly, though, the person of Faust is female.

The novel is narrated in 19 chapters, divided between four sections of unequal length, headed respectively: 'The Granddaughter's Tale', 'The Nurse's Tale', 'The Mother's Tale', and 'The Devil's Tale'. From these section-headings the reader might assume that the narrative perspective will alter accordingly, but in practice it does not. Until we reach the relatively short concluding section – 'The Devil's Tale' – the story is told primarily from the point of view of 26-year-old Ella, who is 'the granddaughter' of the novel and who is, symbolically, both a

Gretchen figure and – as explained to her by the Nurse – a Persephone figure in reverse.[23]

When 'the Devil' addresses us in the final section, we discover that he is not after all His Satanic Majesty Himself, but a subordinate. In Hell, he tells us, he has a master: 'the old prince of all mingling and ambiguity' [138] who had taken him to task once or twice for the length of time he was spending over the conversion of his victim. – Henceforth it will be more convenient for our purposes to refer to this craftily manipulative subordinate simply as Mephisto.

The novel's externals can be summarised as follows. There are five main characters. Four are indicated by the novel's section-headings: 'Granddaughter', 'Nurse', 'Mother', and 'Devil'/Mephisto. The fifth character is actually the novel's central one: the Grandmother, Muriel Twyman (=*Faustine*).

The 'place' is Woodford Manor, home of the fabulously beautiful Lisa Crane – a media star of Marilyn Monroe proportions. This splendid house is situated in the village of Woodford-cum-Slape on the edge of Salisbury Plain, within hearing distance (and almost sight) of Stonehenge. The time is the present – let us say the year of the novel's publication, 1992. And, significantly, the day is Midsummer's Day: echoes of what might be 'Walpurgisnacht' can be heard in the all-night revelling and rioting of the hippie mob who celebrate the summer solstice at Stonehenge despite opposition from the police. The foreground action takes place within one day. Ella, the granddaughter, has returned to England after a 20-year interval to look for her beloved grandmother who had cared for her as infant and young child. She succeeds in locating her quickly but, before she can meet her, she first has to learn what had become of her. The action climaxes when nine o'clock chimes that evening for dinner.

During a brief opening preamble we learn that Ella had been brought up in Australia on a sheep station north of Melbourne; sadly for her as an infant in London, the problem of coping with her had become too much for her single-parent mother and distracted grandmother, so she had been sent away to the care of distant relatives, kindly Maureen and Bill Fisher. The antipodean distance of those relatives' home is necessary to the novel's verisimilitude: the reader has to be persuaded that Ella's loss of contact with her family in England was complete – Australians could be expected to know about the media star Lisa Crane, but not necessarily to know where she had come from.

Despite the eventual loss of contact, Ella never forgot her grandmother. Her only clue as to Muriel's present whereabouts, however, is the place-name Woodford Manor, reluctantly given to her by the aggressively anti-English Maureen, who does not approve of her sentimental journey. Ella reflects on her plan to meet Muriel again:

> My heart was racing – but that wasn't so odd, really, when you consider that love is a rare commodity and I knew enough about what it was like not to have it, to come

> over as faint as a heroine in a romantic novel when there seemed a chance of getting some of it back again. The difference of course, was that my quest wasn't for a dashing young man (and Bill Fisher and Maureen, I'd heard them, thought this pretty weird of me). It was for an old woman. But, as I say, you can no more dictate who you're going to love than sit down and paint or write a masterpiece at the crack of a moneyman's whip. Muriel was all I had. And now I had a clue, at least, as to where I could go to find her. [13].

Section One, 'The Granddaughter's Tale', ends with Ella safely arrived at Woodford Manor, and about to be told what had become of her grandmother. Her informant – the nurse of 'The Nurse's Tale' – is exceptionally well-informed, so much so that she could almost be Muriel Twyman herself. In fact, when Ella first saw her from behind she mistook her for Muriel. They were of an age – Muriel and this, her close friend, Jasmine. So close was their friendship, in fact, that Jasmine had evidently shared looking after infant Ella as intimately as Muriel had done – and yet, curiously, Ella has no memory of her.

Jasmine fills in the story regarding Ella's mother's and grandmother's occupations: Anna, the mother, worked in a publishing house – a women's co-operative, which she had founded herself. The grandmother was a copy-writer for a major fashion glossy. Ella reflects on her childhood perception of their respective occupations:

> What a contrast there was between Muriel's work and my mother's!
>
> Muriel worked, I knew this even so young, so as to be able to buy special presents and treats for me. I was all she had, and she was everything to me.
>
> Anna worked for dear life. She worked to find herself, to create a career, to matter in the world. And I knew, as small children always do, that the person she loved wasn't me. It was something frightening and far away from me: it was theory, and endeavour, and, as I bitterly felt then (for with the cruelty of the very young I knew nothing of the meaning of ideals and wanted only love), she had learned to love herself.
>
> To my mind, Anna loved anything that wasn't me. [43f].

It is about here in this Magic Realist narrative that the reader begins to sense that Muriel Twyman (alias Lisa Crane) is the novel's title-figure: *Faustine*. She is the right age – in her meno-pausal mid-to-late forties. True, she is no frustrated academic, but her job as a copy-writer belongs at the drudgery end of the hack's trade, and academics, too, are notoriously prone to identifying their profession with hackery. Away from the office, Muriel's home-life is no less filled with drudgery – the domestic chores of feeding, washing, bedding and babysitting an infant granddaughter on behalf of an absent, working daughter. In these bored and lonely circumstances Muriel was manifestly an apt target for Mephisto's wiles.

To help him achieve his goal Mephisto took human form in the person of Harry Crane – an irresistibly manly figure – and, additionally, he employed the services of what he calls a handmaiden – Jasmine, this novel's 'Frau Marthe'. At the story's climax Mephisto arrives as a mysterious visitor wearing 'black boots built up at the heel and a dark suit' [131]. When he leaves a short while later, he is seen walking back up the drive. A young woman is on his arm, and 'the effect of light and shade from the moon [...] gives the impression that an old woman, huge in the faint glow from the fires in the woods, is running up the drive after them' [131] – a double reward for his efforts.

Unlike the Mephisto figures in the other four works we are considering, this one remains backstage until the climax – though he is a potent backstage presence. As the innocent and self-absorbed Ella travels from Waterloo down to Salisbury, she becomes uncomfortably aware of a male fellow-passenger:

> a man, I think Maureen would term a 'gentleman' (this with a light laugh, both contemptuous and repressed), a member of a species, at any rate, that we don't have back home, however many mega-millions the Packers and the Murdochs may make or however far-flung their empires. This gentleman was wearing a suit of the deepest black [20].

Arrived at Woodford station, she had just put her hand out to open the taxi door

> when another hand came out from behind me and opened the door instead. I had to look round. I saw the gentleman of the first-class compartment, and I thanked him awkwardly. He obviously had no desire to reply and strode off down the road – though whether he turned away from the town like the hippies, or made for the centre, I have no idea at all [22].

Later on in the story Ella recalls an occasion when, as an infant, she was sitting on the floor in the TV shop where her grandmother was engrossed in the salesman's patter:

> I heard Muriel say, Yes, that's my little granddaughter.
>
> As the man walked past, I distinctly saw that he wasn't wearing socks – only built-up little boots that gave him a funny, strutting air. Being on the floor, I know I saw what his legs were like, between the turn-up of his trouser and the top of his boots. And they were black and shiny, like the coat of a pony or a goat [73].

Infant Ella was a major hindrance to Mephisto: he had to get Muriel to stop caring so much about her. At least once he tried to drown the baby in the river at Woodford.

In 'The Devil's tale' Mephisto explains that his strategy in pursuit of Muriel had been, first, to seduce her daughter, Anna – that strongly woman-orientated leader of a woman's co-operative. Then he would turn his attentions to the jealous mother. He evokes her as:

> my lonely, unloved Muriel [...] darning children's clothes and suffering the agonies of the damned, as she heard Anna and myself making love lengthily and luxuriously in what had until very recently been her own bed.

> Before long my opportunity came, and I was quick to take it. In one of the chains of TV stores with which I have covered the surface of the dying world, I met the sad menopausee and offered her at the flick of a switch, a return of beauty, youth and desire. And – after all, I'm no stinge-merchant – power and money as well. Why not? If a man such as Dr Faustus, was offered such commodities by myself, why, as I'm sure Anna would very strongly agree with me, why not a woman, in this age of equality?
>
> You know the rest [137].

This concluding section is full of sardonic laughter at womankind's expense. Despite that laughter, however, *Faustine* is a relatively bleak, moral fable for our times. It gives no comfort to the reader – least of all to the sub-species 'earnest Feminist'. There is no salvation on offer at the end, whether for Muriel/Lisa/ Faustine or for Ella/Gretchen/Persephone. With barely concealed contempt Mephisto speaks of the Redeemer – 'your Redeemer,' he says to the reader, 'who has nothing now to redeem but the pawn ticket of eternal life' [137].

Whatever became of 'the ever-womanly'? Fay Weldon's *Growing Rich.*[24]

Growing Rich is both humane and artful and very witty. As an ironist, Weldon is the equal of Enright. As a feminist she operates on a different comic plane from Tennant. As a satirically-minded feminist-cum-ironist she is in a separate league. How are we to understand 'men' in the narrator's remark: 'The Devil is often right about things: it helps explain his power over the minds of men' [20]? The life and loves of Faust are certainly of some interest to her – but largely peripheral. Her interest in Gretchen is much more obvious – a thoroughly modern Gretchen, as it turns out, quite strong-willed enough to defy the temptations of the Devil. Where Goethe's Gretchen is an innocent – helpless before male sexual predation – Weldon's certainly is not. As for Mephisto: in matters relating to the Devil Weldon is by common consent a long-experienced expert. All Ruth Patchett's artful plotting in *The Life and Loves of a She-Devil* is meaningless without the metaphor of Hell.

If it is a precarious business offering to comment on Enright's *Faust Book* because of the cycle's pervasive ironies, it is even more of a challenge tackling Weldon's teasing novel, with its echoes of myth and legend including 'the Fall of Mankind', 'the Princess switched at birth' and a 'Judgment of Paris' in appropriate feminist reverse. At least in Enright's case the males behave in a predictable manner and Gretchen is by and large the victim which literary tradition requires her to be. In *Growing Rich* the males may again behave more or less predictably, but the females often do not, and Carmen ("I'll do as I please"-Carmen, this novel's Gretchen) is determined to preserve her virginity. Amazingly, despite all the Devil's wiles, she succeeds – provided we discount that curious dream-like sequence in the woods when the Devil may (or may not?) have penetrated her himself without disturbing the hymen [89]. What is certain is that he'd had his way with her mother some 18 years previously – "You weren't so wrong about your mother ... only it was the black knight not the white" [56]. So who, then (we suddenly find ourselves asking) was Carmen's real father?

In the novel's curious *Catechism* [52-4] the narrator is assured – and thus we are too (or are we?) – that the Devil 'has a sense of fair play. He doesn't move the goal-posts.' – There is something decidedly unconventional about this Devil of Weldon's! In the same *Catechism* we learn even that 'God is his brother.' But then it turns out that the catechizer is the vicar – and who can trust C of E vicars these days on any fundamental matter of dogma?

The novel's action takes place in and around Fenedge, a market town in Norfolk. There are three leading female characters – a trio of latterday Every-women. When we first meet them they are aspiring A-level candidates. Carmen is their leader, Laura is 'the pretty one', and Annie 'is always desperate' [2]. Much like 17-year-olds with a bit of spirit anywhere in the world – be it in 'Dullsville, Tennessee, or Borup, Denmark, or Newcastle, New South Wales, or El Ain in the United Arab Emirates' [2] – this intrepid trio know that they have to get out of Fenedge, or die. When Carmen observed "You can work your way out, you can sleep your way out, you can sell your soul to the Devil", Annie (the daughter of a mortuary attendant father and a spiritualist medium mother dominated by a 14th century Polish Count named Capinski) was quickest to react: "Bags I work" – and she actually succeeded. On her knees laying an attic stair-carpet, she captures the heart of a handsome sheep-farmer visiting from New Zealand.

The time is the present (including a poignant, prescient reference to Princess Di [129]), and the action covers a period of about six years – long enough for Laura ("Bags I sleep") to get pregnant, married, give birth to five daughters, and (we record this with a mite of sadness) without having yet escaped Fenedge – but she'd asked for it, no doubt, by keeping her fingers crossed while she spoke.[25] As Carmen, Laura and Annie were trudging along the road back home from school, a black BMW bearing middle-aged Sir Bernard Bellamy – this novel's Faust – passed them, and he set eyes for the first time on Carmen and fingered her to his chauffeur and factotum, Driver – this novel's Mephisto – as the future love of his life:

> "You get me that girl for a wife, and I'll follow whatever script you put in front of me." — "For a *wife*?" asked Driver. — "For a wife," said Sir Bernard. "I want her body and soul. I am a man of swift decisions. She is my Marguerite." [25f].

Mephisto's startled question prompts the realization that Weldon's males do not in fact always behave predictably – though Sir Bernard's wanting Carmen both body *and* soul is reassuringly male-possessive, even to the point of threatening Mephisto's particular interests.

What sort of a Devil is Driver? He certainly has the requisite supernatural powers: 'he did not need an umbrella: the rain fell all around him but not on him'

[23]. Or consider what happened to Carmen's appearance: a major source of discomfort and embarrassment to her was her unpredictably expanding and contracting waist, legs and bosom – all courtesy of Driver. The episode in the local Job Centre, when he ensured that her figure re-shaped itself before their ravished eyes to suit the vacancy for an air hostess is particularly funny. – So, who says the Devil doesn't move the goal-posts? Or did that catechizer mean just the *moral* goal-posts?

Carmen Wedmore defied Driver, though. She is very strong-willed – which is what preserves her for, again as that eccentric catechizer assures us, 'The Devil's only weapon against free will is self-interest' [53]. Carmen's endearing devotion to her friends' welfare does indeed preserve her from mere self-interest, and she only concedes anything to Driver's machinations vis-à-vis the uxorious Sir Bernard once she is persuaded that her friends' bad luck is the direct consequence of her defiance. Her eventual compliance has the immediate desired effect. On her agreement to a romantic dinner with Sir Bernard everybody's luck changed (for a while). As regards sleeping with Sir Bernard, however, she held out until – as the narrator puts it – she was ready to 'assent to her own female nature' [237] (so everybody's luck ran out again for a time). Sir Bernard, meanwhile, was obliged to improve his appearance – to rejuvenate. His proposal of marriage, when it eventually came, was charmingly old-world: 'He would be honoured if she married him' [226].

The range of Driver's accomplishments is appropriately wide.

> "Now I've given you a little on account," said Driver to Carmen then, "it's time you did one or two things for me." — "What have you given me on account?" — "Item, beauty in the eye of the beholder," said Driver. — "I don't think much of your idea of that," she said. "It keeps changing." — "So does the beholder," said Driver. "I could give you Beauty itself if you're not satisfied." — "So men would look after me in the street?" she sneered. "They do that already." — "That's just sexiness," he said, "with a dollop of prettiness. Any young girl has that. As it is, it's all worry and anxiety: how do you not get pregnant, how do you best use face shaper, did you remember to shave your legs? Are the tops of your arms over-fleshy? It's too much like hard work getting the right look for the right man at the right moment. But Beauty, the Real Thing, you don't have to do anything about. You just carry it round inside you: it shines out from the middle, nothing to do with you. Protects and perfects as it works. No one worries about hairy legs, and they won't be hairy anyway: your body respects the image you and others have of it. Men try to get to the heart of it through you. They have to possess it, they need to own it. It's like gold: it causes fever." — "I don't want it," said Carmen. — "Don't try my patience," he said [82f].

– So much for Beauty in the classical mode of Helen! So much for the blandishments of modern advertising! Mephisto's salestalk had worked successfully with Tennant's Faustine, but this particular Gretchen is made of sterner stuff.

Further on in the same conversation Driver offers her: 'Good luck all round for you and your friends' [84]. He points out that it was he who had relieved her of the presence of her embarrassing parents by enabling them to go on a world cruise. His trump card is that he can make time (and the moon and forest) stand still:

> "Item [...] I can make a moment last for all eternity. Indeed, I can fast-forward and rewind the world, not just put it on pause. Think what that does for sex." — "I'd rather not," said Carmen. "That is disgusting," for Driver either was or wasn't lunging into her as she leaned against the tree [...] — "Do as I say!" snapped Driver in a flurry of sparks, as metal feather scraped on metal feather. — "I'll do as I please", she said [89].

A piece of jewelry plus a promise had been enough to turn Marguerite's head, but one thing which Driver does not tempt Carmen with is jewelry. Admittedly, Carmen wants money in order to get out of Fenedge, but the wealth Driver offers her through marriage to Sir Bernard does not compensate for the distastefulness of Bernard's appearance – until that moment comes when she too, in the way of lovers, sees her suitor's less flattering features with indulgent eyes. Could this defiant Gretchen, we find ourselves wondering, in fact be the real 'Faust' of this novel? We recall that it was she who had said sadly, after Annie and Laura had been quickest to bag their escape-routes: "That leaves me to sell my soul to the Devil" [8]. But this Carmen is stronger than Faust and, in the end (according to Laura), it was her pure tears which saved both Sir Bernard's and her own soul from the Devil's thwarted clutches after Bernard had been rash enough to say exultingly: 'may this day last for ever!' [245].

Acting on Weldon's assurance in *Letters to Alice*: 'You do not read novels for information, but for enlightenment'[26] we are encouraged to reflect on what might be the tendency of *Growing Rich*. Certainly it includes a feminist message, e.g. 'women of spirit do not have to be bound by conventions which assume their social, material or sexual subordination.' This novel is not, however, an artful feminist tract for our times: its re-working of the Faust-myth takes it onto a different plane. 'Gretchen' survives her long pursuit by 'Mephisto' on her own terms. How does she succeed, though ? Is it youthful innocence, coupled with a defiant spirit, which preserves her? Innocence was certainly distasteful to Goethe's Mephisto – we recall Gretchen's instinctive shudder at the sight of him, and he, equally, did not care to deal with her. In this novel there is another instance of female innocence which also disempowers Driver – that of the girls' English Teacher, Mrs Baker, 'a woman he disliked on sight, for all that she wore layers of black. He could not abide a plump woman, and that was that; a plump good woman was anathema to him' [24]. The answer to our question, then, has to be 'yes', i.e. where innocence and selfless devotion were enough to ensure that Goethe's Gretchen is saved – though, finally, only in heaven – as far as Weldon's novel is concerned, youthful innocence and/or altruistic goodness are clearly the key to success in combatting the Devil here on earth.

What this novel does not offer, however, is anything akin to Goethe's 'Ewig-Weibliche' – certainly not as an absolute in itself, and even less as a way of explaining what it might be that keeps males striving along the right path or in pursuit of that which is good – for any such consideration, the twists and turns of 'Luck Bringer's' actions (mirroring the next episode in some video/TV soap perhaps) are too artfully contrived.[27]

At the finish one question still lingers in our minds: what exactly is the role of the novel's narrator? Could she be some sort of handmaiden to Mephisto? Early on we are given a big hint when the narrator says:

> Look at it like this: on the day I summoned Driver out of the flat East Anglian landscape, set him uniformed and gaitered and bright-blue-eyed at the wheel of a black BMW, flickered hell fire through the evening sky to scare the crows, created Bernard Bellamy as both the tempter and the tempted, I did it in response to Carmen, Laura and Annie's desire just to get out of here. I was being helpful, honestly. Creating a window of opportunity for them to leap out of [8].

So who can she be – she who, with the most creative of intentions, summons up the Devil ? Her name is Harriet Upton, and she watches life go by outside whichever window she happens to be placed next to because she is wheelchair-bound – the accidental victim of a surgeon's scalpel. A wasp had stung him while he was completing a repair following a bodged pregnancy termination upwards of a dozen years previously – the knife jerked, and a section of her neural fibre was inadvertently severed [205] (was this just bad luck, or – as her GP opined – just punishment?) For much of the time she watches from the front window of her home in Fenedge, a short way down the road from where our three young heroines also live. At other times she watches from the bay window of the Handicapped Centre (aka the Otherly Abled Centre) in the middle of Fenedge. She has developed remarkable powers of insight. At various moments she is confided in directly by the three young women, at other times she simply knows what is going on in their minds – even when Annie is downunder in New Zealand. She also asks the sort of existential questions which Enright's Faust asked of his Mephisto – but they remain equally unanswered (fiction is not, perhaps, the right context for *theological* answers unless the writer be Dostoevsky[28]):

> what [can] the monstrous sorrow be: the one which lies at the roots of the universe, so that we're left with the poignant echoes of it in our lives, and have to work it through, so patiently and painfully, aeon after aeon; child grieving for parent, husband for wife, each afflicted with grief for the other, not just the self, which, God knows, is bad enough. What happened once to spoil everything so? [95].

– clearly Hattie has a big part in this novel. And by the end she, too, is cured. She does indeed know a great deal about the Devil – on one occasion she felt her useless lower limbs tingling with cheering promise when Driver looked deep into her eyes – but she is not the Devil's handmaiden in the way Frau Marthe or Jasmine were. She turns out to be a kindred spirit for, like him (not for nothing is he also called Videostopheles), she constructs lives:

> My disability allowance had ceased. I would have to find a job, or write a novel: something [249].

Conclusions

How much of his own Mephisto might Goethe have recognised in these modern English manifestations? Driver's knavish persistence and trickery, one suspects, would have reminded him smilingly of his own 'Schalk'. The self-confessed pervert of *Faustine*, on the other hand, preferring to seek his prey amongst middle-aged women, must have struck him as, at least, ungallant: Goethe's Mephisto never asked 'What the hell do women really want?' [139]. Robert Nye's Devil lacks all refinement – not inappropriate in itself, but a far cry from Mephistopheles' subtlety.[29] Enright's Mephisto does have the required wit and also just the right uneasy relationship to the Almighty: 'Sometimes he wondered // Who he was working for' [75], reminding us of Goethe's theological assertion *und stets das Gute schafft*. But it is in respect to the vital aspect of form, i.e. through the fact that his *Faust* is a play – thus under the requirement that characters be authentic for themselves and removing any opportunity for authorial ironisation (other than by dramatic irony) – that Goethe would have known that his version of the Faust-story and his evocation of Mephisto in particular remain supreme.

Not all modern writers who touch on the Faust theme present Hell seriously – as we saw with Nye. Nonetheless the metaphor of Hell continues to glow powerfully, even in a children's book such as *Eric*. C.S. Lewis entitled one of his collections of lectures: 'The Discarded Image',[30] referring to the medieval model of the universe: geocentric, including various Spheres (amongst them a realm for the 'longaevi', i.e. fairies of one sort or another) with the Heavens above and, somewhere or other, Hell. Goethe, although he had outgrown that model himself, was very familiar with it: his *Lemuren* and *selige Knaben* would have made good companions to the various types of Satyr and Faun normally associated with the 'longaevi'. Remarkably enough, although one of the most important theological corollaries of that image, i.e. either the soul's Salvation or its eternal Damnation, may indeed have been discarded by the vast majority of our contemporaries, the strength of Hell as a metaphor in all branches of the visual and literary Arts can still be seen and felt vividly. And, as we have seen especially in the novels by Tennant and Weldon, the evocation of the power of Evil as the work of a potentially malevolent Devil with a host of assistants continues to grip the poetic imagination. Lewis himself provides the example: as critic, his regret at the passing of 'the discarded image' is expressed in relatively pedestrian prose, but as polemical moralist in his *Screwtape Letters* he is brilliantly persuasive. – He, too, might well have concurred with Goethe's aphorism: '*Dagegen brannte sie lichterloh, wenn ich vor drohendem Übel floh.*'

How wise is it to focus on Mephisto, even when done with the disapproval proper to a *homo pedagogicus*? A century and a half ago one of *Blackwood's* critics berated P.J. Bailey for presuming to conjure up the Devil in his *Festus*[31] and – in common with many other, lesser imitators of Goethe – for failing to portray the Devil with sufficient perception of his infinite variety and power:

> In our deliberate opinion they had better have let the Devil alone. [...] It is dangerous meddling with edge-tools. Temptations enough beset even the best of us, without the realisation of the actual corporeality of the tempter.[32]

Such literary-cum-spiritual advice is, no doubt, as wise now as it was when issued a century and a half ago. But it is powerless in the face of 'Dichtergluth'. There is no reason to be alarmed, however, when that 'poetic fire' reflects an optimistic theology such as Goethe's, denying the Devil any ultimate victory, or else finds expression in the artistic vision of two modern English-language women writers who do not equivocate about the Devil's enduring power to corrupt innocence.

Notes and References

1 See W. H. Auden, *Secondary Worlds*, (1962), p.135.

2 Perhaps he should be seen in a more positive light, e.g. 'the archetype of a cultural hero, a champion of individualism emancipating itself from ecclesiastical tutelage' (M. Beddow, *Mann. Doctor Faustus*, 1994, p.12).

3 Attributed to Heine. (I follow Enright's attribution in the epigraph to *A Faust Book*.)

4 e.g. lines 353, 2182, 2321, 2496, 6565, 6577, 6591, 6790, 6817.

5 Page-references are to the Oxford University Press edition, 1979.

6 In *Scrutiny*, vol.13, 1945-6, pp.11-37.

7 See Part I in his collection of shorter pieces, *A Mania for Sentences* (London: 1983).

8 L.W. Forster, 'A Faust Book', in *Life by other means. Essays on D.J. Enright*, ed. by Jacqueline Simms (1990), pp.144-9.

9 'Germans with whom I have discussed this poem were deeply shocked by it; they felt it to be something in the nature of sacrilege, for Gretchen too is a cult figure. I felt and still feel that it is the high point of the whole cycle', *ibid.* p.148.

10 The phrase is Heinrich Böll's, from his novel *Billard um halb zehn*: 'Ironie ist ein Narkotikum für Privilegierte'.

11 D. J. Enright, *Fields of Vision* (1988), p.99.

12 Page-references are to the Hamish Hamilton edition, 1980.

13 Page-references are to the Corgi edition, 1991. Serious-minded students of the Faust myth should skip this section – unless, of course, they accept the proposition that, since the

number of Discworld readers far exceeds that of Marlowe and Goethe put together, it is probably worth their while to be informed about ~~**Faust**~~ *Eric* of Discworld.

[14] Without being an obvious lineal descendant of Ronald Searle's Molesworth, Eric and he do share a not dissimilar sense of humour. Molesworth for example gave his address as: '*St Custards, England, Europe, The World, The Universe, Space*'. Eric's address two generations later is: '*13 Midden Lane, Pseudopolis, Sto Plains, The Discworld, On top of Great A'Tuin, The Univers, Space. nr. More Space.*'

[15] i.e. he uses Faust's, not Aladdin's method which might have been equally effective.

[16] 'wind' pronounced as for 'breeze'. How do we know? – Rincewind turns out to have had a classical ancestor (bearing a certain resemblance to Odysseus) named Lavaeolus, which name being interpreted means 'Rinser of Winds' [100]. Latinists of Molesworth's generation will surely feel at home with that particular etymology.

[17] The Luggage can be imagined as having something in common with an infuriated, multi-legged, express rhinoceros, capable of interdimensional travel.

[18] The framework action's concluding episode has additional piquancy for academics of an allegorizing turn of mind: Astfgl, 'King of Demons, Lord of Hell, Master of the Pit' and perpetrator of endless memos and policy statements (*read*: Principal), is perceived by Duke Vassanego, his right-hand man and surreptitious opponent (*read*: Senior Tutor), as a 'pompous little creature ... a small-minded paper-worshipping nincompoop' [138]. The opposition's strategy for distracting and thus thwarting Astfgl at the story's climax is a cunning ruse, learned from observing what humans do in a similar predicament (*read*: Senate): they promote him – to 'Supreme Life President of Hell' [149]. During the subsequent congratulation-filled confusion the Senior Tutor recommends that Eric and Rincewind (*read*: Author) be allowed to escape.

[19] Why would Eric (or anybody else) wish to be 'Master of Kingdoms' if that entails being tortured to death by a People dissatisfied by their Master's inability to deliver Good Fortune in the manner expected of a God? Later on, after Eric has been smuggled into Tsort in the bowels of a wooden horse and then shown Elenor the most beautiful woman in the world, he whispers "Don't be silly. She looks like my mum" [92]. And at the climax of his next adventure, when he learns that 'living forever' involves starting from the beginning of Time – when there was nobody else around, nor would there be for aeons to come – Eric has no wish to proceed.

[20] Sisyphus the rock pusher, for example, is now obliged first to listen to 'the Unhealthy and Unsafety Regulations governing the Lifting and Moving of Large Objects. Volume 93 of the Commentaries, in fact. The Regulations themselves comprised a further 1,440 volumes. Part 1, that is' [132f].

[21] 'I Meant It For The Best', 'I Thought You'd Like It', 'For The Sake Of The Children', 'We Are Equal Opportunity Employers' [154].

[22] Page-references are to the *faber and faber* edition, 1992.

[23] 'You see, Ella, you have come searching, like Demeter sought Persephone, but it is the wrong way round. You are the maiden who is bound to go under the earth in the autumn and return in spring, for you are the future bearer of children, the mother-to-be of humanity.' [p.115]

[24] Page-references are to the HarperCollins Flamingo edition, 1992.

[25] Regretfully, we can dwell no further on Laura and Annie and their respective families' cart-wheeling fortunes at the hands of that dodgy 'Luck Bringer' [192] aka the Devil, or, in this novel's case, 'Driver' aka Videostopheles [213]: the reader will find time to enjoy the laughter for her/himself.

[26] Fay Weldon, *Letters to Alice on first reading Jane Austen* (1984, Sceptre edition 1993), p.32.

[27] Weldon's most recent survey of the Western Condition invokes the Garden of Eden myth from the outset – 'a new Adam and a new Eve, if the same old Cain and Abel kids' ('The Scotsman Millennium Lecture: Adam and Eve and Tony Blair.' *The Scotsman*, 22.08.98). Of the twentieth century's greatest changes she observes: 'The patriarchy has switched to a matriarchy. ... God is no longer the bearded patriarch in the sky, he has had a sex-change and turned into Mother Nature. ... In the new Garden of Eden ... Nature rules, not God.' Disappointingly for our theme Weldon nowhere touches on what might have become of the Ancient Serpent. Feminist-o-flees?

[28] 'The Karamazow brothers are the best teachers of religion of the late twentieth century; better, I am certain, than contemporary theologians.' – See 'The Karamazov brothers as teachers of religion' in: Donald Nicholl, *The Beatitude of Truth* (London, 1997), pp.65-83, p.65.

[29] The fifth of these 'Mephistos' – Rincewind – is a character whom Goethe might well have excused himself from getting acquainted with, on the understandable grounds of inadequate English: not even the best available bilingual dictionary would have helped with, e.g. 'wossname', 'Iains' [of time], 'boodwah', 'toot sweet', 'mobius Eisteddfod'.

[30] C. S. Lewis, *The Discarded Image* (1964).

[31] First published in 1839.

[32] *Blackwood's Magazine*, vol.71 (1852), p.213.

Shakespeare into Celan: Sonnets 1, 105 and 107

RAYMOND HARGREAVES

Sonnet 107 was the last Celan translated,[1] and in the collection of twenty-one versions he published in 1967[2] it is one of the first in order of fascination, or so it seems to me. Given this predilection, it would be gratifying to write an essay as rigorous and persuasive as Peter Szondi's comparison of Sonnet 105 and Celan's rendering.[3] However, the structure of translation Szondi elicits in this case does not readily transfer on to Sonnet 107, and there seems every reason to accept his view that this structure is peculiar to the poetry of constancy.[4] A relatively brief reading of Sonnet 1 goes some way to supporting a still tentative thesis that Celan's response to Shakespeare is by no means predictable, since to say that he translates through the medium of his own experience and poetic sensibility is not so much to predict as to say what goes without saying.

Sonnet 105

Szondi reads original and version of Sonnet 105 as a poetological encounter, an enactment of the translator's poetic occasioned by his engagement with the different poetic informing the English poem, and he bases this reading on the assumption that fidelity cannot be the criterion.[5] One of the merits of this approach is that it does not assume that the aim of translation is known from the start, we are invited to regard the encounter between original and version as something to be explored and discovered, an approach derived from Walter Benjamin's concept, 'Intention auf die Sprache'.[6] Szondi's definition, which differs from Benjamin's use of the term, includes

> Gerichtetsein des Bewußtseins auf die Sprache, d.h. als die allem Sprechen vorausliegende Sprachkonzeption.[7]

Such theoretical assumptions provide a basis for a working hypothesis which in its turn focuses attention on poetological differences between the two poems and impedes the throw-away gesture indicated, potentially, in the above title: 'Oh well, Celan has simply translated Shakespeare into Celanese'. Szondi's case is built on detailed linguistic analysis. The following simplified and reduced account may provide a context for the gloss I wish to add.

Let not my love be called idolatry,	*Ihr sollt, den ich da lieb, nicht Abgott heißen,*
Nor my beloved as an idol show,	*nicht Götzendienst, was ich da treib und trieb.*
Since all alike my songs and praises be	*All dieses Singen hier, all dieses Preisen:*
To one, of one, still such, and ever so.	*von ihm, an ihn und immer ihm zulieb.*
Kind is my love today, tomorrow kind,	*Gut ist mein Freund, ists heute und ists morgen,*
Still constant in a wondrous excellence;	*Und keiner ist beständiger als er.*

Therefore my verse, to constancy confin'd	7	*In der Beständigkeit, da bleibt mein Vers geborgen,*
One thing confessing, leaves out difference.	8	*spricht von dem Einen, schweift mir nicht umher.*
'Fair, kind and true' is all my argument –	9	*'Schön, gut und treu', das singe ich und singe.*
'Fair, kind and true' varying to other words;	10	*'Schön, gut und treu' – stets anders und stets das.*
And in this change is my invention spent –	11	*Ich find, erfind – um sie in eins zu bringen,*
Three themes in one, which wondrous scope affords.	12	*sie einzubringen ohne Unterlaß.*
'Fair, kind and true' have often lived alone,	13	*'Schön, gut und treu' so oft getrennt, geschieden.*
Which three till now never kept seat in one.	14	*In einem will ich drei zusammenschmieden.*[8]

'All alike' is the explicit statement made in the first quatrain and is there in the shape of parallelism: 'love ... idolatry' in the first line, 'beloved ... idol' in the second; there's a twin expression in the third: 'songs and praises', repetition: 'one ... one' in the fourth, and variation as a foil for sameness: apart from 'one ... one' the whole of the fourth line. All these patterns are taken up and developed in the German version, though not schematically. The parallelism disappears, 'nicht Abgott .../ nicht Götzendienst' is more a case of emphatic repetition, and the emphasis shifts more to 'ich' and its doings with 'was ich da treib und trieb', this pattern of doubling is reduplicated threefold in 'All dieses Singen hier, all dieses Treiben' and the last line keeps returning to 'ihm' or 'ihn' as well as repeating 'i' (four long, one short) in every stress. There is no verb in the last two lines, and 'since' has gone too; this sets the pattern for any conjunctions or argumentative links that occur later, which, like 'since', are lost in the transition from English to German. Shakespeare's discursive statements have thus been commuted into poetic acts, developing or reinforcing any such elements present in the original, with a particular emphasis on repetition and a corresponding erosion of variation. Accordingly, the chiasmus in the first line of the second stanza is replaced by a reiterative pattern, seeming to seek a place in language as remote as posssible from invention and variation with its thrice repeated 'ist' and its style of simple assertion, and the following line, resolutely paratactic, begins with 'und' and repeats 'ist'. In the third stanza 'is all my argument' is replaced by 'das singe ich und singe'; though 'varying' is taken up in 'stets anders' the pattern of repetition is maintained with 'und stets' and the end of the line offers a gesture which denotes a nameless sameness: 'und stets das'. A remnant or two of the English text survive in the next lines, 'erfind' was prompted by 'invention', but undergoes a radical transformation,[9] and 'sie in eins zu bringen' owes something to 'three themes in one'. Apart from these vestiges the German text pursues a line of its own here, while further developing the iterative pattern of the previous lines; in addition, these lines stand out by virtue of their dense word play. Szondi suggests, therefore, that Celan's sense of the possibilities of language is most in evidence here; bringing in, bringing together in one, is his poetic programme in translating this poem; this does not entail treating constancy discursively as a theme but enacting it in language – the German phrase is 'Realisierung der Beständigkeit im Vers':[10]

Szondi concludes as follows:

> In Celan's version the poet does not speak of his 'argument', his 'invention', or his 'scope', but instead the verse is arranged in accordance with the exigencies of this theme and its objective aim. Nor does the poet affirm that his verse leaves out difference; rather he speaks in a language in which differences are simply left out. Celan, writing in the wake of the late Mallarmé and an attentive observer of modern linguistics, philosophy of language and aesthetics drew the logical consequence from the symbolist conception of poetry, in which a poem is its own subject matter and both invokes and describes itself as a symbol. According to Jakobson there exists a certain kind of constancy which is projected from the paradigmatic axis (of which it is constitutive) into the syntagmatic axis and which distinguishes the poetic sequence from the prosaic in this latter axis. If we accept Jakobson's views, then we may say that in translating a poem whose subject matter is that very constancy, Celan, perhaps without knowing of Jakobson's theorem, replaced the traditional symbolist poem – which deals only with itself and which has itself as its subject matter – with a poem which does not *deal* with itself but which *is* itself! He thus produced a poem which no longer speaks about itself but whose language is *sheltered* in that very place that it assigns to its subject matter, which is none other than itself: it is sheltered "in constancy".[11]

This analysis leaves no doubt that here literal accuracy or fidelity to the poetic qualities of the original have been displaced by a poet's need to keep faith with the language he is working in. It is then certainly not a gratuitous courtesy to print original and translation *en face*,[12] if anything it is an act of obeisance a translation of this kind can hardly forego, not because it cannot stand on its own, but because the interaction between the two texts constitutes a third poem, or a third vantage point. Even though the knottier analyses have been omitted from this summary, it is still enough to convey a sense that Celan's use of language is highlighted by comparison with the sonnet he is translating and that this light also falls on the original poem.

As it happens, Szondi disclaims any intention of critically evaluating Shakespeare's sonnet,[13] yet the process of comparison persistently skirts a critical evaluation. Briefly, according to Szondi, 'argument' itself 'suggests discursive, rational argument', 'all' is 'its no less logical qualifier' and 'varying' is a rhetorical term whose deployment rests on the assumption that 'the same thing can be designated by different words' whereas 'Celan's intention toward language, by contrast, may be viewed as the determinate negation of this theoretical linguistic premise'.[14] This presents a difficulty: is a text which negates the linguistic premise of the text it purports to translate still a translation, and if so in what sense? If we accept that Shakespeare's sonnet is firmly embedded in traditional rhetoric whereas in the translation 'we can sense a desire to abolish the distinction between signifier and signified altogether',[15] then the translation is in effect a radically different poem, even though its radical difference is grounded in the verbal realisation of constancy, the theme of the original poem.[16]

Another way of putting this sense of unease would be to say that the seamlessness of this construct is simultaneously persuasive and problematic, and problematic not least because there is so little sense of constraint. Matters of this kind are seldom so neat, so clearly conform to an inner logic – which by the end is the inner logic of a line of poetry leading from Shakespeare to Celan via Mallarmé. Persuasive as this reading is, it is only convincing on the premise that the re-working the sonnet undergoes in translation was latent from the beginning,[17] and I wish to argue that the mode of this latency is not confined to the theme of constancy wedded to the use of repetition.[18] There is only one critical point, in my view, where Celan's version is not derived from a word found in the original, and that is where the difference between his poetic and Shakespeare's is at its most programmatic – when 'is all my argument' is displaced by 'das singe ich und singe' (though even then 'singe' is not alien to Shakespeare's poem which also speaks of 'songs and praises' in the first stanza, generating 'all dieses Singen, all dieses Preisen' in the German, a phrase which anticipates 'das singe ich und singe'). Otherwise there is generally a source in the English for Celan's wording – though it has to be said, with Szondi, that the source may be converted into its opposite; for instance, if 'scope' and 'ohne Unterlaß' are correlated on the grounds that 'scope' may be related to 'compass' and 'ohne Unterlaß' to 'all-encompassing', they are opposed in the sense that 'scope' implies latitude, free play, and 'ohne Unterlaß' has a connotation of rigour, discipline: 'without omission'. Thus, to point to the verbal correspondences is not to disagree with Szondi, it is simply a matter of reversing the direction of his analysis and emphasizing affinity instead of difference. However different 'ich find, erfind' is from Shakespeare's mode of signification, it still takes up 'invention', just as 'stets anders' in the phrase 'stets anders und stets das' takes up 'varying'. Though that exhausts its affinity with the line it is correlated with, there is a degree of semantic and structural parallelism between 'stets anders und stets das' and stanza I, line 4: 'ever such and always so', which is expressed quite differently in the parallel line in Celan's version. Repetition as a poetic enactment of constancy is found in both poems. Celan is taking his cue from Shakespeare,[19] only he is going further. Similarly, the poem commits him to paradox ('stets anders und stets das') because it is founded on the paradox of variation as a figure of constancy, and so, as Szondi demonstrates, he is able to convert the rhetoric of variation, or the variation of rhetorical terms, into words which enact the making of poetry, the poetry of constancy: 'das singe ich und singe', 'ich find, erfind', and 'sie in eins zu bringen, sie einzubringen'.

Evidently, the key issue is not literal correspondence but rhetoric. Again, it is less a matter of unmaking the case Szondi has made than of returning to the ironies and inversions which are Celan's point of departure. So, though there is good reason to agree that 'Shakespeare explicitly mentions *change* (i.e. the replacement of one word by another, while the intended meaning remains the same) whose premise is precisely this traditional conception of language: "And in this change is my invention spent" whereas Celan refuses to concede that words may be interchangeable in this way',[20] since that is manifestly the case, something decisive is missing from this account, which as a rule settles for terms like 'explicitly mentions' and 'this traditional conception of language' and does not consider the possibility that an explicit mention may coincide with an implicit disavowal, a possibility that would bring Shakespeare and Celan closer together.

Indeed, though the discussion is clearly focussed on poetic mode, there is no hint that the mode of the original poem is in a sense playful or that its 'Intention auf die Sprache' has much to do with wit. The wit of the sonnet is that it plays with traditional rhetoric, it invokes argument, invention and scope only to signal their absence. Though the line quoted speaks of change, no change has occurred, though it speaks of invention, nothing is invented; what is being called 'change' and 'invention' is the repetition of 'fair, kind and true'.[21] Similarly, three adjectives in a row, the first and second divided by a comma, the third linked to the other two by 'and' cannot be construed as an argument; which is to say 'is all my argument' is ironic, in the sense that the statement invites and contains its own negation: 'and that's no argument at all'. And again, though 'varying' introduces a rhetorical device, it does so ironically; as the poem insists in the penultimate line, 'fair, kind and true' are semantically distinct, and so the sequence is not an example of variation; and to keep repeating the phrase is not to vary. That there is nonetheless, in terms of the poem's wit, a 'legitimate' sense in which this triad may be construed as a variation emerges only in the conceit of the final line, which establishes a unique – and playful – exception to the rule that each of these three terms has a sense which is not the sense of either of the others. There is no need, however, to attempt to merge these words or to treat them as variants; the poem's closing gambit is that words which are semantically distinct may still converge in one living person, not that these words are interchangeable. 'Fair', 'kind' and 'true' each has a sense of its own, but their point of reference is one and the same person, so the wit of the couplet – which, like a joke explained, by this time does not sound like wit – consists in treating sense as reference.

Apart from that, the use of rhetorical terms may or may not be rhetoric. To invoke argument and invention is not to argue or invent; in Shakespeare's poem, these terms are so many variations on a rhetorical theme and repeat the same pattern: 'scope'[22] and 'invention', together with 'argument', are invoked ironically, to denote their absence, and 'varying', in varying these rhetorical terms, repeats this underlying structure. Rhetoric is an ironic metaphor for the procedures of this poem, the reiterated appeal to its modes, its verbal presence, marks its absence. An absence marked over and over again to give it a kind of pseudo-presence may coincide with a presence that is constant, but implicit, and this presence is made explicit in Celan's version. The terms of rhetoric are used paradoxically, they do not describe what is happening in the poem, and that is their rhetoric; but this brings them close to lyric; 'invention' consists in saying one and the same thing over and over, so many variations on a theme around a refrain.

These paradoxes on a periphery, I would say, are what prompted and enabled Celan to take a step further and translate 'is all my argument' with 'das singe ich und singe', possibly with a sense of staying close to the spirit of the original. The particular way this sonnet plays with technical resources and upturns the traditional *modus operandi* with a quick, ironic wit makes it possible to turn it into an enactment of a different poetic. This poem, in demonstrating that the resources of rhetoric do not meet the occasion and are not meet to it, invites a recognition that what is beyond rhetoric lies within the purview of lyric poetry, particularly when one sonnet after another insists that 'rhyme' is able to rise to the occasion and lift it out of its temporal context.[23]

Sonnet 1

If George's version of Sonnet I is put alongside Celan's, it is evident that both of them keep to the form and metre of the English sonnet.[24] Since George also stays close to the imagery and syntax, his version parallels the English poem line by line. There are, however, points where he appears to have found it impossible to keep all these things up in the air at the same time and has evidently decided that line and rhyme must stay whatever else might have to go – you can hardly do otherwise if you are writing a sonnet. In any case, line and rhyme were for him the syntax of verse, hence the absence of conventional punctuation, and a decided shift towards parataxis. The opening line ends with a strong stress on a monosyllable, 'einen spross', which contrasts with the vowels in the rest of the line and singles out this offspring as the promised blessing if only his friend will put himself about a bit: 'Von schönsten wesen wünscht man einen spross'. A plain man's – or perhaps an unplain man's variation – on the less specific, seductively pleasing, Latinate alliteration cum assonance of 'From fairest *creatures* we desire in*crease*'. George simply gives us alliteration, and an end-stopped line. Conversely, Shakespeare's fourth line is alliterative and has an internal rhyme, whilst George gets a touch of alliteration and a patterned series of assonances: 'Ihr angedenken trag ein zarter erbe'. Both George and Celan rhyme 'sterbe(n)' and 'Erbe', which looks as though it is predestined for this theme, as though language had been shaped here by our fear of death and our generic resistance to mortality. Shakespeare's rhyme for 'heir' is 'bear' which reads as 'carry' or 'wear' and amid thoughts of life and death, beauty and procreation, naturally draws on 'bear' in the sense of 'give birth to'. A possible sense of George's 'trag' is 'be with child', which yields a fitting sense of reciprocity: may your heir, once born, bear your memory.

If 'zarter Erbe' tilts towards 'fragile' as well as 'affectionate', this is not worrying, since a further tilt towards transience goes with the original grain. The phrase recurs in Celan's version (which on the whole dispenses with adjectives), not that he was necessarily working with George in mind, since both 'zart' for 'tender' and the rhyme 'sterbe(n)/Erbe' are literal – or dictionary – translations. Otherwise Celan's first quatrain shows a number of changes. The opening line is less aphoristic, but preserves a level of generality by abstracting, shifting from procreation on to a sublimer plane, and immediately addresses a 'du' (thou) who could be the 'du' of monologue. 'Die Rose Schönheit' is a symbol, not a metaphor for the poet's friend, and 'ein Mehr' (a surplus, and to the ear also 'ein Meer', a sea) is a long way off a common-or-garden 'spross', though it corresponds more closely, with a difference, to 'increase'. In other words, it looks as though the theme has been approximated to later sonnets and their interest in the power of a poem to commemorate beauty that does not last. Consistent with rendering 'beauty's rose' as 'die Rose Schönheit' is the way 'zarter Erbe' is nudged towards a metaphor for a work of art (= 'ein Mehr'?), and if that reading seems questionable, it will seem less so the moment the possessive adjective is noticed; 'ihr zarter Erbe', i.e. the rose beauty's tender heir. Shakespeare's chiding his narcissistic friend, a sort of back-handed reproach, is being converted into concern about withdrawal of another kind.

In the second quatrain the direct references to physical beauty all but disappear; 'bright' goes from 'eyes', the tautology or excess of 'thy light's flame' becomes 'deine Flamme loht', 'thy sweet self' is replaced simply by a reflexive pronoun, whereas 'abundance' becomes ' überreich beschenkt' (superabundantly endowed), which could refer to the gift of poetry. 'Kein solcher Herold' lends itself to this reading without difficulty, but the preceding line in III which presents 'du' as the ornament of ornaments (whilst dropping 'fresh') might pose a problem, until it is seen as recouping the first two lines: 'Kein Schmuck wie du, den sich ein Jahr je gab' corresponds to 'Was west und schön ist', and the greater ornament is then conceivably the poet's beauty, his poetry, which ensures that the rose beauty shall not die. Accordingly, the first line of the couplet elaborates and modifies 'Pity the world', directs 'du' to direct his thoughts on the world, brings forward 'due' and renders it as 'Erbteil', which takes up 'Erbe' in a form that corresponds to 'inheritance' ('das Erbe') and is not used of a person, – anything by nature of 'spross' has receded so far it is virtually out of sight –, and the last line is technically different from the rest of the poem/translation:

From fairest creatures we desire increase,	*Was west und schön ist, du erhoffst ein Mehr*
That thereby beauty's rose may never die,	*von ihm: die Rose Schönheit soll nicht sterben.*
But as the riper should by time decease,	*Und gibt sie, die gezeitigte, die Krone her,*
His tender heir might bear his memory:	*so wahre, was sie war, ihr zarter Erbe.*
But thou, contracted to thine own bright eyes,	*Doch du, ins eigne Auge eingeengt,*
Feed'st thy light's flame with self-substantial fuel,	*verbrauchst dich selbst, daß deine Flamme loht,*
Making a famine where abundance lies,	*du darbst und hungerst, überreich beschenkt,*
Thyself thy foe, to thy sweet self too cruel:	*und bist, der dich am grausamsten bedroht.*
Thou that art now the world's fresh ornament	*Kein Schmuck wie du, den sich ein Jahr je gab;*
And only herald to the gaudy spring,	*kein solcher Herold seiner Farbenfreuden;*
Within thine own bud buriest thy content,	*doch du: die eigne Knospe ist dein Grab,*
And, tender churl, mak'st waste in niggarding:	*ein einzig Knausern bist du im Vergeuden.*
Pity the world, or else this glutton be –,	*Denk an die Welt und was ihr Erbteil ist,*
To eat the world's due, by the grave and thee.	*du, der du dich nicht sattgräbst und es frißt.*[25]

Before turning to the last line and its difference, it is worth recording that there are moments in this poem where poetry ('das Dichterische am Gedicht') and closest proximity to the text ('größte Textnähe')[26] appear to be neither mutually exclusive alternatives nor opposites imperfectly reconciled after taxing and delicate negotiations; they seem instead to be virtual synonyms. The most remarkable of these moments is the phrase 'ins eigne Auge eingeengt'. Given that 'bright' has disappeared in the general purging of epithets, that is, within certain limits, as literal a rendering as you could get, allowing for a routine adjustment of English to German idiom ('das eigene Auge' for 'your/thine own bright eye'). One of the English senses of 'contract' (= enter a legally binding agreement, an engagement, a marriage contract) which survives, vestigially, in George's 'freit', is lost, but the other sense of 'contract' (= shrink) is strongly present in 'eingeengt'. Celan's phrase has a sequence of glottals; there is one before 'engt' in 'eingeengt' as well as before the vowel at the beginning of each word; the assonances are marked and distinct, the sounds of 'eigne' are picked up and pinned down by 'eingeengt' and the glottals, in conjunction with the pattern of 'g' and 'ge', mime a sense of constriction in the throat. This aural and vocal sense of entrapment not only takes off from a literal reading, it may also have been stimulated by the pattern of assonance in the English phrase, 'contracted to thine own bright eyes', with the repeated 'i' binding the sound to 'eyes'.

Another find occurs in the first stanza, though it has evidently been arrived at by a different route. What a literal, and pleasing, rendering might look like is indicated by George's line: 'Ihr angedenken trag ein zarter erbe'. It is possible that this accomplished line prompted Celan to cast about for some other possibility, equally as good, but different, or he may have come upon his version as he was moving away from child as image of father, bearing his memory, to remembrance, preserving the memory. However he came upon it, the remarkable thing, the find, is the coincidence of 'wahre' (preserve) and 'war' (was) as though what was ('was... war') is redeemed from transience and death in the word which expresses 'preserve': 'wahre'. This presence of the past is beautifully realised in the quiet, measured cadence of 'So *wahr*e, *wa*s sie *war*, ihr *zar*ter Erbe', and that sustains and develops the opening phrase: 'Was west und schön ist', articulated as it is on forms of the verb 'to be'. That the find is a discovery, an uncovering, is indicated yet again by the overlapping of 'wahre' and 'war' with 'wahr' (= true): what endures is tested and true.

George straightens out the last two lines by saying:

Gönn dich der welt! Nicht wie ein schlemmer tu:
Esst nicht der welt behör • das grab und du!

Paraphrased: 'Grant yourself to the world, don't behave like a glutton, don't eat the world's portion, the grave and you', which is no doubt intended to convey, 'don't you as well as the grave ...', but equates 'du' and 'grab' syntactically and makes them both equally the subject of 'esst nicht der welt behör'. Shakespeare's syntax is a bit askew, but he does not ask the grave to do anything so unnatural. What is natural for the grave is unnatural in his friend, so that the coupling of 'grave and thee' provides a measure of his friend's departure from nature, and it is this unnatural bracket that yields the forced conceit and wrenched syntax of the final couplet. George's formally correct syntax comes close to conveying something along these lines, but is not as coercive and decisive. Celan responds with a line which is deeply paradoxical and enigmatic and powerfully conveys a sense of strangeness. Most of the words correspond lexically to something given in the original, but they are shuffled about. 'Grave' gives 'gräbt' (= digs), which is close to ' Grab' (= grave) and 'glutton' suggests 'fressen', or 'sich sattfressen', only ' fressen' is separated off and a new verb 'sich sattgraben' is formed instead; '... du der du dich nicht sattgräbst' takes up and develops the stark phrase used in the previous stanza: 'deine Knospe ist dein Grab'. It expresses an insatiable self-consuming, and is juxtaposed, conceivably, with an integration of death into life. Placing original and version side by side points up modernist syncope which in its turn may be seen as a way of responding to the impacting of syntax and metaphor in Shakespeare.

In highlighting these three moments in the poem, I do not wish to suggest they stand out as its three most powerful moments. On the contrary, they arise from the movement of the poem and flow back into it. What is interesting is the degree to which this movement is initiated by the English poem. If 'ins eigne Auge eingeengt' can be construed as a more or less literal rendering of elements in 'contracted to thine own bright eyes', 'so wahre, was sie war' cannot quite be assigned to the original text in like fashion. This is both statement and enactment, a literal grafting of past on to present which connotes their identity, visually and audibly, in a way consonant with Shakespeare's theme, but Celan's ' mode of signification' is different, though this is word play, it uncovers a deep continuity embedded in language, a latent potential made manifest in this poem.

The final couplet stands in a different relationship again to the English text. The parallel between 'the grave' and 'thee' is absorbed into the activity of 'du', delineating strangeness in a neologistic phrase, and focussing on 'du' exclusively: conform with his self-absorption. Though this is a different procedure – neologism instead of wrenched syntax–, it is a response to a strangeness patterned in the angular shape of Shakespeare's last sentence. If fidelity cannot be the criterion in this or the previous instance, that does not altogether undermine Celan's claim that he is aiming at 'closest proximity to the text',[27] since the moments of correspondence and deviation both engage closely with the text of the original. The result is not so much an exact replica, as an exact(ing) reply. If the other half of Celan's translator's confession is then brought into play, it might be argued that no antiquarian rendering is likely to capture what is poetic about the original poem. A historical reconstruction of Shakespeare's poetry in modern German will produce at best a plausible pastiche;[28] and in the latter half of the twentieth century no one is likely to devise a sixteenth/seventeenth century German Shakespeare. Conversely, the insistence on energies and possibilities inherent in the translator's language does not exclude a deep responsiveness to the original. The deeper the response, the greater the possibility of a poetically creative translation.

This leads to the most radical change of all, which departs from the original in a different sense and creates a shift of emphasis that affects the whole poem, the conversion of '*we* desire increase' in the first line to '*du* erhoffst ein Mehr'. 'We desire increase', allied as it is going to be with an 'and you, apparently, don't', is a strong opening gambit and sets up the tensions on which the poem is constructed. To say 'you hope for a something more from it' creates different tensions, they are no longer located in the space between 'we' and 'thou', the poet and the world on the one hand and the poet's friend on the other, but within the one person, the 'du', who hopes for increase from his encounter with 'Was west und schön ist', yet is confined to his own eye. In keeping with this intensified preoccupation with 'du', where the original is possibly ambiguous, Celan's rendering is not: 'making a famine (where abundance lies)' is turned into an emphatic statement, without any periphrasis: 'du darbst und hungerst'. Another and, I think, more plausible reading of Shakespeare's line would be to say that since the friend keeps himself to himself, he makes the famine and it is the world that goes without, starved of the abundance it could otherwise have drawn from him, and then 'famine' comes into its own, as a general state of affairs. As it is, Celan's paradox points up inner contradictions: 'du darbst und hungerst, überreich beschenkt'. This more intense focus on 'du' is also palpable in the few epithets retained. Apart from 'zarter Erbe', pride of place goes to those which specify selfhood: 'ins eigne Auge eingeengt', 'die eigne Knospe ist dein Grab' and exclusivity: 'ein einzig Knausern' (the uninflected form 'einzig' strangely emphasizes the nothing-buttery). As the world recedes from the text – the word itself occurs three times in Shakespeare and once in Celan, in the penultimate line – the effect is to isolate 'du', structure the poem throughout on someone who is solitary and self-absorbed. In short, this 'du' is like Goethe's Tasso:

> *Ich halte diesen Drang vergebens auf,*
> *Der Tag und Nacht in meinem Busen wechselt.*
> *Wenn ich nicht sinnen oder dichten soll,*
> *So ist das Leben mir kein Leben mehr.*
> *Verbiete du dem Seidenwurm zu spinnen,*
> *Wenn er sich dem Tode näher spinnt.*
> *Das köstliche Geweb' entwickelt er*
> *Aus seinem Innersten und läßt nicht ab*
> *Bis er in seinen Grab sich eingeschlossen.*[29]

Emerging from Celan's translation we see the figure of the self-consuming artist, whose talent – 'überreich beschenkt' – turns to ascetic withdrawal and the menace of poetry – 'und bist, der dich am grausamsten bedroht'.[30]

The (auto)biographical potential of certain lines needs no emphasizing:

> *... die Rose Schönheit soll nicht sterben.*
> *Und gibt sie, die gezeitigte, die Krone her,*
> *So wahre, was sie war, ihr zarter Erbe.*

A further consequence of reshaping the first stanza is that it now speaks of only one person initially, 'du', who may be the poet or some other with whom the speaking voice is closely identified. The lines just quoted are preceded by 'du erhoffst ein Mehr/von ihm:' and so what follows the colon, 'die Rose Schönheit soll nicht sterben' articulates the hope expressed in 'erhoffst', and if, despite these tender hopes, the rose beauty succumbs to the fate of all things temporal, then may her gentle heir preserve what she was. It is perfectly possible, and not at all unreasonable, given this structure, to identify 'du' with 'zarter Erbe', indeed, if this identification is not made, the tender heir is left at a bit of a loose end. There is no need to leave him there, however, since the grammatical shift in gender caused by 'die Rose Schönheit' converts masculine: 'his tender heir ... his memory' into feminine: 'so wahre was sie war' and 'ihr zarter Erbe'. It is hoped that the tender heir of the rose beauty may preserve her memory, in fulfilment, despite her mortality, of the hope that this beauty shall not die, which not dying is an excess, goes beyond the supposed normal pattern of life and death. It is 'du' who has this hope, and her tender heir who is called upon to fulfil it, even if she does 'yield the crown'. Together with the other elements of reshaping, particularly the switch from 'we' to 'du', this other gender provides a basis for reading the lines quoted above as words spoken *in memoriam* by a poet when thinking of his mother.

Sonnet 107

'Not minc own fears' goes readily into German as 'nicht die eigene Angst' and the article can be dropped to bring out 'eigene' and give 'nicht eigne Angst', iambic, and a good opening phrase.[31] If 'Nicht Angst, mir eigen' is preferred, this changes the sense, no longer makes a distinction between own and others' fears, but makes fear a personal property, essential to the speaker's make-up. It would be tempting to call that a translation into the twentieth century, only the *Sonnets* are full of a sense of fragility; and violence, including the prospect of a violent death, might be called one of Shakespeare's imaginative properties. Celan's response is initiated by the English phrase and the possibility of rearranging the normal German equivalent to produce that semantic shift; one imagines an ineradicable edginess, a Central European sense of insecurity, or more immediately and specifically 'eine jüdische Angst'[32] set off by this phrase and prompted to restructure it. But if Shakespeare is our witness there are grounds enough for surmising that such fears were not less rooted and endemic in the age of the first Elizabeth:

Not mine own fears, nor the prophetic soul	*Nicht Angst, mir eigen, nicht der weltweiten*
Of the wide world dreaming on things to come,	*Wahrträume Sinn für Dinge, die da kommen,*
Can yet the lease of my true love control,	*kann bemessen meiner Liebe Fristen oder Zeiten,*
Suppos'd as forfeit to a confin'd doom.	*entgrenzt und unverwirkt ist sie, in niemands Bann.*
The mortal moon hath her eclipse endur'd,	*Der Mond, der sterbliche, verschattete: er blinkt!*
And the sad augurs mock their own presage;	*Augurenwort, dir war Augurenspott beschieden.*
Incertainties now crown themselves assur'd,	*Das Schwankende von einst? Gekrönt und unbedingt,*
And peace proclaims olives of endless age.	*Und mit dem alterslosen Ölzweig kommt der Frieden.*
Now with the drops of this most balmy time	*Umbalsamt meine Liebe, bist du, bist umtaut*
My love looks fresh; and Death to me subscribes,	*Von frischer Zeit – kein Tod, dich fortzuschwemmen.*
Since spite of him I'll live in this poor rhyme	*Ich lebe, ihm zum Trotz, im Reim, den ich gebaut,*
When he insults o'er dull and speechless tribes:	*derweil er dumpfen grollt und sprachelosen Stämmen.*
And thou in this shalt find thy monument	*Und du: in diesem hier, da steht es noch, dein Bild,*

When tyrants' crests and tombs of brass are spent.	14	*wenn Gräbererz verwittert und Tyrannenschild.*[33]

There is another context in which the difference in register is more pronounced than anything found in this instance and marks a historical rather than a personal difference in sensibility, and that is the avoidance of anything corresponding to 'sweet' in Celan's version of Sonnet 5.[34] If the two couplets are put side by side a correspondence can be found for each semantic element, apart from 'sweet', always provided changes in syntax are allowed, including the reduction of a clause to a word:

1 2 3 < 4 >
But flowers distill'd, though they with winter meet,

< 5 > 6 7 8 –
Leese but their show: their substance still lives sweet.

1 3/6 5 6 - 8
Doch so, als Geist, gestaltlos, aufbewahrt,

8 2 7 4 7-8
west sie, die Blume, weiter, winterhart.[35]

'Hart' for 'sweet' is indeed a remarkable exchange, the more so since this is the word the poem ends on, echoing in the ensuing silence. Olschner links this change with remarks Celan made on the difference between French and German poetry since 1945:

> Both texts end with the attribute which determines, for each of the respective epochs, the essence of "weiterwesen": "sweet" and "winterhart." In his own time Celan was not able to call the survival even of "das Schöne" "sweet", especially since the German of post-war poetry, as he termed it in 1958, was "eine 'grauere' Sprache".[36]

Though Celan's point about the relative greyness of post-war German poetry is fully taken, it is a general point, not confined to his own work, and, of course, it is Olschner, not Celan, who relates these remarks to his rendering of Sonnet 5, specifically to '(winter)hart' in lieu of 'sweet'. A number of qualifications present themselves on reading Olschner's comment, the first of which concerns the emphasis in the phrase 'even of "das Schöne"' which singles out the survival of 'das Schöne' and gives it privileged status, a position of priority in the order of survival, whereas the said 'greyer language' grants 'das Schöne' no privilege or priority; and there is no such problem in Shakespeare's poem which locates beauty in the context of the seasons, the organic phases of life and death, closely equating 'beauty' with life itself, or the fulness of life, so that 'does beauty survive?' is a way of asking 'what immortality is there?' Further, it so happens that Shakespeare uses 'sweet' eight times in the twenty one sonnets Celan published in this collection, and on each occasion Celan avoids 'süß'.[37] The other instances are: 'Thyself thy foe, to thy sweet self too cruel': 'und bist, der dich am grausamsten bedroht' (I); 'thy sweet self': 'Dein eigen Ich' (IV); 'in heaven's sweetest air': 'Wo Himmel blaun', 'the sweetest buds': 'die Knospe duftet' (LXX); 'in your sweet thoughts': 'in deinem Sinn' (LXXI); 'sweet love': omitted (LXXIX); 'in the blazon of sweet beauty's best': 'da, wo Schön am schönsten war' (CVI). Given that 'sweet' is an adjective and generally accompanies a noun, its prospects are in any case limited. By way of contrast, George, who sees 'die leidenschaftliche hingabe des dichters an seinen freund'[38] as the centre of the sonnets, has no such compunction and on each of these eight occasions says 'süss', perhaps to make his re-creation ('Umdichtung') firmly homo-erotic.

Though Shakespeare uses the word liberally, it is worth remarking that its use in this sonnet, as elsewhere, includes physical properties, suggests taste and fragrance: a sweet distillation of flowers; it also includes more spiritual qualities: 'loved, cherished', 'pure, free of corruption', culminating here in the 'sweet' – or perhaps the 'afters' – of pure spirituality, and so it is 'sweet' which links phenomenon, 'show', 'beauty's effect', and noumenon, 'substance'. In his own way Celan is at least as paradoxical as Shakespeare. A flower preserved as spirit, essence, 'Geist', hence formless, 'gestaltlos' (or structured as a fluid), is not, strictly speaking, a flower any longer, nor is it 'winterhart', since it no longer exists in the shape of a flower exposed to the rigours of winter. The closing line, however, denies and defies that proposition. Not exposed is how Hölderlin sees heavenly beings in 'Hyperions Schicksalslied':

Keusch bewahrt
In bescheidener Knospe,
Blühet ewig
Ihnen der Geist[39]

– lines which appear to have worked their way into the kaleidoscopic correspondences between the original and Celan's version. In short, not only is 'sweet' omitted, 'flowers' become 'sie, die Blume', metaphor turns to symbol in a gesture close to apostrophe, naming, and because the contrast between ephemeral 'show' and eternal 'substance' is elided, paradox turns towards transcendence.

Hardened by the winter, hard as the winter, shapeless, yet retaining name and identity, the flower is now like Hölderlin's 'modest bud', untouched by adversity, not buffeted by earthly events. But this other-worldliness is not simply equated with otherness, no more than in Shakespeare's sonnet, which takes the flowers of summer and gives them a time-proof form for the winter, whereas Celan's final line sounds like a part-revision of this conception, and of his own penultimate line, in that the quality of endurance is defined, not unnaturally, by what it has to endure. Winter leaves its mark, tests the flower's resistance and defines it as a particular kind of hardness, winter-hardiness, so the flower has integrated the cold of winter into its own nature and is no longer only a thing of summer, a configuration which may be heard as a response to Hölderlin's 'Weh mir, wo nehm ich, wenn es Winter ist, die Blumen ...'.[40] This is a flower not withered by the cold blast; it looks set to keep its winter-hardiness to eternity, or its winter-hardiness will so keep it.

It may be said of this closing line that it, too, not only has constancy as its theme but is also an enactment of constancy in language, with its sequence of word (or syllable) and metric stresses beginning with 'w' and ending with 't' and the last stress likewise ending on 't', all of which throws into relief, elevates, the central word, a mystical presence, 'die Blume', surrounded and untouched by the attendant iterations. Though 'winterhart' includes 'grey' in its complex of association, there is in my view nothing grey about this language which integrates death into life and life into death. The words are contained in a syntactic unit and within the framework of the iambic pentameter, at the same time there is a space around each individual word or phrase – the unit defined by a comma –, so that the rhyming couplet here accommodates the movement of free verse. Each unit is weighed, is felt and pondered, in a kind of sober enthusiasm, and the lines have the movement of an unfolding epiphany.

Finally, the comparison of epochs gives rise to misgivings which relate to the subsumption of individual experience into historical generality and to the precarious ground of comparison. A somewhat different emphasis may be found in Edwin Brock's poem which elaborates ways of killing a man in a broad historic sequence and concludes:

There are, as I began, cumbersome ways
to kill a man. Simpler, direct and much more neat
is to see that he is living somewhere in the middle
of the twentieth century, and leave him there.[41]

That emphasis on 'cumbersome' and 'more neat' distinguishes the epochs solely in terms of technological progress, which is equated with increasing economy and efficiency in the technique of killing, but otherwise bleakly assumes a sameness in intent and behaviour. Alongside that we can set Shakespeare whose imagination dwelt on the bloody history of his country and conceived the terrible intimacy of:

See't shalt thou never. Fellows, hold the chair.
Upon these eyes of thine I'll set my foot.

And again, after putting out the first eye, à propos of the second:

Lest it see more, prevent it. Out, vile jelly!
Where is thy lustre now?

And then, with a combination of contempt and managerial know-how:

Turn out that eyeless villain. Throw this slave
Upon the dunghill.[42]

Admittedly, this is *Lear,* not the *Sonnets.* Even so, such imaginings should inhibit the assumption that Shakespeare in his epoch had an altogether more sanguine view of the world than Celan had in ours.

Let us assume, wrongly, on returning to 107, that there is nothing worthy of note in the next two lines and move on to the end of stanza I. The German text does not attempt to sustain the syntax over the whole quatrain and so keep a sense of argument active – 'can *yet* control', *'suppos'd* as forfeit ... ' but simply states 'kann/bemessen' and then introduces another main clause in the fourth line, which no longer operates obliquely, by implication, '[wrongly] suppos'd as forfeit to a confin'd doom'. Instead it offers direct statement, proclamation, with emphatic inversion, each stressed syllable strongly stressed, reaching a climax on 'sie', followed by a pause, and a renewed declaration of independence: 'entgrenzt und unverwirkt ist sie, in niemands Bann'. This anticipates the second line of the third quatrain of the English poem, and even the final couplet, particularly if the triumphant note is given its due. The end begins to show through in Shakespeare's first quatrain, but is kept half-latent, with the full development held over until later, whereas Celan's version has no argument left to develop, all it needs to do is to elaborate and re-state, and that relates to the note of rejoicing as well as the theme, or to the theme as a musical argument. So though the motifs correspond line by line in stanza II, Shakespeare's measured ductus with its beautifully balanced and modulated antitheses gives way to sharper contrasts and rhythms distinctly more abrupt. The syntax profiles, emphasizes, separates out parts of speech, the third line dispenses with a verb, throws up a question in a phrase, which nicely puts the metrical stress on an unstressed syllable, miming what is tottering, 'das Schwankende', and gives an answer in another verbless sentence, two adjectival participles, not quite rhyming, but echoing and reinforcing one another, joined by an 'und' that announces and blends in with the 'un' of 'unbedingt', which establishes the tone, firm, unequivocal, unconditional: 'Das Schwankende von einst? Gekrönt und unbedingt'. It is only in the fourth line that the triumphal trumpet sound grows quiet and the movement flows as calmly and serenely as the English, closing on the attainment of peace, 'Frieden'.

In his rendering of 'Now with the drops of this most balmy time/My love looks fresh' George[43] shows how close you can keep to the original wording and capture something of its music: 'Jetzt in dem träufeln so balsamischer zeit // Blickt meine liebe frisch', though he cannot get anything close to the superb 'and Death to me subscribes' with its touch of *superbia.* Then in the third line he combines the folksong diction of 'mein arm lied' with the sub-Goethean 'mir dauer leiht' for 'I'll live in this poor rhyme'. Celan recasts the first three lines, bringing 'thou' forward from the first line of the final couplet to the first line of this quatrain, keeping Death in the second line, but linked now with 'du': 'no death to sweep thee away', which effects a considerable change in emphasis and attitude. Instead of reporting ' my love looks fresh' he uses apostrophe: 'meine Liebe ... du', followed by a laconic abolition of death, an assertion that death does not have the power to do what he otherwise always does, sweep the loved one (and everyone else) away – in the German it is the sweeping of waters, 'schwemmen'. Thus, if 'thou' is prominent enough in Shakespeare's text, 'du' in Celan's is given even greater prominence, lifted up on high. Taking the cue given by 'spite of him' and possibly George's 'trotz ihm' (though it is difficult to be more literal than that) and bringing in the mood of 'Death to me subscribes', he then turns the next line in the direction of Shakespeare's, a poet's, proud defiance. There is no place here for 'poor' as an epithet for rhyme; quite the contrary, Celan's phrasing echoes lines in Goethe's *Prometheus*:

Mußt mir meine Erde
Doch lassen stehn,
Und meine Hütte,
Die du nicht gebaut[44]

Only what is defied here is Death, not Zeus, and the earth and the hut he has to leave standing are 'the rhyme I built'. This is the house Celan built. It holds the image of 'du', 'umbalsamt ... umtaut', enveloped in the balm and dew of fresh time.

What I intended to convey by forgetting Shakespeare's claims for a moment was not an act of disappropriation but a sense of the naturalness with which Celan is able to inhabit his, Shakespeare's rhyme, as though in saying 'Reim' for 'rhyme' he has come into his own. He makes it his own (perhaps spontaneously) by changing the furnishing, heightening the intensity, expressed in assonance and alliteration, and by repetition, 'umbalsamt' and 'umtaut' containing and enfolding the line, with 'bist du, bist' confirming the mirror pattern the two participles create around (= 'um') 'meine Liebe ... du', themselves in the mirror relation of subject and complement: 'meine Liebe bist du'. Repeated 'bist' heightens the emphasis on modes of temporality, or stresses that temporality is in abeyance and sets the pattern for this line. Its movement returns to and rests on one and the same: 'Umbalsamt meine Liebe bist du, bist umtaut', the *stasis* of ecstasy.

The dash in the next line marks a change in perspective, a laconic comment, like an aside projected from a position of relative sobriety, then follow the proud, defiant words on the power of poetry. The last lines stick close to the original, keeping the adverbial clause of time, whereas George has a wish or invocation and – shade of 'Übermensch' perhaps – translates 'tribes' simply as 'menschen': 'Er schlage menschen stumpf und ohne sprach!', which death, as we well know, has a knack of doing without any exhortation. To say 'sprachelos' as Celan does instead of 'sprachlos' extends 'speechless' from a momentary to a more permanent condition, 'languagelessness', which is, no doubt, an implication of using 'speechless' as a generic epithet, 'speechless tribes'. It is as easy to understand why Celan might have preferred the more explicit epithet (apart from metrical constraints) as it is difficult to imagine him using a word as vague and general as

'Menschen' for 'tribes' in such a context. George's *Sonnette* were first published in 1909, and this word 'tribes' / 'Stämme' evidently had no personal or historical frisson for him. Some thirty years later 'Stamm' or 'Abstammung' is a matter of life or death. By the same token, Shakespeare's contrast between the poet and 'dull and speechless tribes', between monuments of wealth and power and poetry, is a configuration Celan invests with a sense of intense immediacy, exalted and quietly exultant.

'And thou in this', 'Und du: in diesem' – apart from the colon, it could hardly be more literal. After that, the shape is different, with the movement of the line bringing recurrences and a symmetry marked by the punctuation, image and mirror image on the axis of the central comma, 'hier' on one side, 'da' on the other, and so on, and the iterative, binding, equating force of alliteration: 'du', 'in diesem', 'da', 'dein'. If the central comma marks where the mirror stands, the mirror pattern extends in either direction with 'und du' at the beginning of the line and at the corresponding point at the end of the line 'dein Bild' (thine image).

'... da steht es noch' is in the present tense, and until the next line it looks and sounds as though 'noch' refers to the past, an impression reinforced by the syntax and the gestures of pointing, i.e. 'it's still standing there' or 'there it is, still standing', all of which is suddenly projected into the future with the next line, a use of the simple present founded in common usage ('Nächstes Jahr fahren wir nach Paris', etc.), to give 'it'll still be standing there when...'. The present here contains both past and future, and what it holds is constant, 'dein Bild', which no longer plays off 'monument' against 'crests' and 'tombs of brass' – George follows suit and says 'gedächtnismal' – but uses a word that means 'image', 'picture', 'portrait' and includes poetry; 'Bild' is the common word for image or metaphor, in keeping with 'Reim'. This is not the first time in Celan's version that a present has been used instead of a future, and in the earlier instance there is no sense of a present with a future sense, or only to the extent that the present is a continuous present: 'Ich lebe, ihm zum Trotz, im Reim, den ich gebaut': 'I live, in defiance of him, in the rhyme I built'. The future tenses concede too much to transience. Whatever is not touched by death is immortal now. This consistent use of the present accords at a deep level with the proud humility of 'Death to me subscribes'.

Politics must be involved in the 'things to come' / 'Dinge, die da kommen', and one of the consequences of recasting the last line of the first quatrain in the way Celan does is that allusions to the grave recede and a phrase is used that anticipates 'tyrants'/ 'Tyrannen' at the end: 'in niemands Bann'. Admittedly, the phrase may still be read as 'under no one's sway, (not even Death's, and he is the greatest tyrant of them all)', but a shift towards political power (tyranny) is detectable in 'Bann', a potent word. Besides 'sway' it also contains 'spell', 'power' and 'banishment'; 'unter Acht und Bann' is an old formula for 'outlawed', and 'verbannen' is 'to ban, banish, exile', so 'unter niemands Bann' could fairly be paraphrased as 'free from tyranny' or 'not tyrannized by anyone'. Parallelism links the couplet with the last two lines of the quatrain:

Since spite of him I'll live in this poor rhyme (11)
And thou in this shalt find thy monument (13)

While he insults o'er dull and speechless tribes (12)
When tyrants' crests and tombs of brass are spent (14).

Celan profiles the symmetries even more. The eleventh line belongs, emphatically, to 'ich' and the thirteenth raptly to 'du', just as the adverbial clauses of time in 12 and 14 both bring the verb forward to mid-line, even placing it in 12 between the two adjectives to create a considerable degree of tension between this and normal usage, with the verb signalling the end of the sentence whilst the sense is still palpably incomplete, so that first 'grollt' is amplified, and then the expected conclusion follows in a sharp, shuddering cadence. Two enemies are flouted in Shakespeare's sonnet, death and the world, which enables George to end with a fine flourish, an ominous, weighty final note:

Und dir wird hierin ein gedächtnismal
Wenn herrscherreif verfiel und gruft von stahl.

In Celan's version the political and existential strands are parallel throughout the poem, and the slow, static-ecstatic movement of the penultimate line stands out against the unimpeded movement of the final line, in which the monuments of power come tumbling down:

Und du: in diesem hier, da steht es noch, dein Bild,
wenn Gräbererz verwittert und Tyrannenschild.

A consummation devoutly to be wished: translation is implicit criticism, it allows you to approach the world of another's imagination in a way which is intuitive and technical, where technique is often intuitive and intuition works through technique. I do not know at what point Celan found iambic pentameters would not work for him in this poem and decided he needed an extra foot, not here or there but throughout the whole poem.[45] I imagine that, once a crucial line or two had assumed this shape, the rest followed. The earliest sonnets in German were written by the Baroque poets, usually in alexandrines, often with the caesura in mid-line:

Derweil er dumpfen grollt und sprachelosen Stämmen
Das Schwankende von einst? Gekrönt und unbedingt
[It sounds appropriate, so metaphysical]
Ich seh' wohin ich seh / nur Eitelkeit auff Erden.[46]

Whatever occasioned this departure from pentameters in Celan's version, its results are manifest throughout, in the bipartite (mirror) structure of the lines, with their caesura, and in those lines that are dwelt in intensely, which have the space to move in, to invoke, state and return.

One of the benefits of translating into German, as with other European languages, is that 'du', unlike 'thou', is not a historic presence, a memory preserved in older literature and in the Authorized Version, it is there now all the time under everyone's nose, on the tip of the tongue, and is intrinsically more affectionate and intimate than 'you'. The word is central to Celan's poetry; even when he is addressing himself 'du' is derived from the other, the founding presence without whom there would be no utterance other than an inarticulate cry.[47] The second person singular has no truck in the present context with quaint and endearing archaism and instead emphasizes, or re-emphasizes, the force of 'thou' as the apostrophe of love: 'And thou ...'. In Celan's line the colon after 'du' makes for a brief pause, a moment's suspension, holding up 'du', strengthening the monumental effect of apostrophe, and the holding is sustained through the recouping, iterative pattern of the line. Far from trying to identify the historical person addressed in Shakespeare's *Sonnets,* whether friend or dark lady, it is better to accept the poetic identity we are given, the features and attributes ascribed by the poems, inseparable as they are from the sonneteer's feelings. For him, true, the gifts of accident are all-important, but what he has not translated into poetry can only be laboriously reconstructed, or not, as the case may be. For us, much that was accident is lost, fallen away, the particulars of time, place and person, and what is transmitted and translatable is the figure of the loved one, this *alter ego,* in the friend's case, who is so disposed to waste his beauty and his sexuality, this comrade in time seemingly careless of time and mortality. He is the poetic figure of these concerns, elaborated in response to his apparent unconcern, and he is the living, breathing beauty of body and mind which starts words up, gives them their movement, energy and staying power. The beauty perishes, and the poetry lasts (at least some of it), yet the latter is grounded in the former and would have no meaning without it.

The *Sonnets* would have us believe they will preserve what has to perish, and if that claim is valid, they will always be immediate, create an image or a presence out of their own inherent energies. Celan's poetry, on the other hand, does not anticipate the moment of loss but is remembrance and lament from the beginning. His translation of Sonnet 107 is a passionate indwelling and meditation,[48] an act of gratitude and homage, confirming that something in this poem has come to life and is being reenacted in his thoughts and feelings. Without limiting the openness or indeterminacy of the lyrical 'I'[49] we can recognize that the transition from 'I' to 'ich' in this translation is potent and vital and that its potency is most tangible and explicit in 'Ich lebe, ihm zum Trotz, im Reim, den ich gebaut'. This emphasis on 'ich' is different from the emphasis on the prison of selfhood in the first sonnet, which Celan's version does not mitigate. Here it is sustained by the rhythm of defiance and self-assertion; poetry is the living space he has created for himself, in defiance of death. The biographical basis of this emphasis is well known and needs no elaboration. This intense occupation of 'ich' naturally affects 'du'. The more the translator inhabits the 'I' offered by the original, the more the corresponding 'thou' is relocated or redefined. In the dialogue which is translation there is a moment when 'du' naturally appears to be the original poet:

Aber du: in diesem hier, da steht es noch, dein Bild.

Marked stresses, frequent cola and alliteration of 'd' all beat time, and time beaten, all is presence, 'hier', 'da'. In the suspension of this line 'da steht es noch' is a firm affirmation, insisting on the image's staying power, and so the translation confirms, some three and a half centuries later, what the original sonnet predicted, and all that in its turn powerfully supports an intuition that the oscillations of 'du' include the original poet: 'And thou, in this here, there stands it still, thine image'. Translating – or translating as Celan does here – confirms that Shakespeare's sonnet has endured, is still a vital structure of words. If this translation is regarded as a would-be replica of the original, the mode of the latter's survival might appear shifting and fluid, even uncertain; but if it is seen as a way of expressing a response to the life embodied in this poem, then we recognize that the original poem is still flowing in the stream of life,[50] and the two texts side by side, facing one another across the spine of the page, are like mirror images that reflect their inevitable difference, whose nature is as difficult to define as it is manifest. In the distance between being difficult to define and being manifest lies the *raison d'être* of poetic translation.

There are several passionate definitions of poetry in *Der Meridian* which come to mind in the present context, amongst them 'diese Unendlichkeitssprechung von lauter Sterblichkeit und Umsonst'[51] ('this immortalization of sheer transience and futility'), which is close to the central theme of the *Sonnets*. A little later poems are possibly paths, 'Um-Wege, Umwege von dir zu dir... Wege einer Stimme zu einem wahrnehmenden Du' ('roundabout ways, detours from thou to thou... ways of a voice to a perceptive thou'), and then, in a single phrase-sentence at the end of the same paragraph, 'Eine Art Heimkehr' ('A kind of homecoming').[52] Shakespeare's 'I' and 'thou' prefigures Celan's 'ich' and 'du', and – there is a point in keeping to the German word, whose territorial implications are confined here to words on a page – a kind of 'Heimkehr' is an open paradigm, it is what the translation offers the poem and the poem the translation and what either or both offer their reader.

Notes and References

[1] Cf.: Leonard Moore Olschner: *Der feste Buchstab: Erläuterungen zu Paul Celans Gedichtübertragungen.* (Göttingen; Zürich, 1985; <*cited as*: OLSCHNER, 1985>), p.296.

[2] William Shakespeare: *Einundzwanzig Sonette,* übertragen von Paul Celan (Frankfurt am Main, 1967).

[3] 'Poetry of Constancy – Poetik der Beständigkeit' in *Peter Szondi: Celan-Studien*, (Frankfurt am Main, 1972; <*cited as*: SZONDI>), pp.13-45 ; translated into English by Harvey Mendelsohn in: 'Peter Szondi, "On Textual Understanding and Other Essays"', in *Theory and History of Literature*, vol. 15 (Manchester University Press, 1986; <*cited as*: MENDELSOHN>), pp.161-214.

[4] 'Kommt Celans Übertragung von Shakespeares 105. Sonett dem Grenzwert durchgängiger Realisierung des Äquivalenzprinzips in der syntagmatischen Abfolge näher als jedes Gedicht zuvor (sieht man einmal von der konkreten Dichtung ab), so nicht, weil Celans Gedicht – und seine Übertragung ist eines – poetischer wäre als andere Gedichte von ihm und als Gedichte anderer (dies folgern hieße Jakobson mißverstehen), sondern weil Beständigkeit das Thema seines Gedichts, seiner Übersetzung ist.' (SZONDI, p.42f.). 'Celan's translation of Shakespeare's sonnet 105 approaches more closely than any previous poem to the limiting value of a thoroughgoing realization of the principle of the equivalence in the syntagmatic sequence (if one leaves concrete poetry aside). This is so not because Celan's poem – and his translation is a poem – is more "poetic" than other poems by him or by others (to conclude this would be to misunderstand Jakobson), but because constancy is the theme of his poem, his translation.' (MENDELSOHN, p.176f.).

[5] 'In der Differenz der Intention auf die Sprache, der Art des Meinens, von Original und Übersetzung hat Benjamin die Legitimität, ja die Notwendigkeit des Übersetzens gesehen, die zugleich der Frage nach Treue oder Freiheit von Übersetzungen die Prämissen entzieht.' (SZONDI, p.20). 'Thus Benjamin saw the legitimacy, indeed the necessity, of translating as lying in the different intentions toward language and the modes of signification displayed in the original text and its translation. This very difference, moreover, invalidates the premises underlying debates over the issue of fidelity versus freedom in translating.' (MENDELSOHN, p.165).

[6] Walter Benjamin: 'Die Aufgabe des Übersetzers', in *Walter Benjamin: Schriften* Bd IV.I. (Frankfurt am Main, 1972; <*cited as*: BENJAMIN>), pp.9-21. 'Intention' occurs repeatedly, and Benjamin also uses 'intentio'. The term Mendelsohn uses is 'intention towards language' (see e.g. the previous note), which is a direct, single-phrase equivalent. Some caution is required, however, since 'Intention' and 'intentio' are not identical either with 'Absicht' or English 'intention', as e.g. in the following passage: 'Ihre Intention [d.h. die Intention der Übersetzung] geht nicht allein auf etwas anderes als die der Dichtung, nämlich auf eine Sprache im ganzen von einem einzelnen Kunstwerk in einer fremden aus, sondern sie ist auch selbst eine andere: die des Dichters ist naive, erste, anschauliche, die des Übersetzers abgeleitete, letzte, ideenhafte Intention' (BENJAMIN p. 16). 'Its intention [i.e. the intention of translation] is not only directed at something different from that of poetry, that is to say, at a language as a whole starting out from a single work in a foreign language, it is also something different in itself: that of the poet is naive, primal, tangible, that of the translator derived, ultimate, conceptual intention' (my translation). 'Der Dichter', 'der Übersetzer' are here generic, not specific – i.e. personifications of 'die Dichtung' (= poetry) and 'die Übersetzung' (= translation) – there is no ground here for assuming that an individual poet is necessarily aware of being naive, primal, just as there is no ground for assuming that a translator consciously aims at 'language as a whole'. At such moments 'bent' or 'inbuilt tendency' has the advantage of excluding any suggestion of an individual poet's (conscious) intention.

[7] SZONDI p.19, footnote 5: 'the directedness of consciousness towards language, that is, [...] the linguistic conception preceding all speech', (MENDELSOHN, p.212). At the beginning of this note Szondi also says "'Intention" heißt in Benjamins Aufsatz nicht "Absicht"' (p.18) and then quotes Fritz Mauthner's comment on the medieval use of 'intentio': 'darum war [...]

intentio das Gerichtetsein der Aufmerksamkeit oder des Bewußtseins auf ein wahrgenommenes oder wahrzunehmendes Objekt': 'hence for them *intentio* was directedness of attention or of consciouness to a perceived or perceptible object' (MENDELSOHN, p.212). My reading of Benjamin would bracket out 'oder des Bewußtseins' where it could be taken to mean individual awareness. 'Aufmerksamkeit' (= attention, attentiveness) contains the possibility of being completely wrapped up in something, of seeing only the object, not oneself, of being intent without intention.

[8] Paul Celan, *Gesammelte Werke in fünf Bänden* (Frankfurt am Main, 1983), Bd V, p.345. The text of Shakespeare's poem is the text given on p. 344 of this volume.

[9] [In] *Ich find, erfind* 'wird [...] die Kulisse der Sprachperformanz, der parole, durchlöchert und der Blick auf das Gestänge des Sprachsystems, der langue, freigegeben. Was man erblickt, sind Teile des Konjugationsparadigmas, das eine Mal unter dem Gesichtspunkt des tempus (was ich da treib und trieb), das andere Mal unter dem der Person: ich find, erfind (= er findet) ...' (SZONDI, p.32f.) '... with the phrase *Ich find, erfind* Celan pierces the façade of linguistic performance, that is of *parole* (speech), making it possible to glimpse the inner workings of the linguistic system, of *langue* (language) ... What is thereby revealed are parts of the conjugation paradigm, once with respect to tense (was ich da treib und trieb) and once with respect to person: ich find, erfind (= er findet).' (MENDELSOHN, p.171).

[10] SZONDI, p.38.

[11] MENDELSOHN, p.178: 'Nicht mehr läßt Celan den Dichter von seinem *argument*, seiner *invention,* seinem *scope* sprechen, sondern sein Vers ist so gefügt, wie es dieses Thema und diese Absicht verlangen. Celan läßt den Dichter nicht behaupten, ein Vers lasse Unterschiede aus, sondern er läßt ihn eine Sprache sprechen, in der Unterschiede ausgelassen sind. Aus der Konzeption, welche die Symbolisten von der Poesie hatten, die sich selbst zum Gegenstand wird, sich selbst als Symbol beschwört und beschreibt, hat Celan in der Nachfolge des späten Mallarmé wie als Zeitgenosse und aufmerksamer Beobachter der modernen Linguistik, Sprachphilosophie und Ästhetik die Konsequenz gezogen. In der Übertragung eines Gedichts, dessen Gegenstand jene Beständigkeit ist, die nach der Definition Jakobsons als von der Achse der Paradigmatik, der sie konstitutiv ist, auf die Achse der Syntagmatik projizierte in dieser die poetische Sequenz von der prosaischen unterscheidet, hat er – vielleicht ohne Jakobsons Theorem zu kennen – an die Stelle des traditionellen symbolistischen Gedichts, das von sich selber handelt, das sich selbst zum Gegenstand hat, ein Gedicht gesetzt, das von sich selbst nicht mehr handelt, sondern es ist. Ein Gedicht, das nicht mehr von sich selbst spricht, sondern dessen Sprache in dem *geborgen* ist, was es seinem Gegenstand, was es sich selber zuschreibt: *in der Beständigkeit,'* (SZONDI, p.44f).

[12] George is more literal than Celan and still calls his translation of the *Sonnets* an 'Umdichtung', a translation of poetry into poetry; that he does not give the English text may denote several things, i.e. that the versions are poems capable of standing on their own, not glosses, that they are meant for readers who know their Shakespeare, and that readers interested in the relation between ' Umdichtung' and original will consult an English edition, all of which would indicate a relatively low level of interest in the interplay between original and version.

[13] 'Die Fragestellung dieser Arbeit erlaubt es nicht, dem Sonett Shakespeares in einer von dessen eigenen Gegebenheiten her erfolgenden Analyse Gerechtigkeit widerfahren zu lassen.' (SZONDI, p.24; note 9). 'An analysis of Shakespeare's sonnet that would do justice to it would have to proceed from its own distinctive features, but that would carry beyond the bounds of the present essay.' (MENDELSOHN, p.212).

[14] MENDELSOHN, p.170. The corresponding phrases in Szondi are: 'das schon von der Wortwahl her an die diskursive räsonierende Sprache gemahnende *argument* und dessen nicht minder logische Bestimmung *all*' (p.30), 'Nur deshalb kann dasselbe mit verschiedenen Wörtern bezeichnet werden' (p.31), 'Celans Intention auf die Sprache darf hingegen als die bestimmte Negation dieser sprachtheoretischen Prämisse verstanden werden' (p.31).

[15] MENDELSOHN, p.171. SZONDI: 'die Absicht, eine Unterscheidung von signifiant und signifié zu negieren', p.32.

[16] The rewriting might then be comparable to the rewriting of lines in Brecht's poem 'Schlechte Zeit für Lyrik' in 'Ein Blatt, baumlos, // für Bertolt Brecht', Paul Celan, *Schneepart* (Frankfurt am Main, 1971) p.59 = *Gesammelte Werke*, Bd II, p.385. See Winfrid Menninghaus, *Paul Celan: Magie der Form* (Frankfurt am Main, 1980) who moves from 'fast vollständig ein Zitat und doch ganz ein Gedicht Celans' to 'diese auf eine kategorial andere Ebene transponierte Sprachkritik' and 'die dialektisch gedachte Intra-Kommunikation der sprachlichen Form', pp.37-39: from 'almost completely a quotation and yet entirely a poem of Celan's' to 'this criticism of language transferred onto a categorically other level' and 'the dialectically conceived intercommunication of linguistic form'.

[17] A remark in Benjamin's essay (see Note 4) is particularly suggestive at this point: ' In [der Übersetzung] wächst das Original in einen gleichsam höheren und reineren Luftkreis der Sprache hinauf, in welchem es freilich nicht auf die Dauer zu leben vermag, wie es ihn auch bei weitem nicht in allen Teilen seiner Gestalt erreicht, auf den es aber dennoch in einer wunderbar eindringlichen Weise wenigstens hindeutet als auf den vorbestimmten, versagten Versöhnungs- und Erfüllungsbereich der Sprachen' (BENJAMIN, p.14f): 'In [the translation] the original grows as it were into a higher and purer atmospheric region of language in which admittedly it is not able to live permanently, just as it is far from reaching to this height with every part of its form, but to which it nonetheless at least points, with a wonderful incisiveness, as the predestined, unattained zone in which the languages are reconciled and fulfilled'.

[18] The following discussion might be compared with: 'Nur in der anaphorischen (und insofern rhetorisch konsakrierten) Wiederholung von *Fair, kind and true* geht Beständigkeit in die Sprache selber ein. Anders bei Celan. Konsequent läßt er die Stellen unübersetzt, in denen Shakespeare das eigene Gedicht, den eigenen Stil, das Ziel seines Dichtens beschreibt, oder er übersetzt sie so frei, daß sie nicht mehr davon zu handeln scheinen' (SZONDI, p.43f.). 'Only in the anaphorical (and thus rhetorically consecrated) repetition of "Fair, kind and true" does constancy enter the very language. In Celan's version we find something very different. Consistent with his overall approach, Celan leaves untranslated those passages in which Shakespeare describes his own poem, his own style, and the goal of his writing: or else he translates so "freely" that they no longer seem to deal with those topics' (MENDELSOHN, p.177).

[19] This comment concurs entirely with SZONDI: 'Bereits Shakespeares Text zeichnet sich durch eine große Anzahl von Wiederholungen aus. Celan hat sie, wie "frei" er im übrigen auch verfährt, stets wiedergegeben' (p.27): 'Shakespeare's own text contains a large number of repetitions, which Celan always retains, however freely he may proceed in other respects' (MENDELSOHN, p.168).

[20] 'Darin wird der *change,* die Auswechslung des Wortes bei gleichbleibendem Gemeinten, deren Voraussetzung eben jene Sprachkonzeption bildet, beim Namen genannt: *And in* this *change is my invention* spent. Celan weigert sich ebenso, die Möglichkeit solcher Austauschbarkeit von Wörtern zu konzedieren', (SZONDI, p.32).

[21] For Szondi the repetition of this phrase is anaphoric, hence rhetorical (see note 18). The poem, however, is claiming the opposite, i.e. that its subject is not amenable to the devices of rhetoric. Insofar as what it does is rhetoric, then only to act out rhetoric's undoing.

[22] This is a point at which the commentary most evidently misses something in the original: 'Sowenig Celan dem Dichter erlaubt, daß er von seiner Inventionsgabe spreche, sowenig darf dieser bei ihm den Spielraum seines Dichtens *(scope)* erwähnen oder ihn gar als *wondrous* kennzeichnen' (SZONDI, p.35). Mendelsohn's translation, in its turn, omits the emphasis of 'gar als *wondrous*': 'Celan, as we have seen, does not allow the poet to speak of his own inventive gifts; similarly, he forbids the poet to mention the *scope* of his poetry or call it "wondrous"' (p.172). – To continue in this idiom, though it feels incongruous, Shakespeare allows the poet to use these words on the understanding that 'scope' is said where there is none, 'wondrous' is said and its opposite meant; meaning here is of the ironic kind (= die Art des Meinens ist hier ironisch). So, what otherwise might seem a weak repetition, the friend's 'wondrous excellence' followed by the poet's 'wondrous scope', is a contrast, with the 'wondrous scope' standing ironically for the monotony induced by the friend's truly wondrous (and unfailing) excellence.

[23] Regrettably, this reading of Sonnet 105 is not informed by Shakespeare criticism. One foray into that domain brought some corroboration: 'In recurrence, love's writing finds its end. So repetition, that essential protracted tautology, became, for Shakespeare, perfect eloquence [...] A poem like 105 is scrupulously and Shakespearianly dull, but it is dull nonetheless... The text is stripped of metaphor; there are no false comparisons [...] In so far as Shakespeare exceeds the Erasmian *copia,* shunning 'variation' for the sake of tautologous recurrence, his verse palls'. William Shakespeare, *The Sonnets and A Lover's Complaint* (Harmondsworth, 1986), edited by John Kerrigan, 'Introduction', p.29.

[24] Von schönsten Wesen wünscht man einen spross
Dass dadurch nie der schönheit rose sterbe:
Und wenn die reifere mit der zeit verschoss
Ihr angedenken trag ein zarter erbe.

Doch der sein eignes helles auge freit
Du nährst dein licht mit eignen wesens loh·
Machst aus dem überfluss die teure-zeit·
Dir feind und für dein süsses selbst zu roh.

Du für die welt jezt eine frische zier
Und erst der herold vor des frühlings reiz:
In eigner knospe gräbst ein grab du dir
Und· zarter neider· schleuderst weg im geiz.

Gönn dich der welt! Nicht wie ein schlemmer tu:
Esst nicht der welt behör· das grab und du!

Stefan George: *Gesamt-Ausgabe der Werke* (Berlin, 1931), Bd XII: *Shakespeare. Sonnette. Umdichtung*; <*cited as*: GEORGE>, p.7.

[25] Celan, *Gesammelte Werke* V, p.324f.

[26] Celan named two criteria in translating poetry in a letter to Gleb Struve, dated 29.1.59, i.e. closest proximity to the text and preserving the poetry: '...glaube ich sagen zu dürfen, daß meine Übersetzungen auch von meinen ständigen Bemühungen um philologische Genauigkeit zeugen. (Ich habe an der Sorbonne Germanistik und Sprachwissenschaft studiert.) Freilich ging es mir vor allem darum, bei größter Textnähe das Dichterische am Gedicht zu übersetzen, die Gestalt wiederzugeben, das Timbre des Sprechenden'. See Leonard Olschner: 'Anamnesis:

Paul Celan's Translations of Poetry', in *Translating Tradition: Paul Celan in France,* edited by Benjamin Hollander. Acts 8/9. Acts: A Journal of New Writing (San Francisco, 1988) <*cited as*: OLSCHNER, 1988>. 'I believe I may rightly say that my translations also bear testimony to my constant endeavor towards linguistic precision. [...] To be sure, I was chiefly concerned, not only with staying as close to the original text as possible, but also with translating the poetry in the poem, with rendering form and timbre of the voice speaking in the poem' (OLSCHNER, 1988, p.69). The degree of latitude afforded by 'as close ... as possible' is naturally not defined, just as what is poetic about 'the' poem is naturally left open, as are ways and means of translating it.

[27] See previous note.

[28] I find something of this kind in Hanno Helbling: *William Shakespeare: Die Sonette* (Zürich, 1983). These versions are smooth, pleasant, often at first sight closer to the literal sense than either George or Celan, but bland. The essence seems to have been distilled out of them. The first quartet of the first sonnet must suffice as an example: 'Das Holdeste, wir wünschen es vermehrt, // damit der Schönheit Rose nie vergehe // und alsbald, wenn das Reife sich verzehrt, // sein Bild im zarten Erben neu erstehe' (*ibid.*, p.7).

[29] Goethe, *Torquato Tasso,* V, iii. *Werke*, Bd.5 (Hamburg, 1952), p.156.

[30] For a searching meditation on 'Poetry as Menace and Atonement', see G. W. Hill, *The Lords of Limit* (London, 1984), pp.1-18.

[31] GEORGE: 'Nicht eigne angst noch der prophetische geist // Der weiten welt ...', p.113.

[32] '– ach in wortreichen Nächten, wie oft verschwieg ich // meine jüdische Angst, von der ich behaupte // daß ich sie habe ...': 'ah, in nights full of words how often // I kept silent about my Jewish fear which I claim // to have ...'. Wolf Biermann in 'Gesang für meine Genossen', translated by Michael Hamburger in: *East German Poetry, An Anthology,* edited by Michael Hamburger (Oxford: Carcanet, 1972), p.176f.

[33] Celan, *Gesammelte Werke*, Bd V, p.348f.

[34] See OLSCHNER, 1988, p.84, note 26. The phrase of Celan's Olschner is referring to, 'eine "grauere" Sprache', occurs in a reply Celan sent to the Librairie Flinker when asked about work in progress in 1958. See *Gesammelte Werke*, Bd III, p.167.

[35] Celan, *Gesammelte Werke*, Bd V, p.324f.

[36] OLSCHNER, 1988, p.84.

[37] One instance of the difficulties 'sweet' has occasioned in this century, though not a casual one, is the 'old Lie' in Wilfrid Owen's 'Dulce et decorum est', half hidden in a Latin tag, which indicates its age and a possible evasion. See Wilfrid Owen, *War Poems and Others.* Edited with an Introduction and Notes by Dominic Hibberd, (London, 1974), p.79. Owen's own comment is enough: 'Here is a gas poem, done yesterday. [...] The famous Latin tag means of course *It is sweet and meet to die for one's country. Sweet!* And *decorous!'* (Letter 552, 16 October 1917). See *ibid.*, p.120.

[38] GEORGE: p.5.

[39] Friedrich Hölderlin: *Sämtliche Werke,* edited by Friedrich Beißner,Bd I, i (Stuttgart, 1946), p.265.

[40] Hölderlin, 'Hälfte des Lebens', *ibid.*, Bd II, i (Stuttgart, 1951), p.117.

[41] Edwin Brock, *Five ways to kill a man.* New and selected poems. (Petersfield, 1990), p.17. The poem with this title appeared in *With Love from Judas* (1963), and also in *Penguin Modern Poets 8* (1966).

[42] William Shakespeare: *The Tragedy of King Lear.* The New Cambridge Shakespeare, (CUP, 1992), III, 7, pp.201-203.

[43] Nicht eigne angst noch der prophetische geist
Der weiten welt der künftige dinge ahnt
Auf meiner treuen liebe ablauf weist
Und an verfall zu fester frist gemahnt.

Der menschen mond strahlte nach finsternis
Und trübe magier spotten eignen spruchs.
Das reich der schwankungen ward nun gewiss •
Friede ruft palmen aus von ewigem wuchs.

Jezt in dem träufeln so balsamischer zeit
Blickt meine liebe frisch und Tod gibt nach
Da trotz ihm mein arm lied mir dauer leiht . .
Er schlage menschen dumpf und ohne sprach!

Und dir wird hierin ein gedächtnismal
Wenn herrscher-reif verfiel und gruft von stahl.

[44] Goethe, *Werke*, Bd I (Hamburg, 1948), p.45.

[45] Celan uses an occasional alexandrine amongst his pentameters. See e.g.: II: 'und deiner Jugend Kleid, dran soviel Augen hängen'; IV: 'Die Schönheit, ungenutzt: mit dir muß sie verwesen'. LVII has alexandrines in the quatrains and pentameters in the couplet; LX, with its baroque theme, alternates pentameter and alexandrine in the quatrains – with the exception of the third, which has an alexandrine in the first as well as the second and fourth lines – and ends with pentameters in the couplet. Here the spirit of seventeenth century German poetry does stalk the page: 'Der Jugend Blust: die Zeit durchbohrt ihn, gräbt // der Stirn der Schönheit ein die Zeilen und die Zeichen'.

[46] The first two alexandrines are taken more or less at random from Celan's version of Sonnet 107, the third is my comment and the fourth is the opening line of Gryphius's sonnet 'Vanitas, Vanitatum, et omnia Vanitas. Es ist alles gantz eytel. *Eccl.* I. v. 2.' Andreas Gryphius, *Gesamtausgabe der deutschsprachigen Werke*, Bd I (Stuttgart, 1963), p.7.

[47] In the light of Buber's fundamental distinction between the 'Grundwort Ich-Du' and the 'Grundwort Ich-Es' 'no utterance' might be rephrased as 'no poetic utterance' which would be implicitly distinguished from functional language: 'Das Grundwort Ich-Du kann nur mit dem ganzen Wesen gesprochen werden. Das Grundwort Ich-Es kann nie mit dem ganzen Wesen gesprochen werden', Martin Buber, 'Ich und Du', *Werke*, Bd I (München and Heidelberg, 1962; <*cited as*: BUBER>), p.79: 'The basic word I-Thou can only be spoken with the whole being. The basic word I-It can never be spoken with the whole being' (my translation).

[48] Cf.: 'Solang der Himmel des Du über mir ausgespannt ist, kauern die Winde der Ursächlichkeit an meinen Fersen, und der Wirbel des Verhängnisses gerinnt' (BUBER, p.83): 'As long as the heaven of thou is extended above me, the winds of causality cower at my heels and the vortex of destiny clogs up' (my translation).

[49] Or 'the split 'I'. Jakobson talks of 'a split addresser ... a split addressee and ... a split reference' as characteristic of the poetic function: Roman Jakobson, 'Linguistics and Poetics', in: *Style in Language* (Cambridge, Mass., 1960) edited by Thomas A. Seboek, p.371. Similarly, Gadamer's reading of the sequence 'Atemkristall' is oriented on the indeterminacy of 'ich' and 'du': 'Wir wissen nicht vorher und nicht aus einem distanzierten Überblick oder Vorausblick, was Ich oder Du hier meint und ob Ich das Ich des Dichters ist, der sich selbst meint, oder das eines jeden von uns. Wir haben es zu lernen'. Hans Georg Gadamer, *Wer bin Ich und wer bist*

Du? Kommentar zu Celans 'Atemkristall' (Frankfurt am Main, 1973, revised and augmented 1986), p.12f.

[50] See 'In ihnen [= in Übersetzungen, die mehr als Vermittlungen sind] erreicht das Leben des Originals seine stets erneute späteste und umfassendste Entfaltung' (BENJAMIN, Bd IV, I, p.11): 'In these [= translations which are more than mediations] the life of thc original attains its constantly renewed, most recent and most extensive development' (my translation).

[51] Celan: 'Der Meridian', *Gesammelte Werke*, III, p.200.

[52] *ibid.*, p.201.

RE-WRITING, RE-CYCLING:
Friedrich Dürrenmatt and *The Tragedy of King John*[1]

SYDNEY G. DONALD

By 1967, Friedrich Dürrenmatt's long-standing but often stormy relationship with the *Schauspielhaus*, Zürich, had almost reached breaking point. In that year, however, he met Werner Düggelin, sometime stage-lighter at the *Schauspielhaus* but more recently returned as guest director of *Die Wiedertäufer*, Dürrenmatt's re-write of his first play, *Es steht geschrieben* (1947). The friendship between Dürrenmatt and Düggelin was instantaneous; the ensuing Dü-Dü partnership, though shortlived – it lasted precisely half of the three years which were originally envisaged – was intense and productive, but it ended in acrimony and recriminations all round.[2] Shortly after the première of *Die Wiedertäufer* in March 1967, Düggelin was appointed artistic director of Basel's two theatres, the *Stadttheater* and the *Komödie*. He seems to have had little difficulty in persuading Dürrenmatt to join him as co-director. Thus began the ill-fated 'Basler Theaterexperiment'. Dürrenmatt rented a flat behind the Barfüsserplatz in Basel and threw himself body and soul into his new venture, writing programme notes and monthly articles for the new theatre magazine, attending rehearsals, regaling his new colleagues into the small hours with shipments of claret from the legendary cellars of his home in Neuchâtel, and making do with two or three hours' sleep a night. But the arrangement was altogether too vague for Dürrenmatt's liking. He was paid token expenses of SF 100 per day, but no salary; he was never quite sure of his role, and as time went by he felt increasingly marginalised. Then came his heart attack in April 1969, his enforced convalescence in Neuchâtel and the Engadin, the arguments and the final break with Düggelin in October 1969. 'Ich bin mir noch jetzt nicht im klaren, ob ich als Arzt oder als Patient in dieser Institution meine Zeit vergeudete,' he wrote shortly after his departure from Basel [*WA* 24, p.156].

Yet they had hoped for so much. For Dürrenmatt, the move to Basel promised to be the fulfilment of a dream, the dream of having his own theatre which had haunted him since the fifties when he had turned down Brecht's invitation to join him as *Dramaturg* in the Berliner Ensemble. He hoped that his contributions to the theatre magazine might eventually form the basis of a *Basler Dramaturgie* to rival Lessing's *Hamburgische Dramaturgie*. But most immediately, perhaps, the break with Zürich held out the prospect of fresh inspiration and revitalisation for the jaded author:

> Auch ich brauche Pausen. Ich brauche neue Ansätze, neue Zeit zum Überlegen. Ich habe gerade in der letzten Zeit ziemlich viele Theaterstücke aufeinander folgen lassen, und ich brauche einen neuen Anreiz, um weiter zu schreiben.[3]

Despite the resounding success of *Die Wiedertäufer*, Dürrenmatt was still deeply depressed following the failure of *Der Meteor* a year earlier, and was desperately in need of a fresh start.[4] The straight run of adaptations and productions of classics which followed *Der Meteor* during this, 'Dürrenmatt's dramaturgic phase', suggests that he was going through a creative crisis:[5] after *Die Wiedertäufer* and *König Johann* (1968) came *Play Strindberg* (1969); *Urfaust* (Zürich) and *Titus Andronicus* (Düsseldorf), both 1970, premiered within two months of each other, and punctuated by his only original work during this period, *Porträt eines Planeten* (Düsseldorf); then in Zürich *Woyzeck* (1972) and *Emilia Galotti* (1974, in the original text). And besides these adaptations, two others were planned which, though they never actually took place, nevertheless played their part in the break-up of the Dü-Dü team: first of all, the atmosphere in Basel was severely strained when Düggelin broke his promise to stage a Dürrenmatt production of Frisch's *Biedermann und die Brandstifter*; and finally, Dürrenmatt returned from his convalescence to discover that Düggelin had replaced his adaptation of *Minna von Barnhelm* with Lessing's original text without a word of consultation.[6]

Together, Dürrenmatt, Düggelin and his young *Dramaturg*, Hermann Beil, had planned an ambitious repertoire, including *The Acharnians*, *Woyzeck*, *Troilus and Cressida*, *Kasimir und Karoline*, and much more besides. Staging Shakespeare's *King John* was Beil's idea, but was also much favoured by Düggelin.[7] He had arrived in Basel 'mit einem zu 90 Prozent aus allen Windrichtungen neu engagierten Ensemble' [RÜEDI, *loc.cit.*], and this first production was conceived, Dürrenmatt told Rainer Litten, as much as an exercise in team-building as anything else:

> Es ist eine Auftragsarbeit, wenn Sie so wollen. Es handelt sich ja darum: Wie kann man einen Schriftsteller in ein Ensemble einbauen? [...] Ich kann die Vorteile ausnützen, innerhalb eines Kollektivs zu arbeiten. Man kann schon früh mit den Leuten diskutieren, denn Schreiben ist ja nicht nur eine Arbeit am Schreibtisch. Es ist eine Arbeit mit der Bühne für die Bühne.[8]

Considering that *King John* is one of Shakespeare's least-performed plays, and that it has never once been staged in the Schlegel translation in the Federal Republic, it is a testimony at least as much to Dürrenmatt's skill (and, as we shall see, his ruthlessness) in adaptation as to the topicality of its subject-matter that *König Johann. Nach Shakespeare* was an immediate box-office success, and went on to become the most frequently performed Shakespearean history play in Germany.[9] The play opened at the *Stadttheater* on 18 September, 1968, only days after the Soviet invasion of Prague, which Dürrenmatt himself had attacked in a speech, 'Tschechoslowakei 1968', at a matinée in the same theatre on 8 September [*WA* 28, pp.35-42]. As outlined above, subsequent events indicate that its success in team-building was rather more limited than its success on the stage.

As well as examining Dürrenmatt's response as a playwright to the challenges posed by the Shakespearean original, the present analysis of *König Johann* will seek to show that, even if in the late sixties Dürrenmatt's ideas for novel *plots* had temporarily dried up, the inventiveness and skill of his stage-craft remained largely undiminished. In the absence of a supply of new *Stoffe*, he drew, as we shall see, on his extensive experience as a dramatist for inspiration, particularly by developing his latest characters out of creations from his earlier plays, and by re-cycling themes, ideas and tricks of the trade which had served him well in the past.

Beyond general agreement that *The Tragedy of King John* is one of Shakespeare's earliest works, there is much conjecture about the origins and date of the play; scholars are even divided, for example, on whether Shakespeare's source was the anonymous and much longer *Troublesome Reign of John, King of England*, or *vice versa*.[10] Dürrenmatt followed the majority view, that Shakespeare's play was an adaptation of the earlier work, and since his only source, for all practical purposes, was *King John* in the Schlegel translation, we have no need to explore the matter of provenance further.[11]

King John is a bloodthirsty thirteenth-century tale of skulduggery and treachery in high places. King John (nicknamed Lackland) rules England precariously by virtue of his dying brother's will rather than by lineal descent: King Richard the Lionheart had been persuaded on his deathbed by his mother, Queen Eleanor, to name John, his youngest brother, as his successor instead of the rightful heir by primogeniture, his deceased brother Geoffrey's child Arthur. John impetuously embarks on an ill-judged war with France, assisted by his new-found nephew, Philip Faulconbridge, an illegitimate son of King Richard who turns up towards the end of Act I. Once knighted and dubbed Sir Richard Plantagenet, the Bastard Philip becomes the real hero of the play. As King John's right-hand-man he supports him through thick and thin and, as John's fortunes begin to slide and his character begins to crumble, he assumes control and does what little is possible to ward off disaster. When John finally dies of poisoning, it is the Bastard who delivers the last words of the play, a rousing call for national unity in the face of foreign aggression:

> Now these her princes are come home again,
> Come the three corners of the world in arms,
> And we shall shock them. Nought shall make us rue,
> If England to itself do rest but true. [*TKJ*, p.169]

Shakespeare's drama traces the dynastic struggle between King John and King Philip of France over the crown and the English right to certain French territories. Philip backs the minor Prince Arthur's ambitious mother, Constance, in pursuit of her claim to the English throne on her young son's behalf. When faced with attack by the combined forces of both opposing armies because of their unwillingness to take sides in the dispute over sovereignty, the citizens of Angers propose a diplomatic marriage between the Dauphin and John's niece, Blanche. John readily agrees to this, because it implies French endorsement of his position as monarch and abandonment of Arthur's cause, whilst Philip for his part agrees because of the extensive lands which Blanche brings with her to the marriage.

No sooner have hostilities been called off, however, than John proceeds to make an enemy of the Pope, by refusing to acknowledge Rome's authority over him. The papal legate, Cardinal Pandulph, calls on Philip to defend the faith by declaring war once more on John. In the ensuing fracas, Prince Arthur is taken prisoner by the English forces and placed in the custody of Hubert de Burgh. This custodian is encouraged by the King to blind the boy or worse, but instead takes pity on him and decides to give out a tale that the Prince has been killed. Meanwhile John has himself crowned a second time, by his peers and without the ministrations of a priest, in open defiance of the Pope, but also in order to secure the fickle allegiance of the English nobles, who in return, suspecting that the King has designs on the boy's life, demand the liberty of Prince Arthur. When Hubert (pretending) and John (believing) announce that Arthur has died, the nobles turn against the King.

With the enemy invading and his peers rebelling, John is forced to pay homage once more to the Pope. As a reward for his penitence, he receives his crown back from Pandulph 'as holding of the Pope' [*TKJ*, p.148], along with a promise from the Cardinal that he will now call off the French. But no sooner have his fortunes thus taken a turn for the better than the Bastard brings the news that Arthur has died accidentally in a fall whilst trying to escape from the tower in which he has been imprisoned, whereupon John, devastated by this turn of events, places himself and his fortunes in the hands of the Bastard.

Things now go rapidly from bad to disastrous. The French refuse to retreat and John, poisoned by a monk, expires in agony amidst the tidings that most of the Bastard's remaining forces have been drowned in the Lincolnshire Washes. But the play ends, against all odds, on a positive note, for the papal legate has at last persuaded the French to treat for peace with the new King Henry, John's son, under whom England shall be united once more. What is left unsaid is that the land is well rid of a tyranny so autocratic and detested as to spawn that early declaration of human rights, the Magna Carta.

It is not difficult to see how such a tortuous plot, brimful of duplicity, intrigue, misunderstandings and downright bad luck, might appeal on the one hand to Dürrenmatt's dark sense of humour, and on the other to his profound distrust of power-brokers and the powerful. Whitton recalls Dürrenmatt's remarks at the time:

> In 1969, shortly before his 'departure', he told me in Neuchâtel: '*König Johann* war eine Theatergelegenheitsarbeit. Es war ein ewiger Traum, das zu machen', that is to

> present a poor Shakespearean play from a modern point of view and show that it could be made to be relevant [WHITTON, p.135].

King John treats of the political and constitutional issues of the day: legitimacy and legality; the nature, scope and limitations of kingship; religion, particularly reflecting the anti-Catholic sentiments prevalent at the time; nationalism and patriotism. The plot caters amply for the Elizabethan love of stage battles and bloodshed, of rhetoric and pathos, and indeed 'the styles of acting in the late eighteenth and nineteenth centuries also account for much of *King John*'s appeal, for nearly every minor character has a passionate speech of some sort.'[12]

Some five years after Dürrenmatt's *König Johann* opened in Basel, John Barton's production of *King John* at Stratford-upon-Avon was roundly criticised by R.L. Smallwood for trying to incorporate material from *The Troublesome Reign* and from John Bayle's *King Johan* into the script. In short, 'by adding to the material given by Shakespeare, Mr Barton had created difficulties for himself.'[13] Dürrenmatt went in the opposite direction, for the dramatic challenge, as he saw it, was not (despite the current vogue for such things) to create a documentary or chronicle play, but – *pace* Tiusanen [p.336] – a parable; and the ideological challenge was to make his audience hear echoes of their own time in the cadences of his medieval characters:

> Ich stellte mir die Aufgabe, die dramaturgische Dialektik des vorhandenen Spielmaterials reiner herauszuarbeiten, die ständigen Peripetien beizubehalten, die auch bei Shakespeare vorhanden sind, und zu einem eleganteren Endspiel zu kommen; das Spiel zu verkürzen, statt des mühsamen Kleinkrieges, mit dem Shakespeare und sein Vorgänger ihr Matt erzielen, es mit wenigen Spielzügen zu erreichen und so die Handlung durchsichtig zu machen. Aus einer dramatisierten Chronik wird ein Gleichnis: Die Komödie der Politik, einer bestimmten Politik.[14]

His method, then, was to rethink the *dénouement* and then work backwards through the plot, streamlining in places, but also freeing up space for new scenes of his own. The success of the play as political commentary lies beyond the scope of this study, but certainly one is inclined to agree that the author doth protest too much, as Tiusanen clearly implies when he writes that 'the playbill *did its best* [my italics] to clarify the political parallels of *König Johann*: there were photographs published of historical [*sic*] peace conferences, including those of Versailles 1919, Yalta 1945, Paris and Bratislava 1968' [TIUSANEN, p.337]. Although Dürrenmatt, surprisingly, dropped the most famous passage in the original, the Bastard's Commodity speech, the pictures chosen for the *Programmheft* show various world leaders coming to a series of self-serving accommodations (commodity); but Dürrenmatt's thinking about politics, in this play as in earlier ones, is mostly abstract and general rather than concrete and particular.[15]

In this study we shall concentrate primarily on how Dürrenmatt set about recasting the plot of the pre-text, Schlegel's *König Johann*, for it is perhaps in the assurance with which he went to work pruning and shaping Shakespeare's tangled tale, and his skill in grafting his own – often tongue-in-cheek – blank verse on to the Schlegel rootstock, that his ability and authority as a dramatist are most immediately evident. Dürrenmatt took the work of a fledgling playwright and, bringing two decades of experience to bear on the material, lent new focus, tautness and direction to the original. The resulting drama is not so much an adaptation as a re-write, but whether that constitutes a valid *criticism* is a moot point. Neither Dürrenmatt nor Barton had much respect for 'the usual restraint of the sanctity of the text' [SMALLWOOD, p.84], the justification for their wholesale reconstruction of the original being, interestingly, the same in each case: Shakespeare's immaturity at the time of writing it. Thus Dürrenmatt commented:

> Aus einer Bearbeitung wurde eine Umarbeitung. Nun halte ich es für sinnlos, einen *Macbeth* oder einen *Lear* umzuarbeiten, wohl aber einen *König Johann* oder einen *Titus Andronicus*; sie sind mehr Rohstoff für Stücke als Stücke [*WA* 11, p.212].

And Barton:

> I would never tamper with mature Shakespeare, but with this early and imperfect work I hoped that alterations would increase rather than cloud the force of the best Shakespearean sections.[16]

Dürrenmatt retained much of Schlegel's blank verse unaltered, or interwove it with skilfully written passages of his own, so as to give the overall impression of a successfully executed pastiche that is in several ways, but especially in terms of clarity of purpose, an improvement on Schlegel's version.[17] By simplifying and slimming down the plot he focussed the audience's attention more sharply on the issues at stake, as he saw them; and by introducing humour where previously there was none, he both lightened the tone and prepared the ground for his own version of the events of the play as a 'Komödie der Ohnmacht', a genre first developed in *Die Wiedertäufer* and discussed more fully below.

First, however, an examination of Act I in some detail may yield insights into Dürrenmatt's general approach to adapting the classics. Two major weapons in his arsenal are the explanatory gloss, and modernisation and/or simplification of vocabulary and syntax. The tricky dynastic matters broached in the first scene present a considerable challenge to a twentieth-century dramatist, and their exposition calls for the use of both devices, so that Schlegel's

> CHATILLON. Philipp von Frankreich, kraft und laut des Namens
> Von deines weiland Bruder Gottfried Sohn,
> Artur Plantagenet, spricht rechtlich an
> Dies schöne Eiland samt den Ländereien,
> Als Irland, Poitiers, Anjou, Touraine, Maine,
> Begehrend, daß du legst beiseit das Schwert,
> Das dieses Erb anmaßendlich beherrscht,

> Daß Artur es aus deiner Hand empfange,
> Dein Neff und königlicher Oberherr. [*KJS*, p.95]

is given a linguistic short-back-and-sides and sent on its way with four new lines of explanation:

> CHATILLON. Philipp von Frankreich sieht das Recht verletzt.
> Drei Brüder starben dir, vor dir geboren:
> Der erste Heinrich, Gottfried dann und endlich
> Der edle Richard Löwenherz.
> [...]
> Philipp von Frankreich fordert an im Namen
> Arthur Plantagenets, des Sohnes deines
> Ums Reich geprellten ältern Bruders Gottfried,
> Dies schöne Eiland samt den Ländereien
> Von Irland, Poitiers, Anjou, Touraine, Maine. [*KJD*, p.11f.]

The shakiness of the *de facto* monarch's claim to the throne – his 'borrowed majesty' [*TKJ*, p.63], so nicely hinted at by Shakespeare in a whispered aside between John and his mother –

> KING JOHN. Our strong possession and our right for us.
> ELEANOR. Your strong possession much more than your right,
> Or else it must go wrong with you and me. [*TKJ*, p.64]

– once again requires a word of explanation, along with some simplification of the syntax. Schlegel's

> KÖNIG JOHANN. Uns schirmt Besitzes Macht und unser Recht.
> ELEONORE. Besitzes Macht weit mehr als Euer Recht,
> Sonst müßt es übel gehn mit Euch und mir. [*KJS*, p.96]

becomes

> KÖNIG JOHANN. Uns schirmt, was ich besitze und mein Recht.
> ELEONORE. Uns schirmt, was du besitzest, nicht dein Recht,
> Sonst müßt es übel gehn mit dir und mir,
> Denn Recht hat Arthur ebenso wie du. [*KJD*, p.13]

The ingenious scene in which King John is asked to judge between the Bastard Philip Faulconbridge and his younger brother Robert's claim to inherit the old Sir Robert's estate enables Shakespeare to develop the theme of legitimacy and draw the audience's attention to the unspoken affinity between King John and the Bastard. Dürrenmatt retains much of the Schlegel original, but coarsens the tone and heightens the humour by the occasional introduction of incongruous slang or the juxtaposition of an unadulterated line of Schegel's with his own brand of scurrilous blank verse, as when, for example, the rather arid

> ELEONORE. Was willst du lieber sein? ein Faulconbridge,
> Der Lehnbesitzer wie dein Bruder, oder

> Des Löwenherzens anerkannter Sohn,
> Herr deines Adels, und kein Lehn dazu? [*KJS*, p.99]

gives way to the altogether racier

> ELEONORE. Wohlan denn, wähle:
> Was willst du lieber sein, ein Faulconbridge,
> Ein reicher Herrscher über Kraut und Rüben,
> Vermistet, ohne Bildung, ruhmlos, oder
> Von meinem Sohn ein anerkannter Sohn,
> Plantagenet wie wir. [*KJD*, p.19][18]

Lady Faulconbridge, who appears in the final scene of Act I and meekly owns up to her adulterous transgressions and her son's paternity, is conceived as a foil to Queen Eleanor, pointing up the contrast between her own feebleness and the Queen's steely character, but also raising doubts about the integrity of mothers in general. Dürrenmatt leaves Lady Faulconbridge's small part intact, but his Queen's role is subsequently developed well beyond that of the original.

Besides the French challenge to the legality of Johann's claim to the throne, and his mother's dark hints, both of which are present in Shakespeare, Dürrenmatt goes a step farther in his exposition of the King's dilemma: it seems that he is beset on all sides, and like autocratic rulers throughout history, he needs a war to rally the nation behind him:

> Durch meines Bruders Richard genial
> Verschlampte Heldenwirtschaft kam
> Das Land in Unordnung. Der Adel murrt.
> Er liebt nicht meine starke Hand. Er will
> Die Freiheit, England auszuplündern,
> Für sich allein, drum neigt er Arthur zu.
> Die Kirche sucht mich zu erpressen, pocht
> Auf ihre Pfründe, und des Himmels Gnade
> Fließt bloß für bares Geld. Das Volk ist dumpf,
> Gesund ist nur das Heer, und diese Waffe,
> Bevor sie rostet, muß ich brauchen. Krieg
> Den Lords wär Bruderkrieg, er schwächte mich,
> Doch Krieg mit Frankreich eint die Nation
> Und zwingt den Adel sich zu unterwerfen. [*KJD*, p.13f]

This new speech neatly lists the threats surrounding the King, which are in turn the factors that will be instrumental in his downfall: the dire state of the country and the hostility or indifference of nobility, Church and subjects.

Up to the end of Act I, Shakespeare's plot and Dürrenmatt's approaches to it and to the questions it raises, are more or less identical: as well as introducing the central issues of legitimacy and the legality of John's claim to the throne, both playwrights are at pains to establish the impetuous nature of John's character (e.g. declaring war on France without a moment's reflection), and hence the value of a level-headed companion such as the Bastard. In addition, however, Dürrenmatt makes more explicit through the character of the Bastard – but also, by implication, through that of the King – that illegitimacy, or the lack of sound title, is itself no bar to fame and fortune in this corrupt world:

> BASTARD. Nach außen adlig, ganz ein echter Ritter,
> Weiß doch mein Sinn, daß alles Hurerei,
> Was diese noble Welt in Ehren treibt.
> Verstellend mich, um mich nicht zu belügen,
> Bleib ich, die Welt belügend, mir so treu,
> Erklettere mit kühnen Heldentaten
> Der Ehre Hühnerleiter voller Dreck. [*KJD,* p.21]

The first rung on that ladder is a dalliance with the King's niece, Blanka von Kastilien, whom Dürrenmatt endows with a sensuality nowhere in evidence in the Shakespearean original:[19]

> BLANKA. Verzeiht, Sir Richard. Ich gestand, daß Ihr
> Mir sehr gefällt. Warum nicht, ich bin reich. [...] *Blanka ab.*
> BASTARD. Die Lady amüsiert sich gut mit mir.
> Sie denkt ans Bett. Ich denke, was mir blüht. [*KJD,* p.20]

In Act II, Dürrenmatt wittily conveys 'his' Blanka's interest in sex to the well-read spectator by the merest alteration of the Schlegel original. Thus

> BASTARD: Wenn muntre Liebe nach der Schönheit geht,
> Wo fände sie sie holder als in Blanka?
> Wenn fromme Liebe nach der Tugend strebt,
> Wo fände sie sie reiner als in Blanka? [*KJS*, p.116]

becomes:

> BASTARD: Wenn heiße Liebe nach der Schönheit geht,
> Wo fände sie sie heißer als in Blanka?
> Wenn keusche Liebe nach der Tugend strebt,
> Wo fände sie sie keuscher als in Blanka? [p.42]

– with the added joke that these tongue-in-cheek lines are delivered by the very man who has been bedding her, the Bastard!

Having, with the exceptions mentioned, followed the pre-text more or less faithfully thus far, Dürrenmatt begins to reshape the original from Act II onwards in pursuit of his general aims: to unravel some of the baroque complexity of the plot; to create an atmosphere in which callousness, brutality, duplicity and self-seeking are accepted unquestioningly as the norm; to introduce the audience to the concept of *Macht/Ohnmacht* and establish, as major themes, the unbridled abuse of power and the notion that commerce makes the world go round. But his particular, overriding objective, from this point forward, is to present the Bastard as ambitious, to be sure, but first and foremost as a pragmatist and an isolated advocate of rational behaviour, struggling against all odds to beat a reasonable path through an increasingly impenetrable jungle of unreason:

> Was den Ratgeber König Johanns betrifft, den Bastard Philipp Faulconbridge, so ist er bei Shakespeare und mir ein Außenseiter. [...] Mein Bastard ist weder Ideologe noch Moralist, für ihn sind die Könige die Machthaber und die Völker die Opfer dieser Machthaber. Was er von den Königen verlangt, ist allein, daß sie vernünftig regieren, er versucht Johann vernünftig zu machen. [*KJD*, 11, p.203][20]

One casualty of the Bastard's character shift, as we have seen, is the Commodity speech which concludes Act II:

> That smooth-faced gentleman, tickling Commodity,
> Commodity, the bias of the world. [*TKJ*, p.98]

Dürrenmatt discards this monologue, presumably because it presents the Bastard as being just as grasping and venal as the nobles around him –

> And why rail I on this Commodity?
> But for because he hath not wooed me yet.
> [...]
> Well, whiles I am a beggar I will rail,
> And say there is no sin but to be rich;
> And being rich, my virtue then shall be
> To say there is no vice but beggary. [*TKJ*, p.99]

– and therefore too uncompromisingly self-seeking for the new-drawn character. It is nevertheless curious, given that this is the most famous speech in the play, that Dürrenmatt dispenses with it entirely, rather than finding some other way of retaining it, such as by giving it to some other character. Instead he simply transfers the Bastard's self-interest and cynicism to the monarchs and the townspeople of Angers, and subsumes the notion of 'commodity' under the wider umbrella of 'Geschäft' [WHITTON, p.136].

Generally speaking, Dürrenmatt's alterations to the plot and his adjustments of the given characters are interdependent, as one might expect. Thus, for example, the main plot change in Act II concerns the proposal of a wedding between Louis, the Dauphin and King John's niece Blanche/Blanka. In *King John*, the idea comes [*TKJ*, p.92] from the Citizen of Angers as a last-ditch attempt to stave off the attack on his town by the combined English and French armies which the Bastard has proposed as punishment for their refusal to settle the dispute between the two countries by declaring one or other of the rival claimants – King John or Prince Arthur – as their rightful sovereign. Dürrenmatt turns the Citizen's diplomatic reluctance to take sides (which in *King John* very nearly backfires on him) into a first essay in diplomacy for the Bastard, but one which is also underpinned or indeed dictated by his new character, for Dürrenmatt's Bastard could not 'reasonably' suggest anything as wasteful and pointless as razing a city to the ground. Instead – and here, as we shall discover, we are already witnessing the Bastard sowing the first seeds of disaster for his king, or, in Dürrenmatt's terms, the playwright making the first move in his endgame – the Bastard goes one step farther and (to Blanka's lasting fury) convinces the two kings of the advantages to both parties of a double wedding: if Louis marries Blanka, he will gain Poitiers, Anjou, Touraine and Maine, whilst by marrying Philipp's niece Isabelle von Angoulême (an invention of Dürrenmatt's) who is presently betrothed to the Dauphin, Johann will be seen to win Philipp's blessing and, with it, something much more important to him than land – the French King's endorsement of his right to the English throne:

> Ich brauche
> Legalität und nicht Besitz in Frankreich. [*KJD,* p.46].

And so, in Dürrenmatt's version, it falls to King Philipp to order, quite unreasonably, the destruction of his newly acquired city:

> Doch weil ihr keine der Parteien wähltet
> Und weder warm noch kalt wart, laue Hunde,
> Seid jetzt bestraft. (*ibid.*)

It is a significant feature of Dürrenmatt's approach that here he makes explicit what is left unsaid by Shakespeare:

> KÖNIG PHILIPP. Der Handel klappt. Ich gebe Isabelle
> Zur Mitgift Irland, es sei damit dein.
> Ich anerkenne dich zum König Englands. [*KJD,* p.46]

In a programme note written for the première of *Die Wiedertäufer*, Hugo Loetscher identifies another important aspect of Dürrenmatt's methodology:

> Die Parallel-Lektüre von *Es steht geschrieben* und *Die Wiedertäufer* ist zunächst eine vorzügliche Schule für Dramaturgen. Dafür, wie man aus einem Text, der fürs Theater geschrieben ist, Theater macht. Dadurch nämlich, daß Dürrenmatt in seinem zweiten Stück [i.e. *Die Wiedertäufer*] alles in konkrete Situationen bringt; also nicht mehr von der Bühne herab fürs Publikum schreibt, sondern für die Bühne. Das heißt im einzelnen, daß der Autor nicht mehr mitteilt, was geschieht, sondern das Geschehnis in Szene setzt. [*play Dürrenmatt*, p.196]

The new shaving scene which concludes Act II is a good example of this visual approach. The idea is obviously borrowed from Büchner's *Woyzeck*, itself the driving force behind *Achterloo* (1983-88), and it occurs again and again in successive versions.[21] The function of this scene, the prototype, is not only to demonstrate the Bastard's continued subservience to the King, as Dürrenmatt suggests (and as reflects the situation in *Woyzeck*),[22] but also to bring home to the audience the *intimacy* of their relationship. The Bastard's attempt to persuade Johann to talk Philipp out of razing Angers to the ground fails, not because the King wishes to show who is in charge, but because the Bastard's own logic runs counter to his plea for sanity:

Mein König, Tollheit ist's, Angers zu strafen!
Wofür? Weil es in Eure Händel sich
Nicht mischen wollte, wird es ausgelöscht!
Wozu der Unfug? *König Philipp straft*
Sich selber. Diese Stadt ist sein, die Steuern
Gehören ihm. [*KJD,* 48, my italics]

That there is more intimacy than subservience between the two men becomes clear from the discussion which ends the scene, during which the King symbolically releases the Bastard from his subordinate role by taking over his own shaving. Their dialogue concerns Blanka, whom the Bastard has manoeuvred into marrying the Dauphin with such unseemly haste. But the Bastard reveals to Johann that, far from being rash and ill-conceived, his decision to discard Blanka instead of marrying her himself was a move carefully calculated to save him from being cuckolded, in due course, by the King, for he has discerned that 'die schöne Nichte, Lady Blanka // Ist mehr für Euch als eine Nichte' [*KJD*, 11, p.49].

Johann, for his part, has made a shrewd assessment of the complementary, indeed symbiotic, nature of their relationship. The Bastard needs the King, for, as Johann reminds him,

Ein Bastard findet diese Welt im argen.
Der Makel seiner Abkunft macht ihn so.
Er will die Welt verbessern. Doch das Werkzeug
Zum beßren Bau kann nur ein König sein
Wie ich. Drum bin ich Euer Werkzeug nun jetzt,
Ihr habt kein andres. [p.50].

But Johann is prepared to relinquish some of his advantage, for he, having no one else he can trust, also needs the Bastard. It is a partnership, or a bonding, of a kind seen many times before in Dürrenmatt's dramas, starting with the Bockelson-Knipperdollinck pairing in *Es steht geschrieben*, where the charlatan prophet Bockelson attains immense wealth and power at the expense of the richest man in Münster, who is convinced that he will find grace by parting with all that he owns. In *Die Ehe des Herrn Mississippi* (1952), the public prosecutor Florestan Mississippi and the communist reformer, Frédéric René Saint-Claude, are two sides of the same coin: both began in the gutter, one found a copy of the Bible, the other *Das Kapital*, and now each of them wants to change the world according to his particular lights. A more whimsical example of the same phenomenon occurs in *Ein Engel kommt nach Babylon* (1953) in the form of the two kings of Babylon, Nebuchadnezzar and Nimrod, who alternate as monarchs for periods of nine hundred years at a time, the other acting meanwhile as the reigning monarch's footstool. There is again much doubling of a rather superficial kind in *Der Besuch der alten Dame* (1956), with Toby and Roby, Koby, Loby and Moby, and psychological doubling on a grand scale in *Die Physiker* (1962) when the physicists Beutler and Ernesti don the *personae* of Newton and Einstein and, ultimately, the mantle of insanity. In *Der Meteor* (1966), Dürrenmatt stands the idea of symbiosis on its head, by making all the secondary characters meet their end, one by one in the course of the play, as a result of their encounters with the principal character, Wolfgang Schwitter, ironically the one character who desperately wants to die and cannot. Still to come, following *König Johann*, was a portrayal of the love-hate symbiosis of marriage in the relationship between Alice and Edgar in *Play Strindberg* (1969); and finally, far removed from the Johann-Bastard partnership, we have that apotheosis of pairing, doubling and trebling *Achterloo*, in which each and every character has a *Spielrolle*, a *Wahnrolle* and a *Person*, e.g. one character is at various times Napoleon Bonaparte, Holofernes and a Professor: 'So we now have characters like those Russian *babushka* dolls, a succession of smaller characters within a larger' [WHITTON, p.155].

Dürrenmatt's version of Act III shows a number of significant changes affecting not only characters and relationships, but also plot and mode of presentation. By curtailing or excising some of the longer passages – notably Blanche's eloquent plea for peace between England and France:

> Which is the side that I must go withal?
> I am with both, each army hath a hand,
> And in their rage, I having hold of both,
> They whirl asunder and dismember me. [*TKJ*, p.113]

–, and by condensing the more protracted parts of the action, he makes room for two entirely new scenes.

The first of these, Scene 3, though strikingly original in conception, displays numerous familiar Dürrenmattian features. The action resumes after the interval in a chapel in Le Mans, with King Philipp, the Dauphin and Konstanze kneeling in an attitude of prayer, and Cardinal Pandulpho seated in a sedan-chair which serves as a confessional. This device recalls *Der Besuch der alten Dame* [*WA* 5], in which Claire Zachanassian has herself carried everywhere in a sedan-chair by her two ex-Sing-Sing bodyguards, and Emperor Charles V in *Die Wiedertäufer*, who likewise favours a sedan-chair; but also, by contrast, the hapless Bishop of Münster in the same play, who is anachronistically confined to a wheelchair. Just as the wheelchair obviously signifies impotence, so, conversely, a sedan-chair is emblematic of servants, power and majesty.

As first the King, then Konstanze, and finally the Dauphin kneel before the Cardinal to make their 'confession', the glaring discrepancy between the religious setting, the characters' devout poses and their ostensible preoccupations, on the one hand, and their profane, cynical, scheming dialogue on the other, becomes increasingly apparent. Kings and prelates, it seems, are above such petty concerns as human suffering and death, and the overacted exchange between Philipp and Pandulpho attests to their shared indifference towards their subjects and their flock:

PANDULPHO. Wieviel Mann verloren wir?
KÖNIG PHILIPP. Wieviel Mann verloren wir?
LOUIS. An fünfzehntausend.
KÖNIG PHILIPP. Entsetzlich. Fürchterlich. Ein schlimmes Blutbad.
PANDULPHO. Die Seelen sind bei Gott. (p.68)

But Philipp reserves his chief contempt for his English counterpart's unregal conduct on the battle-field. The crowned heads of Europe belong to one big family ('Wir sind dieselbe Rasse, wenn auch Feinde' [p.27]), and certain courtesies must be observed. In III, 1, Philipp was horror-struck by Johann's naive suggestion that they would meet again on the battle-field like common soldiers:

KÖNIG JOHANN. Frankreich, wir werfen Unsere eigene
Person in diese Schlacht. Wir hoffen dich
Zu treffen, wo man Männer trifft, im Kampf.
KÖNIG PHILIPP. Im Kampf? Du bist beleidigt? Nimmst persönlich,
Was unumgänglich durch die Politik?
Das kann dein Ernst nicht sein, mein lieber Freund,
Im Kampfe wäre scheußlich. Doch von einem
Zum andern Feldherrnhügel grüßend, wollen
Wir sehen, welchen von uns zwein bevorzugt
Die Hure Glück.[23] [p.62]

Now, in the aftermath of battle, he is unable to contain his disgust at Johann's unprincely behaviour, taking quarrels too personally and getting his hands dirty:

Bin schwer enttäuscht. Da hat man Differenzen
Mit einem Freund, hochadlig wie wir selber,
Führt etwas Krieg, was tut er? Tötet, mordet,
Stößt Menschen nieder! Eigenhändig, als
Wär er ein Henker, Feldherr oder Söldner;
Und hat die Frechheit noch, mich zu besiegen,
Als ob ich ihn nicht fair behandeln würde,
Fiel er in meine Hand. Bin degoutiert.
Bei Gott! Am nächsten Fürstentage rede
Ich mit dem Kerl kein Wort mehr, keine Silbe. [p.68f]

The running gag, pointing up the cynicism of rulers the world over, echoes the words and manners of 'Die Fürsten' in *Die Wiedertäufer*, who sneeringly dismiss the Bishop's heartfelt pleas on behalf of their suffering subjects as 'peinlich' and 'ordinär', who find nothing to fire their enthusiasm except their hobby, the private theatrical troupes they each maintain, and who are only stirred to action against the Anabaptists at last by the threat posed by 'Gütergemeinschaft'.

Cardinal Pandulpho, with his ineffectual platitudes – the only counsel he can offer Konstanze, distraught at the news that her son has been taken prisoner by the English, is exhortations to accept God's will and pray –, is the latest in a line of feeble clergymen, *qua* clergymen: it is probably the lame pastoral efforts of the

Pfarrer in *Der Besuch der alten Dame* which spring most readily to mind, but we also recall the weak-willed Pfarrer Lutz in *Der Meteor*, who ironically dies of ecstasy when confronted with a genuine miracle, and the minister in *Mondfinsternis*, who doggedly goes on preaching his sermon to the pews in an empty church, in honour of a God in whom he too has lost all faith.[24] But Pandulpho, unlike these other characters and his fellow-prelate, the Bishop of Münster, is first and foremost a scheming politician who bends, sways, applies pressure and yields as the occasion demands. He is, in fact, the Bastard's secret adversary, and being cleverer and longer in the tooth, he outwits him in the end.

In *King John*, as in *König Johann*, Prince Arthur falls into enemy hands, but whereas Shakespeare's Queen Eleanor is feared captured for only a fleeting moment [*TKJ*, p.114], Dürrenmatt has the Queen not only taken prisoner by Philipp's men, but executed on his orders. Shakespeare, who clearly has no further use for them, lets both Queen Eleanor and Constance fade quietly out of the picture: in IV 2, a messenger reports to King John that

> the first of April died
> Your noble mother; and, as I hear, my lord,
> The Lady Constance in a frenzy died
> Three days before. [*TKJ*, p.120]

In III 4, the powerful new scene which concludes this Act, Dürrenmatt contrives a showdown between Eleonore and Konstanze, two women who, though on opposing sides, have lived by the same rules and must now face the consequences. Their grim encounter in Eleonore's cell, which ends with the Queen exiting with the executioner and Konstanze dying by her own hand, serves to show what fate holds in store for women who presume to play the male game of political intrigue in this men's world. The ironical outcomes of their scheming on their sons' behalf are that Arthur is rendered so dangerous to Johann that he cannot be allowed to live, and Philipp is provoked to execute Eleonore as part of an elaborate double-double-cross instigated by her own son. With very few exceptions –, such as Ottilie Frank in *Frank der Fünfte* [*WA* 6], Dr Mathilde von Zahnd in *Die Physiker* [*WA* 7] and, in one sense only, Claire Zachanassian –, Dürrenmatt's women are either losers, pawns or victims of male cruelty. One thinks, for example, of Anastasia in *Die Ehe des Herrn Mississippi* [*WA* 3], Queen Julia in *Romulus der Große* [*WA* 2] and Ann in *Der Mitmacher* [*WA* 14], as well as the nameless women in early stories like *Der Sohn* and *Die Falle* [*WA* 18]. In *König Johann*, too, although Dürrenmatt 'modernises' the female characters (for example by portraying Blanka as sexually emancipated), their lot is unremittingly grim – as Blanka discovers when, despite her protest that she loves the Bastard and is 'keine Ware, // Die man verhandelt' [p.44], she still ends up being thrown to the Dauphin

wie ein
Stück Fleisch dem ersten besten Köter, der
Aus Zufall über Euren Weg lief. [p.60]

Eleonore's final words, spoken just as Konstanze stabs herself, must surely rank amongst the bleakest lines from the pen of an author often accused of pessimism:

ELEONORE. Wir liebten
Gewalt und Männer, schworen, brachen Treue.
Betrügend wurden wir betrogen. [...]
Mein Ende ist das deine. [...]
Ich sterbe gern, doch du mußt weiterleben
In dieser leeren Welt, ein Leib,
Der nur gebar, um Schlächtern Fleisch zu liefern,
Ein Opfer deiner Tat wie ich der meinen. [p.74f]

As *König Johann* progresses through the last two acts, the plot undergoes increasingly radical alterations at the hands of Dürrenmatt. His Act IV is reduced from three scenes to two, and although they depict the same basic events as in *King John* (the threat to and the sparing of Arthur's life, the King's second coronation and Arthur's fatal accident), the focus and tone are fundamentally shifted – notably by dispensing with the character of Hubert, who is merged into that of the Bastard, but also by drastic shortening, from over 560 lines in the original to ca. 250; and most strikingly, by injecting a series of slapstick elements into the second (coronation) scene.

In ordering Queen Eleonore's death, Philipp hopes that Johann will be prompted to kill Prince Arthur in revenge, thus giving the Dauphin a legitimate claim to the English throne through Blanka, whose late mother was Johann's sister. And indeed Prince Arthur's life is no less threatened by Dürrenmatt's King than by Shakespeare's, so that in the first scene of Act IV he is only saved from execution by an act of *lèse-majesté* on the part of the Bastard, who holds Johann at the point of a sword for long enough to persuade him of the strategic advantages in sparing the boy's life:

Ein jeder sinnt auf Euren Untergang.
[...] Die Liebe
Und Hoffnung aller: Arthur. Arthur habt Ihr.
Er ist ein Pfand in Eurer Hand. Er schützt
Euch vor dem Aufstand aller. [...]
Ihr seid verloren, wenn Ihr Arthur tötet. [p.80]

Johann decides to let Arthur live but – like Shakespeare's Hubert – to give out the tale that the young Prince has been murdered. Johann's perverse plan is to have himself crowned for a second time by his peers, and with his position thus assured, magnanimously to produce his 'lieben, treuumhegten' [p.81] – and politically neutered – nephew for all to see. Unfortunately his plan will backfire, in this version as it did in the original, when the boy falls whilst trying to escape.

The idea of a coronation scene (IV 2) is loosely based on fact:

> Historically this was King John's fourth coronation, [...] shortly *after* Arthur's death [my italics]. Among the Angevin kings this oft-repeated ceremony allowed the king and nobles to reaffirm their oaths of trust and service, patching up differences after a crisis. In [Shakespeare's] play John asks for loyal support in anticipation of a crisis, and the nobles become suspicious, treating it as an occasion for complaint [BEAURLINE, p.177].

In Dürrenmatt's version, as we remarked, Johann's ulterior motive for wanting a second coronation is to consolidate his position *vis-à-vis* the nobility, although his stated reason is to demonstrate to the Pope that he no longer owes him any allegiance:

> Die Krönung war zum zweitenmal notwendig,
> Weil bei der ersten Uns ein Priester krönte.
> Jetzt setzen wir Uns selbst zum König ein,
> Nur Gott gehorsam und nicht einem Papst. [p.83]

Shakespeare's peers consider this coronation 'superfluous'; Dürrenmatt's think the whole idea is simply stupid: 'eine Schnappsidee' [p.82], 'eine Posse' [p.84]. But as Johann anticipated, the peers suspect him of killing Arthur, and presently we learn that the French have invaded England to claim the throne and to avenge Arthur's murder. Johann, playing his trump card, calls on the Bastard to prove that Arthur is alive, but instead he comes in bearing the boy's corpse: 'Ein Unglücksfall' [p.88]. Needless to say, no one believes Johann's protestations of innocence, and in a vivid demonstration of just how precarious Johann's rule is, the lords depart *en masse* for Kent, there to defect to the French.

The essential gravity of the events portrayed in this scene is, however, undercut by a display of characteristically Dürrenmattian black humour. Perhaps taking up a hint of inclement weather in *TKJ*, or perhaps (as in the later scene in Swinstead Abbey, V, 1) just playing on the English reputation for an inhospitable climate and uncivilised living,[25] Dürrenmatt reduces the first part of the scene to farce by making Johann's coronation take place in a storm of thunder, lightning and hailstones which leaves the peers soaked to the skin and frozen to the marrow. Needless to say, the King has spent the two-hour ceremony under the shelter of a canopy, unlike Bigot, who has had to kneel in a puddle for the entire time. The lords are reduced by the elements to a teeth-chattering level of banal humanity, their fine new armour is starting to rust and chafe, and they have to send for a *Schlosser* to release them. The bathos of this scene is reminiscent of that produced by a similar device in *Es steht geschrieben* when the commanders of the two opposing mercenary armies, Ritter von Büren and Ritter von Mengerssen, confront one another. They are both clad in all their martial finery, including full suits of armour, but whenever either of them speaks he has to lift up his visor, which promptly falls down again when he has finished. There, as in this coronation scene, the humour derives from the discrepancy between these self-important characters and the way in which their ceremonial, warlike armour, which is any case so ungainly as to be funny, seems to rule them.

But the audience's laughter at the lords' predicament is silenced only moments later by the sobering entrance of the Bastard bearing Arthur's shattered body. Such shock tactics are not uncommon in Dürrenmatt, but perhaps used to best effect in the famous mock trial during the banquet scene in *Der Besuch der alten Dame*, when Claire Zachanassian brings the Gülleners' self-congratulary speeches to a sickening halt with her revelations about her past and her demand for Ill's life.

The news of Arthur's death shatters Dürrenmatt's Johann (IV, 2) almost as much as it does Shakespeare's John (V,1). Both Kings turn instinctively to the Bastard for counsel, but whereas this, the moment when John relinquishes control – 'Have thou the ordering of the present time' [*TKJ*, p.151] –, marks the beginning of the end for him, his counterpart Johann's despair, denoted by his repeated entreaty, 'Was soll ich tun?' [p.89f], occurs earlier in the play and constitutes only a brief setback for a character endowed with far greater reserves of resilience and a strong sense of self-preservation – in Dürrenmatt's terms, a decidedly more political animal –, so that just moments later we see him shrewdly weighing up the merits of the Bastard's strategy: Johann must enlist the dual support of the Church and his subjects in order to bring the rebel peers to heel. The two-point plan requires Johann to submit to the authority of Rome, which will so impress the Pope that he will promptly re-instate him as King; and to grant new rights to the people in the form of the Magna Carta.

Johann's profound contempt for his subjects rapidly turns to cynical posturing in response to the Bastard's curt interjection:

> KÖNIG JOHANN. Das Volk!
> Es lebt dahin in Stumpfsinn, ungebildet,
> Legt sich ins selbe Stroh zum Zeugen und
> Zum Sterben, vegetiert nur, ist Gesindel.
> BASTARD. Gesindel? Sir, es stellt die Mehrheit dar.
> *Schweigen.*
> KÖNIG JOHANN. Mein Volk! Auf einmal wird mir warm ums Herz,
> Denk ich an meine Bauern, meine Bürger,
> Das gute Volk! Geduldig, froh, genügsam. [p.91]

Johann's words parody those of the fastidious Kaiser Karl V. in *Die Wiedertäufer*, whose ideal vision is of an empire

> Sauber aufgeräumt von meinen Landsknechten und reingefegt von jeder Ketzerei durch die heilige Inquisition

> Ohne Menschen meinetwegen,
> [...]
> Auf die Untertanen kann ich verzichten, Untertanen stören nur die erhabenen Spiele der Macht. [*WA* 10, p.72]

Thus at the close of Act IV Johann, much as he detests himself for it, finds himself following the Bastard's 'reasonable' advice. But there is more than a touch of dramatic irony in his observation that reason will yet be his undoing, for by concentrating on the immediate threat posed by Arthur's death, both the King and the Bastard fail to anticipate the crucial element in their author's game plan, the political consequences of Johann producing a son and heir.[26]

The brief final Act of *König Johann*, with its jarring combination of knockabout humour and high seriousness, bears the sure stamp of Dürrenmatt. In a radical shortening and reconstruction of the original, Shakespeare's seven scenes are reduced to a mere three, two of which nicely reflect the mounting chaos in the land by being cast as farce.

Scenes 1 and 2 are entirely of Dürrenmatt's invention, whilst the closing scene bears at best a passing resemblance to the original. In the first, Cardinal Pandulpho has taken refuge in Swinstead Abbey, which is the worse for the Bastard's looting. Extending the running gag introduced in the coronation scene, the Italian prelate makes numerous jibes about the heathen English and their weather, which in turn gives rise to another running gag which has the monks continually trotting in and out with a supply of hot-water bottles to help Pandulpho combat the freezing cold and constant rain and mist. When Johann first appears, complete with the Bastard, Pandulpho thinks, not unreasonably, that they have come to kill him, and in a move borrowed directly from *Romulus der Große* (1949), his terrified secretary takes refuge under the bed.[27] But Johann, following the Bastard's advice, is clad in a hairshirt. Dürrenmatt makes the two men engage in some entertainingly ambiguous kneeling and grappling before the prelate realises that Johann has come to do penance. Pandulpho then accepts the proffered crown with alacrity, forgives Johann his sins and and restores to him, in Schlegel's very words,

> Aus dieser meiner Hand als Lehn des Papstes
> Die königliche Hoheit und Gewalt. [p.99]

Whereupon – neatly capping the gag about hot-water bottles and at the same time graphically underlining the calculated mutual self-interest behind the surrender of the crown and its return – the King and the Cardinal climb into bed together. In a dramatic turnaround, Pandulpho will now threaten the French with excommunication if they do not call off their invasion of England; and Johann will proclaim his new law protecting the rights of his subjects.

But once Johann has confided in Pandulpho that he has a son and heir, it becomes clear to the audience that the Cardinal is not to be trusted. No sooner has he packed the King and the Bastard off with assurances that this will allow hostilities to cease than he dictates a secret letter to the traitor Pembroke, urging him to poison Johann. In an ingenious, ironic twist to this tale of challenged majesty and flawed legitimacy, the birth of a son and heir to Johann is precisely the opening which will bring about checkmate, for with Johann dead, England will once more have the infant monarch the French desired in Arthur. Henceforth France and the Church will rule England jointly through Queen Isabelle as Regent and, *de facto*, through her adviser Pembroke, working hand-in-glove with Pandulpho. The stage directions and Pandulpho's words in V, 3 make the new arrangements abundantly clear:

> *Die Herzogin erscheint verschleiert mit dem Säugling Heinrich dem Dritten. Setzt sich auf den Thron, zur Linken der Kardinal, zur Rechten Pembroke. Pandulpho salbt das Kind.*
> PANDULPHO. Sei König über England, Heinrich. Graf
> Pembroke wird dich erziehen, wir, die Kirche,
> Dir beistehn. [p.112]

Dürrenmatt uses Scene 2 partly to prepare the ground for this *dénouement*, but also, as in the preceding scene, to add to the confusion of the audience, who must by this stage in the proceedings be expecting tragic *gravitas* rather than a vision of King Philipp and the Dauphin each in a separate bathtub and Blanka reclining in the background in a state of undress, luxuriantly anointing her body. And indeed, the introduction of scurrilous slapstick elements at this point creates an experience that is at once both farcically entertaining and grotesquely disconcerting.

Whilst a page scrubs Philipp's back and lathers his hair, Pandulpho and Pembroke report that Johann is near death but now has an heir – the significance of which is not lost on the French king:

> KÖNIG PHILIPP. Genial!
> Das ist die Lösung des Konflikts. Ein Kind
> Ersetzt das andre Kind. Wir dürfen
> Gott danken, daß die Angoulême gebar. [p.106]

Thus hostilities between France and England can cease forthwith.

But the highlight of Scene 2, and for that matter one of the most dramatic moments of the play, is the brief but decisive confrontation between Blanka and the Bastard. Because Philipp can now control England more directly through Isabelle, he no longer needs to pursue his claim to the throne through his daughter-in-law. Yet again, Blanka has been used and cheated, and she takes her bitter revenge on the Bastard:

> Es sei. Der Friede ist geschlossen. Doch
> War England mein, durch mich kam Frankreichs Anspruch
> Auf Land und Krone der Plantagenet.
> Verzichtend will ich dennoch nicht verzichten
> Auf meine Rache für die Schande, die
> Ein Mann mir brachte. Er sei mein: der Bastard.
> PANDULPHO. Er sei der Eure, Fürstin.
> BLANKA. Nehmt ihn fest.
> *Soldaten verhaften den Bastard.*
> [...]
> Führt ihn hinaus. Peitscht ihn wie einen Hund.
> Dann laßt ihn fahren. [p.108f]

The echoes of Claire Zachanassian in *Der Besuch der alten Dame* are unmistakeable, for

> Heav'n has no rage, like love to hatred turn'd,
> Nor Hell a fury, like a woman scorn'd

– or rather, betrayed – by the love of her life. Alfred Ill pays the ultimate price for adandoning the sweetheart of his youth, and thereby attains something approaching tragic stature. Blanka's libertine life-style, like Claire's, is an expression of her utter contempt for the male sex, but the Bastard, unlike Ill, is cut out to be a survivor, and sparing his life is both a more subtle and a more appropriate response to the realities of this tawdry world of commodity they both inhabit. In this scene she literally has the last word, albeit that hers is a Pyrrhic victory.

The final scene of the play begins with a glaring contradiction between the ghastly appearance of the dying King Johann, '*im Nachthemd und blutbesudelt* [...] nach frischem Blutsturz' (109) and his optimistic words. It ends with Pembroke ordering the unceremonious disposal of his body:

> Ihr Lords, verscharrt den König irgendwo
> Wie irgendeinen. Auf zum Staatsgeschäft.[28] [p.113]

Central to the scene, however, is not Johann's death, but his final speech, the moment of anagnorisis in which he confronts his own death and what has brought it about: the Bastard's all-too-reasonable advice. Far from being tragic, his death, as he realises, is absurd and ridiculous, for he has been ousted by a babe-in-arms,

> Gefällt
> Durch Pipi und Gekacke meines Sohns. [p.111]

Johann's thoroughly untragic discourse is entirely appropriate to his lot. His fate is a variation on that which might have befallen Scott of the Antarctic, as described in the *Dramaturgische Überlegungen zu den 'Wiedertäufern'*, written in 1967 and still fresh in Dürrenmatt's mind. Shakespeare, Dürrenmatt writes, would have made Scott's death a tragedy of character, Brecht would have adduced factors of class and economics to account for his end, whilst Beckett would have reduced his story to an absurd endgame in which Scott and his companions are frozen into uncommunicating blocks of ice. But supposing Scott accidentally gets shut in a cold-store in the middle of town whilst purchasing provisions for his expedition? This Robert Falcon Scott, the victim of 'ein läppisches Mißgeschick', at first lighting a cigarette to kill the time until he is released, then calling out, hammering on the door, etc., and finally expiring in disbelief and frustration a few feet away from freedom; *this* Robert Falcon Scott cannot be construed as a tragic figure, for

> aus einer tragischen Gestalt ist eine komische Gestalt geworden, komisch nicht wie einer, der stottert, oder wie einer, der vom Geiz oder von der Eifersucht überwältigt worden ist, eine Gestalt, komisch allein durch ihr Geschick. Die schlimmstmögliche Wendung, die eine Geschichte nehmen kann, ist die Wendung in die Komödie.[29] [*WA* 10, p.127f]

And similarly, what audience could possibly perceive as tragic a death that is motivated by such a natural occurrence as siring a son, and accompanied by references to such banalities as the contents of a baby's nappies?

When Johann dies, the Bastard declines Pembroke's offer of a role within the new regime. For the best of motives he has tried and failed to make reason prevail in a world of unreason, and now he will retire. To be sure, he has done enough damage in the process, not least because he has repeatedly failed to realise that he is not the only clever and scheming character in the play. Little wonder that the dying Johann curses him: 'Die Welt verbessernd, machtest du sie nur verdammter' [p.112]. He leaves behind him a land that will be little better off under Johann's successors, apart from the token concessions of the Magna Carta. Pembroke's intention is

> Dies Land durch unsre Zeit hindurch zu karren,
> Im alten Gleise, ungestört von Narren. [p.113]

These are the dismal words of the *Realpolitiker*, which neither Johann nor the Bastard ever was, and they bode ill for the people of England. The Bastard's closing speech, announcing his defeat at the hands of unreason and his retreat from the diplomatic stage into a simple, self-imposed exile in the country, there to bed as many rustic wenches as possible and beget a tribe of bastards like himself, smacks of defeatism, although admittedly he has no real alternative. During his brief sojourn in high places he has striven for the greater good according to his own lights,

> Doch Dummheit zog den Wagen des Geschicks,
> Und Zufall. Was ich hoffte, das blieb aus,
> Nach soviel Feilschen, Morden und Verrat
> Kam statt Vernunft ein Pembroke bloß heraus. [p.113]

But what else could he expect, for this, after all, is a Dürrenmatt 'Komödie', not a classical tragedy? And so the Bastard, like Augias, or Candide, either of whom could have served as his prototype, bows out. In *Herkules und der Stall des Augias,*[30] a satire on Swiss parochialism, a unique opportunity is missed when Herkules is prevented from performing his Fifth Labour, the Cleansing of the Augean Stables, by inertia, small-mindedness and fear of change. Augias, the advocate of progress and reason, finally gives up the unequal struggle and, following Candide's example, retires to cultivate his garden, 'weil die Vernunft große Zeiträume braucht, sich durchzusetzen, und weil Ausmisten nicht die Sache eines Geschlechtes, sondern die vieler Geschlechter ist' [p.113]. The Bastard, it seems, comes to a similar conclusion.

In Dürrenmatt's play, the ruling classes are all alike, grasping, calculating and self-seeking. They are also all supremely *unlike* their subjects, and aloof from them. The former point is neatly made by the emphasis placed on the many and complex ties – blood-ties, marriage-ties – that bind them to one another in space and time, crossing the English Channel and the battle-field, but also transcending the short-lived quarrel or the expedient stratagem and placing them, in a sense, above politics. There is a continuity of kingship that consists quite simply in the long-term preservation of the *status quo*. The gulf between the monarchs and their subjects is manifest on numerous occasions, but perhaps most notably in the callousness with which they raze Angers to the ground, and presently enjoy a wedding feast against the gruesome backdrop of the ruined city:

> PEMBROKE. Der Ratshaustisch, gedeckt zum Fest. Er macht
> Sich gut vor der zerstörten Kathedrale.
> Bloß stört der Brandgeruch, und Leichen liegen
> Auch noch herum, schleppt sie davon, marsch, marsch!
> *Soldaten schleppen Leichen über die Bühne.* [p.52]

As observed earlier, the Basel programme note, with its photographs of world leaders at decisive moments in history, invites comparisons, though only generalised ones, between the dictators and politicians of our time and the monarchs of the play. The abuse of power by those in powerful positions had been a central theme of *Die Wiedertäufer*, and was in any case a topic of major concern in 1968. Topical, too, was the idea most trenchantly formulated by Brecht in *Mutter Courage*, that

> Der Krieg ist nix als die Geschäfte
> Und statt mit Käse ists mit Blei.[31]

The mighty are interested in their nations primarily as businesses: Charles V talks of his ancestors establishing 'ein Weltgeschäft' [*WA* 10, p.71], whilst King Philipp reminds Johann quite explicitly that 'uns, die wir einander hart bedrängen, // Trennt nur Geschäft, nicht Haß' [p.27].

Despite remarking to Whitton that 'Das Eigenartige bei Shakespeare ist das Fehlen des Volks' [WHITTON, p.135], Dürrenmatt likewise keeps the monarchs' subjects largely off-stage, although they are, as we have seen, referred to from time to time, mostly in disparaging terms. In the original script of *König Johann*, when the Bastard is about to retire from politics he declares that his hopes for the future of his country lie with the common people:

> Zeug ich Bastarde, wie ich selber einer,
> Und senke in das Volk die Kraft des Löwen!
> Nur so ist diesem England noch zu helfen. [pp.113, 223]

When the *Werkausgabe* was published in 1980, the last two of these lines were removed and replaced by:

> Ihr habt gesiegt, ihr Lords, zerfleischt euch selber,
> Was schert mich England noch, was die Geschichte?
> Ein Ungeheuer starb, es bleiben Wichte. [p.113]

The accompanying notes bore the caustic comment that 'Mein Vertrauen in das Volk ist in letzter Zeit zu arg erschüttert worden' [p.223].

If the kings look down with disdain upon their subjects' way of life, Dürrenmatt makes it clear that their own conduct is also far from commendable. Philipp sanctimoniously dismisses the loss of fifteen thousand men as 'Entsetzlich. Fürchterlich. Ein schlimmes Blutbad' [p.68], the rival kings discuss a battle in the language of football fans:

> KÖNIG JOHANN. Gib's, königlicher Bruder, zu: Der Angriff
> Des rechten Flügels unsrer Reiterei
> In deine linke Flanke, das war Klasse.
> KÖNIG PHILIPP. Wir geben's zu, wenn England zugibt:
> Als unsre Söldner durch die Mitte brachen,
> Mit wildem Ungestüm, das war gekonnt. [p.40]

But it is Konstanze who brings their callousness most tellingly into focus when she rebukes Philipp with:

> Ihr
> Habt eine Schlacht verloren, weiter nichts.
> Für Euch nicht schlimmer als ein Pferderennen,
> Bei dem Ihr falsch gewettet. Ich verlor
> Den Sohn. [p.69]

And to be sure, as the mighty in *König Johann* are repeatedly revealed as all-too-base and all-too-human, any residual mystique that may have surrounded them is systematically debunked. This is accomplished primarily through a running gag centring on Leopold, Duke of Austria, a glutton and a boor (modelled on the Kurfürst in *Die Wiedertäufer*) who scoffs and boozes his way through the most serious of negotiations with loud demands for ever more food and drink: 'Was gibt es denn zu essen? [...] Keine Knödel? [...] He! Wein! Füllt mir den Humpen! [...] Der Ochse schmeckt fantastisch' [pp.52-58], and so on.

Like other mercenaries of Dürrenmatt's invention, such as the narrator in *Der Winterkrieg in Tibet* [*Stoffe I - III*, pp.11-190] and the *Landsknechte* von Büren and von Mengerssen in *Die Wiedertäufer*, Leopold has a vested interest in maintaining hostilities, and even goes behind the two kings' backs to start the battle: 'Es stinkt nach faulem Frieden. Ich muß handeln' [p.35]. Shortly afterwards, he reproaches Philipp and Johann in words which clearly echo the ironic title of a scene from *Die Wiedertäufer*, 'Der Krieg wird gerettet' [*WA* 10, p.105]:

> Wozu der Unsinn? Es ist Krieg, ihr Fürsten!
> Soll denn der Friede stets gerettet werden? [p.42]

In both versions of the play, the Bastard has a personal score to settle with Austria after the latter found his wife in bed with King Richard the Lionheart and slew him. Dürrenmatt replaces the Shakespearean Bastard's repeated taunts – 'And hang a calf's skin on those recreant limbs' [*TKJ*, pp.105-112] with more explicit sexual insults concerning Leopold's cuckolding by the virile King Richard, which reach their climax in the Bastard's spine-chilling pledge to avenge his father, in which he fuses death on the field of battle with that 'little death', coitus, to form one humiliating, and grotesquely disturbing, image:

> Treff ich dich in der Schlacht, so spring ich um
> Mit dir, als wärst du deine stramme Gattin
> Und ich mein Vater; wälzend uns in einem
> Gar tollen Bett voll Kot und Blut und Därme,
> Soll dir erkalten deines Leibes Wärme! [p.38]

The Bastard duly keeps his promise and, as in Shakespeare, appears with Österreich's severed head [*TKJ*, p.114; *KJD*, p.63], but Dürrenmatt goes one step farther than Shakespeare by making the Bastard place the head in a soup tureen, there to be discovered a few moments later by King Johann: a *Henkersmahlzeit* with a difference![32]

Neither the Bastard nor any of the other characters in *König Johann* emerges with honour. Even the Bastard's passionate speech on the folly of war – 'Und Helden gibt es nicht. Nur Opfer' [p.42] –, is driven by strategic rather than humanitarian considerations. The bestowal of his knighthood catapults him straight into the midst of a callous, scheming gaggle of kings, prelates and nobles. He is no less callous and calculating, which is why he is able to give up Blanka so easily, and probably why he gets into bed with her in the first place (*pace* Rudolf Stamm, who thinks that 'he has got sex on the brain').[33] His twin, and probably incompatible, objectives are to further his own career and to persuade his King to act sensibly. But whereas Shakespeare's John tends to pass the buck and allow the Bastard to take charge, Dürrenmatt's Johann is forceful, decisive and headstrong, a man of action who, as we have seen, bitterly reproaches himself whenever he allows himself to be swayed by the Bastard's rational advice. The tension between the two men is therefore simultaneously productive and destructive; that is, highly dramatic, but also highly unstable.

But Dürrenmatt's treatment of *King John* – his new plot, leading to a new outcome – turns ultimately, like his 1962 runaway success *Die Physiker*, on the proposition that, in the words of Robert Burns, 'the best-laid plans of mice and men gang oft agley.' In *Die Physiker*, the ultra-methodical physicist, Möbius, convinces his fellow-scientists Einstein and Newton by rational argument that the only way to save mankind from the consequences of his world-threatening inventions is for all three men to remain in self-imposed isolation in a lunatic asylum, but their careful calculations are finally thwarted by the unforeseeable chance that the very director of the asylum, Dr von Zahnd, is herself a megalomaniac who has long since taken possession of Möbius's formula and is hell-bent on using it to destroy the planet. In the words of Point 8 of the *21 Punkte zu den Physikern*, 'Je planmäßiger die Menschen vorgehen, desto wirksamer vermag sie der Zufall zu treffen' [*WA* 7, p.91].

In Shakespeare's play, the Bastard is depicted somewhat confusingly as the pragmatist who, having balanced out self-interest against loyal support for even the King's wildest actions throughout the play, emerges at the close as the patriotic champion of national unity at all costs. Dürrenmatt's Bastard tries to live by the dictates of reason, yet ironically he is ultimately *defeated* by the forces of reason, reason of a higher order than he himself commands. For it is not chance, as is so often the case in Dürrenmatt's plays, that brings about Johann's downfall, but the unplanned-for consequence of the Bastard's rational advice that he should marry Isabelle. Even when the King's son and heir is born, neither he nor the Bastard appreciates the implications, but Pandulpho, with his superior powers of reasoning and diplomacy, does so immediately, and Dürrenmatt ensures that the audience grasps the causal link between Johann's death and the Bastard's counsel, long before the King's dying denunciation of his aide, by giving Pandulpho the heavily ironical lines:

> Ein Sohn! Ein Kronprinz!
> *Springt aus dem Bett.*
> Kerle, meine Kleider!
> Sofort nach London, alles neu zu regeln,
> Dem Krieg ein Ende und Vernunft an Stelle
> Der Unvernunft zu setzen! [p.100]

To a degree we may also liken the Bastard to the Bishop of Münster, Franz von Waldeck, whom we first met in *Es steht geschrieben* (1947) and whose character Dürrenmatt had only recently revisited when writing *Die Wiedertäufer*. This frail old man is given the last words in the latter work. Crushed by the selfish manoeuvres of the Princes, he has watched helplessly as injustice is heaped upon injustice, the innocent are punished and the guilty rewarded. Now he laments: 'Diese unmenschliche Welt muß menschlicher werden. Aber wie? Aber wie?' [*WA* 10, p.122]. The Bishop was both the first and the latest in a line of *Weltverbesserer* and altruistic *Narren* created by Dürrenmatt during his two decades of writing for the stage. They included Bernhard Knipperdollinck in *Es steht geschrieben* who, taking Christ's precept concerning the rich man, the camel and the eye of a needle, gives all his possessions away in order that he may enter the Kingdom of Heaven, and ends up humiliated and broken on the wheel; and Romulus Augustulus, the last Emperor of Rome, who seeks to destroy his Empire to atone for its centuries of iniquities. *Die Ehe des Herrn Mississippi* (1952) boasts three such characters: Graf Übelohe von Zabernsee, a Don Quixote-like figure who sacrifices everything for the love of a woman and love of mankind; the eponymous hero of the play, a public presecutor who wishes to set the world to rights by imposing strict observance of Mosaic Law; and his sometime friend and arch-rival, the communist crusader Frédéric René Saint-Claude. The Bastard has also a good deal in common with Augias in *Herkules und der Stall des Augias*, who capitulates before his fellow-citizens' prejudice and pigheadedness, steps down from public life and retires to cultivate his own garden.

Dürrenmatt gives us a tantalising clue as to the ancestry of his Bastard in *Der Brudermord im Haus Kyburg*, a fragmentary sketch about the peace-loving, long-suffering Eberhard, who finally gives up the unequal struggle to make his belligerent brother Hartmann see reason:

> Er stößt im Schloß Thun den verwundeten Hartmann, der seinem humanen Bruder ein derart robustes Vorgehen nicht einmal im Traume zutraute, mit dem Schwert nieder. [...] Wie Eberhard will auch der Bastard Phillip Faulconbridge die Vernunft in die Politik einführen und scheitert, weil die Vernunft in einer unvernünftigen Welt zur Unvernunft wird.[34]

But another part of the Bastard is self-seeking and opportunistic, and he owes this part of his nature to another of Dürrenmatt's creations: Akki in *Ein Engel kommt nach Babylon* (1953). Unlike the Bastard, this street-wise beggar – one of Dürrenmatt's most engaging characters –, has no desire for fame and fortune; indeed, his highly successful philosophy of life is to have neither material nor spiritual aspirations. He lives by his wits, he has a profound, refreshing and highly entertaining disregard for rank and ceremony, but he has no desire to change the world, and so he is spared the painful lessons which the Bastard is forced to learn.

It can be seen, then, that the characters in *König Johann* are constructed from a wide range of sources within Dürrenmatt's *oeuvre*, and their preoccupations, habits and aspirations reveal a continuity which in some cases stretches back as far as his earliest writings for the stage. Similarly, the antecedents of much of his humour and the situations and the devices on which it relies can readily be identified in previous works; yet there are also, as always with Dürrenmatt, moments of striking originality and inventiveness, as for example in the confessional and bathtub scenes at the beginning of Act V.

It is interesting, and sad, but perhaps inevitable, that the much-heralded stimulation of the Dü-Dü partnership should have yielded, not completely new plays, but only adaptations; for with hindsight it appears that at this particular stage in Dürrenmatt's career, when the wellspring of creativity had begun to run dry, neither Werner Düggelin nor any other collaborator would have been capable of restoring the flow. The stimulus of collaborating with Charlotte Kerr following their marriage in 1984 produced a brief flurry of activity centred on *Achterloo*, which Dürrenmatt was working on when they met, but apart from this he would never again write a major play. He continued to be involved with the theatre, to be sure, but from about 1978 onwards his energies were devoted increasingly to a rich stream of autobiographical, philosophical and narrative prose and to the real love of his life, painting.[35]

The fact that Dürrenmatt was able to turn this little-played and inherently difficult Elizabethan play into such a huge box-office success is testimony not only to his reputation with the theatre-going public at that time, but also to his skill as a writer and as a *Theatermann*. As Tiusanen rightly observes, 'Dürrenmatt is clearly the same man as a dramatist and as a dramaturge, both creative and critical, both skilled and whimsical, both ingenious and a victim of his own idiosyncrasies' [TIUSANEN, p.365]. This study traces the sources and the forms of this ingenious creativity, and finds that it consists particularly in an ability to perceive affinity and difference, both as between Dürrenmatt's own time and Shakespeare's and as between the language of the Schlegel translation and the modes of modern discourse; but essentially, too, in the ability to generate out of such affinity and difference a productive dynamic which allows him, using his own inimitable voice and his unique brand of whimsy, to see the ridiculous in the sublime and so to give the English playwright's unremittingly grim plot a lighter, contemporary, but nonetheless serious touch, and one that is altogether more appropriate to the mood of the late sixties: that of the tragi-comic grotesque.

Notes and References

1 References to the primary texts discussed in this article are given in parentheses after the quotation as follows: William Shakespeare, *[The Tragedy of] King John*, ed. L.A. Beaurline (Cambridge, 1990) <*Text cited as*: *TKJ*; *editorial matter cited as*: BEAURLINE>; William Shakespeare, *König Johann*, übers. von August Wilhelm von Schlegel, hrsg. von Hans Matter (Zürich, 1979) <*cited as*: *KJS*>; Friedrich Dürrenmatt, *König Johann: nach Shakespeare* <*cited as*: *KJD*>, in Friedrich Dürrenmatt, *Werkausgabe in dreißig Bänden* (Zürich, 1980; <*cited as*: *WA*>), 11, pp.9-113, 201-7 and 212-229. With the exception of Angiers/Angers which has been

standardised as Angers, spellings of names follow Shakespeare's usage or Dürrenmatt's as the context requires.

[2] Numerous more or less partisan accounts of the events surrounding the Dü-Dü partnership exist, including Dürrenmatt's own bitter 'Mein Rücktritt von den Basler Theatern', published in the newspaper he owned at that time, the *Sonntags Journal*, 18-19 October 1969, see *WA*, 24, pp.155-161. Perhaps the most authoritative is that of Peter Rüedi, *Die Weltwoche*, 21 February 1991 <*cited as*: RÜEDI>.

[3] Interview with Rainer Litten, *Tages-Anzeiger* (Zürich), 21 November 1967, in *Friedrich Dürrenmatt, Gespräche 1961-90 in vier Bänden*, hrsg. von Heinz Ludwig Arnold in Zusammenarbeit mit Anna von Planta und Jan Strümpel (Zürich, 1996), I, p.305.

[4] See K.S. Whitton, *Dürrenmatt. Reinterpretation in Retrospect* (New York, Oxford and Munich, 1990), pp.132-6 <*cited as*: WHITTON>.

[5] Timo Tiusanen, *Dürrenmatt. A Study in Plays, Prose, Theory* (Princeton, 1977), p.364f <*cited as*: TIUSANEN>.

[6] RÜEDI, *loc.cit.*; TIUSANEN, p.346f; WHITTON, p.135. According to Dürrenmatt, 'Die *Minna von Barnhelm* stellte sich nicht als meine Minna heraus, auch nicht als jene Lessings, sondern als jene Düggelins' (*WA* 24, p.158).

[7] Hermann Beil, ' "Du mußt mich kritisieren!" ', in *play Dürrenmatt*, hrsg. von L. Bolliger und E. Buchmüller (Zürich, 1996), p.217; TIUSANEN, p.336.

[8] *Tages-Anzeiger* (Zürich), 14 September 1968.

[9] See H. Zander, *Shakespeare 'bearbeitet'. Eine Untersuchung am Beispiel der Historien-Inszenierungen 1945-1975 in der Bundesrepublik Deutschland* (Tübingen, 1983; <*cited as*: ZANDER>), p.247f.

[10] See BEAURLINE, pp.194-210.

[11] Dürrenmatt: 'Was nun meine Bearbeitung [...] betrifft, so benutzte ich die Übersetzung Schlegels' (*WA*, 11, p.201).

[12] BEAURLINE, p.7. See also Dürrenmatt, *WA* 24, p.191f. – 'sie mordeten, weil die Truppen klein waren und Doppelrollen notwendig machten' – and 11, p.216: 'Shakespeare benötigte für seine Stoffe so viele Schlachten, weil das Publikum noch an diese Schlachten glaubte; heute sind die Schlachten der Schrecken jedes Regisseurs. Ich habe noch keiner geglaubt, die ich sah.'

[13] R. L. Smallwood, 'Shakespeare Unbalanced: The Royal Shakespeare Company's *King John*, 1974-5,' in *Jahrbuch der deutschen Shakespeare-Gesellschaft West*, 1976, pp.79-99 <*cited as*: SMALLWOOD> (p.86).

[14] Dürrenmatt, *Programmheft der Basler Theater*, 12 September 1968; also in *WA* 11, p.201.

[15] For a discussion of this aspect, see A. Subiotto, 'The "comedy of politics": Dürrenmatt's *King John*,' in *Affinities. Essays in German and English Literature. Dedicated to the Memory of Oswald Wolff*, ed. R.W. Last (London, 1971), pp.139-153, <*cited as*: SUBIOTTO>.

[16] Programme note for the 1975 Aldwych production of *King John*, see SMALLWOOD, p.82f.

[17] Melchinger goes rather too far when he suggests that Dürrenmatt's rendering of Shakespeare is closer to the original than Schlegel's: S. Melchinger, 'Grimmiger Dürrenmatt,' in *Theater heute*, 9, Heft 10 (October 1968), pp. 15-18, p.17.

[18] The bawdy uncouthness of provincial squiredom is identified as a prime characteristic of Dürrenmatt's Bastard by W. Ranke: 'Adaption und Intertextualität. Friedrich Dürrenmatts *König Johann* und die Tradition der deutschen Shakespeare-Bearbeitungen,' in *Jahrbuch für internationale Germanistik*, 23, Heft 1 (1991), pp.8-36 (p.17, fn.). SUBIOTTO (p.149f) also comments on Dürrenmatt's fondness for farmyard imagery.

[19] Curren-Aquino notes that 'the Bastard's love for Blanche was part of *The Troublesome Reign*': see D. T. Curren-Aquino, '*King John': An Annotated Bibliography* (New York & London, 1994), p.670. Curren-Aquino (*loc. cit.*) and White scarcely exaggerate when they dub Dürrenmatt's Blanka a 'nymphomaniac': see A.D. White, 'History and its Adaptation: Shakespeare, Brecht, Dürrenmatt,' in *Modern Languages. Journal of the Modern Language Association*, 58, No.3 (Sept. 1977), pp.195-200, p.197.

[20] See H. Beil, 'Provokation zur Vernunft,' in *Programmheft der Basler Theater*, 12 September 1968: 'In der Figur des Bastards äußert sich eine praktische Vernunft, die ohne System, ohne Ideologie, ohne Dogma auskommt, eine Vernunft, [...]. die auf den praktischen Versuch zielt.'

[21] I: *Achterloo. Eine Komödie in zwei Akten* (Zürich, 1983). III: *Rollenspiele: Protokoll einer fiktiven Inszenierung und Achterloo III,* with Charlotte Kerr (Zürich, 1986). IV: published in 1988.

[22] 'Wir entschieden uns für eine Rasierszene. Der Bastard hat sich hervorgetan, seine Ratschläge sind akzeptiert worden. König Johann beschließt instinktiv, ihn zu demütigen, indem er ihn als Lakaien behandelt' (*WA* 11, p.206).

[23] Shakespeare's 'that strumpet Fortune' (Schlegel: 'Buhlerin', *KJS*, p.61) was originally Constance's line, but was clearly too good a metaphor to discard altogether.

[24] *Stoffe I – III* (Zürich, 1981), pp.251-302 (p.281).

[25] ZANDER, p.254, mentions Shakespeare's 'rainbow' and 'a time unseasonable' (IV,2), but both terms are used metaphorically. Pandulpho (*KJD*, p.93) bemoans his misfortune in being posted to England: 'Trostloses Klima und die Speisen Fraß.'

[26] The historical Henry III was nine when he succeeded his father; in Shakespeare he is still a boy, but evidently one capable of assuming command. By making him a babe in arms, Dürrenmatt clearly shifts the fulcrum of power to an entirely new location.

[27] On the Ides of March – in a pastiche of the assassination scene in *Julius Caesar* (III, 1) – Romulus discovers one-by-one his inept would-be assassins concealed under a divan, under his bed, in the wardrobes, etc. (*WA* 2, pp.85-9).

[28] The indignity of anonymity in death was already a topos in *Es steht geschrieben*, where the two principal characters, Johann Bockelson and Bernhard Knipperdollinck, are reduced by the guards to 'Numero 524' and 'Numero 523' respectively as they lie dying, broken on the wheel (*WA* 1, p.143f.)

[29] The theory of 'Komödie der Handlung' expounded in the *Dramaturgische Überlegungen* as a corrective to the classical tragedy/comedy of character is based on the notion of the 'schlimmstmögliche Wendung', which in turn is a development of Points 3 and 4 of the *21 Punkte zu den 'Physikern'* (1962): '3. Eine Geschichte ist dann zu Ende gedacht, wenn sie ihre schlimmstmögliche Wendung genommen hat. 4. Die schlimmstmögliche Wendung ist nicht voraussehbar. Sie tritt durch Zufall ein.' (*WA* 7, p.91).

[30] *Hörspiel*, 1954 and *Komödie*, 1963: *WA* 18, pp.179-226 and 9-117.

[31] B. Brecht, *Mutter Courage und ihre Kinder* (Frankfurt a.M., 1963), p.87.

[32] If 'a severed head was a stock property' in Shakespeare (BEAURLINE, p.114), then it is scarcely less so in Dürrenmatt, who devotes an entire scene of *Die Wiedertäufer* to a confrontation between the Bishop of Münster and the head of his adversary, Jan Matthison (*WA* 10, p.69f); and before the curtain rises on the present play, the audience hears three dull thuds, the sound of three beheadings.

[33] Rudolf STAMM, '*King John – König Johann.* Vom Historienspiel zur politischen Moralität,' in *Jahrbuch der deutschen Shakespeare-Gesellschaft West*, 1970, pp.30-48 (p.41).

[34] *Turmbau. Stoffe IV - IX* (Zürich, 1990), pp.59-61.

[35] Dürrenmatt was an accomplished and prolific artist: his drawings and paintings were exhibited in Bern (1981) and Neuchâtel (1985). and posthumously, in a major event, in Zürich in 1994. The autobiographical works *Stoffe I-III* and *Stoffe IV-IX* appeared in, respectively, 1981 and 1990 (the year of his death); new collections of essays and speeches in 1988 (*Versuche*) and 1992 (*Gedankenfuge*); and the novels *Justiz*, *Der Auftrag* and *Durcheinanderthal* in 1985, 1986 and 1989.

Josephine Butler's campaign against the double moral standard in England, and its repercussions in Germany

INGRID SHARP

Public attitudes to 'the role of women' in nineteenth century England and Germany.[1]

Victorian England has been seen traditionally as a prudish age where sexuality was repressed and its discussion taboo. Yet Foucault argues that the Victorian age was in fact characterised by an 'explosion of discourse' on sex, the location and function of which had undergone a qualitative shift. By the end of the 18th century sex (he claims) had been freed from its link with the Church.

> Through pedagogy, medicine and economics, it made sex not only a secular concern but a concern of the state as well; to be more exact, sex became a matter that required the social body as a whole, and virtually all of its individuals, to place themselves under surveillance.[2]

In the 19th century, then, instead of the strong link between sex, sin and damnation, sex came under the scrutiny and control of medical science and the state. The concept of 'normality' in sexual instincts and behaviour and its equation with health and life was contrasted with the diseases and degeneracy which could afflict individuals through the unchecked development of 'deviant' sexuality. Sex became fraught with dangers, an aspect of life to be controlled and corrected. Sexuality for the bourgeoisie assumed a position centre stage and the bourgeois model of sexuality, constructed to promote what were essentially class interests – the protection of health and heredity of class members – was gradually extended to apply to all sections of society.[3]

Women were characterised as being entirely governed by their sexual and reproductive organs, more or less at the mercy of their womb and ovaries which could as often be the seat of disease and instability as of health. Any disorder, whether physical or mental, whether or not in any way connected with sexuality or the reproductive organs was seen as having its origins in the womb or ovaries, and treatment was liable to involve clitoridectomy or ovariotomy, even in quite young patients.[4]

It is in this context that Josephine Butler's campaign for the repeal of the Contagious Diseases Acts must be viewed. This campaign, motivated as it was by strong moral and religious convictions and linked in the public mind with the development of the sexually repressive National Vigilance Association [NVA] has been viewed as belonging to the problematic arena of social purity.[5] Yet Butler's analysis of the relations between men and women as power relations, her rejection of the double standard of sexual morality and her attack on male morality place her more properly in the radical tradition and provide a link with late twentieth-century feminist concerns with sexuality as a site of power and the domination of women by men.

In her refusal to accept either the double moral standard or the dual model of female sexuality, Butler was attacking the whole basis of separate sphere ideology, whereby men claimed the public sphere as their own, confining women to the private sphere of home and family. In denying the moral rectitude of the male sex and in highlighting the self-interest of the male legislators, Butler called into question the right of men to legislate on behalf of women and thus in effect the validity of the whole social order. Moreover, Butler's position exercised a direct influence on the development of the women's movement in Germany from the 1890s onwards. Her ideas were adopted and developed by Abolitionists in Germany, and for over a decade discussions centred on sexuality-dominated debate within the hitherto cautious, conservative women's movement.

In both England and Germany, a broadly similar view of the nature of the sexes was held and gradually reinforced by advances in the scientific and medical fields from the mid 19th century onwards. In Germany ideas of *Geschlechtscharakter* [the character of the sexes] were expressed in terms of the essential polarity and complementarity of the sexes. This theory arose in the 18th century and was developed throughout the 19th and early 20th centuries. The theory was extrapolated from the social role of the sexes and yet was seen as expressing their quintessential nature. Encyclopaedias throughout the century give definitions of *Geschlechtscharakter* in terms of a series of opposites, locating men in the public, women in the private sphere:

> Constantly recurring characteristics were, for the man, activity and rationality, for the woman, passivity and emotionality, in which the dual concept activity-passivity was derived from the sexual act and rationality-emotionality from the social arena.[6]

In the context of the nineteenth-century belief in progress, in an underlying rational plan within which mankind had a destiny to fulfil, the role and destiny of woman was to complement, support and succour man by providing a place of sanctuary unsullied by the taint of the outside world. She was fitted by her nature for a domestic life, in need of the life-long protection of men and unfit for an independent existence. Her strength came from her dependence, which called forth qualities of chivalry, generosity and love in her male protectors. Men were destined to live a public life, to provide the link between family and state and, by dint of their greater intellectual capacities, rationality and strength of character, to legislate on behalf of women. As Campe put it, writing in 1789:

> Es ist also der übereinstimmende Wille der Natur und der menschlichen Gesellschaft, daß der Mann des Weibes Beschützer und Oberhaupt, das Weib hingegen die sich ihm anschmiegende, sich an ihm haltende und stützende treue, dankbare und folgsame Gefährtin und Gehülfin seines Lebens seyn sollte – er die Eiche, sie der Epheu,

der einen Theil seiner Lebenskraft aus den Lebenskräften der Eiche saugt, der mit ihr in die Lüfte wächst, mit ihr den Stürmen trotzt, mit ihr steht und mit ihr fällt – ohne sie ein niedriges Gesträuch, daß von jedem vorübergehenden Fuß zertreten wird.[7]

[It is therefore both the will of Nature and of human society that the husband should be the woman's protector and master, the wife the loving companion and helpmeet of his life, yielding to him, supporting herself through his strength – he the oak tree, she the ivy that sucks part of its own life force from that of the oak, that grows with it to the heights, braves the storms with it, stands and falls only together with the oak – without it a lowly shrub, trampled by every passing foot.]

For Fichte, as for Rousseau, the sexual nature of male and female is essential to an understanding of their social roles. While Rousseau took over the seventeenth-century view of women's sexuality being naturally stronger than that of men and thus in need of greater social control, Fichte uses his model of male activity and female passivity in the sexual act to justify the complete disenfranchisement of women in the public sphere: through their sexual nature they are disqualified from citizenship and cease to exist as individuals in civil society.

In his *Grundlage des Naturrechts*, published in 1796, Fichte identifies the role of woman as *leidend*, meaning 'passive' or even 'suffering', while the man is described as *tätig* or 'active'.[8] Fichte believed that the principle of activity lay at the basis of the whole of life. By identifying this very quality as essentially masculine, he was placing men at the centre of the historical stream and women at the margins.

As all human beings are rational, it is impossible that a woman would willingly act against her own interests by acquiescing in sexual activity, so Fichte drew the conclusion that her acquiescence in practice must express the essential nature of woman in some way. Fichte identified this as love. It was in the nature of woman to love, and her participation in the sexual act expressed a readiness to self-sacrifice for the sake of love. Through loving, she was fulfilling her true nature, but this entailed ceasing to lead life as an individual in her own right.

> Let me state it concisely: in an uncorrupted woman the sexual impulse does not manifest itself at all, but only love; and this love is the natural impulse of a woman to satisfy a man [...] Her only requirement is to love and be loved. Only thus does the impulse which the woman feels to sacrifice receive that character of freedom and activity which it must have in order to be rational. [FICHTE-KROEGER, p.399]

Fichte believed that a woman could only love one man and that she had to give herself up entirely to the object of her love: 'The woman who gives herself up once, gives herself up forever.' [FICHTE-KROEGER, p.401]

Her fulfilment was to be found in total self-sacrifice and her reward was the knowledge that she was giving him pleasure: her pleasure was his pleasure in her. Any assumption that women had sexual needs to fulfil was dismissed by Fichte as both absurd and shameful for both sexes. Marriage for women meant giving themselves up to the will and rule of the husband. Men responded to the woman's freely chosen and total submission with 'Großmut' [generosity]: she inspired his tenderness and his readiness to consider her feelings and consult her wishes. In this way, women could gain an influence over public life indirectly through their influence on their husbands. Marriage, however, entailed the loss of any more direct influence, as the married woman gave up any rights as a citizen:

> The conception of marriage involves the most unlimited subjection of the woman to the will of the husband; not from legal, but from moral reasons. She must subject herself for the sake of her own honour. The woman does not belong to herself, but to the man. The state [...] abandons all claims to consider the woman as a legal person. The husband supplies her place; her marriage utterly annuls her, so far as the state is concerned [...] The husband becomes her guarantee in the eyes of the law; or becomes her guardian. He lives in all her public life, and she retains for herself only a house life. [FICHTE-KROEGER, pp.417-8]

True happiness and freedom for women could only be found in their dependence and subordination in marriage. Alternatives to marriage were seen as a poor substitute, since the woman would not have the opportunity to fulfil her destiny. On this view, inequalities between the sexes were based on the innate natures of the sexes and, as such, were rational and justifiable.

These ideas were reflected in the Prussian *Allgemeines Landrecht* of 1794, which remained in force, subject to numerous revisions, until 1900, only changing as the century progressed to become even less liberal, for example in changes to the laws regarding divorce and responsibility for illegitimate children. It is striking that while the progress of 'the bourgeois century' was generally in the direction of greater liberty and freedom of thought for the individual, women were an exception to this, and the laws relating to them form a little island of feudalism within which women were bound to obedience and political impotence, confined and restricted in every sphere of their lives.[9]

The concept of *Geschlechtsvormundschaft* was common to all legal systems in Germany, as indeed in Britain, to a greater or lesser extent. This meant that a woman was not a legal entity in her own right, but had to be represented in all her business and legal affairs by a male guardian [*Vormund*]. The husband was the head of the household and the legal guardian of his wife. Without his permission she could not take a job, sign a contract or engage in litigation; she was not a 'legal person' in civil law. Unless a special contract was drawn up, the wife's property passed to the husband on marriage, her earnings also being seen as the property of the man. The rights of the parents over their children were laid down in law. The father had full control over his children, he made decisions about their education, could give or withhold permission to marry and could even decide when the babies were to be weaned. If they were daughters, he was their legal representative and held their property until they passed out of his control on their marriage. If a woman remained unmarried, there was no upper age limit at which the father's power over her ceased. Unless he chose otherwise, he retained the right to administer her fortune, keep her in the family home and forbid her to undertake any work outside the home or train for any profession until his death. While some concessions were made regarding unmarried women, particularly those engaged in trade, the position of the man as 'Herr der Familie' was reaffirmed each time, even in the *Bürgerliches Gesetzbuch* [Civil Code] of 1900 which largely upheld the man's rights over his wife and children.

In some parts of the German empire, women had limited voting rights at local level, but nowhere did they have the right to stand for election to public office. Often the woman had to vote by proxy and the proxy was under no obligation to vote as she had chosen, provided he believed that, had she known the full political circumstances, she would have changed her mind. These restricted voting rights were attached to a high property qualification. If the woman lost her property, as most women did on marriage, for example, she also lost the right to vote.

In Britain, too, a similar view of women's nature was common currency and found comparable expression in the law. Here too women's subordination to men in the private sphere and exclusion from the public sphere were justified by an appeal to 'Nature'. Geddes and Thompson, in *The Evolution of Sex*, placed this at the most primitive level of human development: male and female roles had been decided at the earliest stages of life and '[w]hat was decided among the prehistoric Protozoa cannot be annulled by act of Parliament'.[10]

This exclusion from public influence was supposedly rendered less bitter by a belief in the private influence women wielded over men through their capacity to love and inspire love. Campe was only restating a common belief when he dubbed women as the 'allgewaltiges, obgleich schwaches Geschlecht' [all-powerful, albeit weak sex].[11] Women's private influence over men was seen as spilling over into the public sphere and thus mitigating the seeming inequality of women's legal situation. Illustrative of the negative effect on legislation of this reliance on female influence is the following statement made by J.G. Schlosser, Goethe's brother-in-law:

> Wenn die Frau ihrem Mann den Leib, ihre Ehre, ihre Kinder, ihre ganze Glückseligkeit, ihr Leben und alle ihre Kräfte anvertrauen muß, so ist es, dünkt mich, eine Kleinigkeit, daß sie ihm auch ihr Vermögen anvertraue. Es sei daher nicht unbillig, daß dem Mann das vollständige Recht über das ganze Vermögen eingeräumt werde, und übte er das zu streng, die Frau auf die Kraft ihrer Liebkosungen und der nächtlichen Umarmungen verwiesen werde.[12]
>
> [If woman must place into the hands of her husband her body, her honour, her children, her entire happiness, her life and all her qualities, it seems to me a trivial matter that she should also give up her fortune to him as well. It is not unseemly that the husband should be given exclusive rights over the entire marital fortune, and should he be too strict in his administration, the woman is reminded of the power of her caresses and their nightly embraces.]

Because of this indirect but powerful emotional influence over men, and because of what was seen to be women's greater moral purity, women came to be held responsible for the moral welfare of society: 'Wie die Quelle, so der Bach' [as the source is, so the stream will be] wrote Campe in 1789. Ruskin, writing in 1865, held women responsible for such expressions of masculinity as war and bloodshed, as they had not used their influence to prevent them:

> There is not a war in the world, nor an injustice, but you women are answerable for it: not in that you have provoked, but in that you have not hindered. There is no suffering, no injustice, no misery, in the earth, but the guilt of it lies with you.[13]

This idea of women's indirect influence was further developed in the later decades of the century in response to feminist demands for direct influence in the public sphere. Any activity which placed them in competition with men would 'unsex' them, reducing their influence and at the same time rendering them vulnerable to male brutality otherwise held in check by the chivalrous instincts aroused by female innocence and helplessness. Paradoxically, then, the more women sought to enter the public sphere and compete with men there – something which they were by nature ill-equipped to do – the less influence and power they were likely to have, as these activities rendered them unfeminine and distasteful to men and indeed to all 'true' women.

A woman was in danger of 'unsexing' herself if she engaged in any activity deemed suitable exclusively for the male sex. Lorenz von Stein, writing in 1886, categorically states that a woman engaging in spheres of traditionally male activity – as well she might, should circumstances or inclination compel her to do so – ceases to be a woman:

> Die Frau kann zuletzt, wenn die Dinge sie äußerlich oder ihre Individualität sie dazu innerlich zwingen, alles, was der Mann kann. Ob besser oder schlechter, darauf kommt es hier nicht an. Es gibt *nichts*, das sie nicht wie ein Mann durchzuführen vermöchte. Aber, und das ist es, was wir für uns festhalten müssen, während wir das nicht bestreiten, ist es andererseits ebenso gewiß, daß die Frau, sowie sie das Männliche wirklich thut, nur eine weibliche Form des Mannes und *keine Frau mehr ist*.[14]
>
> [If put to it, a woman can do anything a man can do – when external circumstances or her own inner inclination compel her. Whether she does them better or worse is not the point. There is *nothing* which a man does that she cannot do. But, and this is what we must hold on to at all times, while we do not challenge this point, it is nonetheless equally true that a woman, when she is in reality doing male things is, to that extent, only a man in female form and *she ceases to be a woman.*]

Acting out of role did not serve to cast doubt on the appropriateness of the prescribed role for women, it simply showed that the woman was not a 'true woman', in other words, the ideal took precedence over the reality. This mechanism was particularly important in the field of sexuality, where 'true' women were, in W. Acton's words, 'happily for [them/]society not very much troubled by sexual feeling of any kind.'[15]

The strength of the biological argument increased towards the end of the century as the feminist assault on the male view of the world became more vocal. Despite what women and their misguided champions may have *thought* they wanted, biological necessity and the health of the race *demanded* that women be excluded from certain influential areas of life in order to prevent them from causing damage. Medical theory postulated a limited reserve of energy, which, in the case of women, could not be diverted away from their reproductive function without seriously impairing that function. This would have dire consequences for the individual woman, her sickly offspring and ultimately for society. Maudesley used this argument in his 1874 article 'Sex in Mind and Education' to justify women's continued exclusion from Higher Education:

> Whatever aspirations of an intellectual kind they [women] may have, they cannot be relieved from the performance of those offices [work as mothers and nurses of children] so long as it is thought necessary that mankind should continue on earth. Even if these be looked upon as somewhat mean and unworthy offices in comparison with the nobler functions of giving birth to and developing ideas [...] it still must be confessed that for the great majority of women they must remain the most important offices of the best period of their lives.[16]

Woman's role is to complement that of man and any attempt to 'contend on equal terms with men for the goal of man's ambition' is doomed to failure,[17]

> If she is to be judged by the same standard as men and make their aims her aims, we are certainly bound to say that she labours under an inferiority of constitution by a dispensation which there is no gainsaying. This is a matter of physiology, not a matter of sentiment [...]. It may be a pity for woman that she has been created woman, but, being such, it is as ridiculous to consider herself inferior to man because she is not man, as it would be for man to consider himself inferior to her because he cannot perform her functions. [NEWMAN, p.86]

So we see how in both countries assumptions about the nature of the sexes served to provide a justification for women's continued confinement to the private sphere and her continued inequality before the law. The arguments used show clearly that this was held to be in the best interests, not only of society, for whom stable families with the male at the head mirrored the order of the state, but for the men and women themselves: only through acceptance of their differing functions could individual men and women fulfil the destiny of the human race.

As the discourse of fundamental difference rested largely on biological differences, it comes as no surprise that the sexual natures of men and women were seen as similarly opposed. The Victorian view of the sexual nature of middle-class women has been characterised as 'passionlessness' by Nancy Cott, and this amounted to the assumption of sexual anaesthesia in most women and the pathologisation of any women displaying unnatural sexual urges.[18]

Acton again:

> there can be no doubt that sexual feeling in the female is in the majority of cases in abeyance, and that it requires positive and considerable excitement to be roused at all; and even if aroused (which in many instances it never can be) it is very moderate compared with that of the male.[19]

Men, on the other hand were seen as possessing a strong sex drive, the regular relief of which was necessary for health. Healthy males needed regular but not excessive sexual release or untold damage could be done to their organisms. This relief could not be found in the practice of 'the solitary vice', as masturbation was held to provoke a whole range of debilitating moral and physiological effects. On the whole then, this mismatch of sexual desires presented men with a dilemma: where to satisfy their legitimate manly sexual urges without besmirching and defiling women of their class?

The answer lay in the construction of a divided sexuality for women. As well as the 'pure' or 'uncorrupted' woman there existed another category of women who were innately vicious and degraded and, thus, a legitimate outlet for male sexual urges: the prostitute.

Prostitution in Britain and Germany.

The dominant 19th century image of the prostitute in both Britain and Germany is remarkably similar and it emphasises the corrupted, deviant nature of the women themselves. The theory of Cesare Lombroso that some women, through an innate moral defect, are simply born to be whores was highly influential in Germany.[20] In England, too, the women involved in prostitution were seen as innately degraded, most often placed in a separate category altogether from that of 'pure' women who were deserving of the consideration of men. Once a woman 'fell' and became sexualised, she left the category of 'true' women altogether:

> What is a prostitute! She is a woman who gives for money that which she ought to give only for love; who ministers to passion and lust alone, to the exclusion and extinction of all the higher qualities [...]. She is a woman with half the woman gone, and that half containing all that elevates her nature, leaving her a mere instrument of impurity; degraded and fallen she extracts from the sin of others the means of living, corrupt and dependent on corruption, and therefore interested directly in the increase of immorality – a social pest, carrying contamination and foulness to every quarter to which she has access, who
>
> *like a disease,*
> *Creeps, no precaution used, among the crowd,*
> *Makes wicked lightenings of her eyes,*
> *and stirs the pulse,*
> *With devil's leaps, and poisons half the young.*[21]

This categorisation of certain women as being innately predisposed towards sexual promiscuity, and thus prostitution, was reflected when it came to allocating blame and prescribing social or legal sanctions for this form of illicit sex. The prostitute as individual was seen as preying on the sexual nature of men for personal satisfaction and financial gain. The role allocated to the male in all of this was most often that of weak and helpless victim, whose sexual make-up rendered him incapable of resisting the lure of the prostitute:

> Such women, ministers of evil passions, not only gratify desire but also arouse it. Compelled by necessity to seek for customers, they throng our streets and public places, and suggest evil thoughts and desires which might otherwise remain undeveloped [...]. Prostitutes have the power of soliciting and tempting. Gunpowder remains harmless till the spark falls upon it; the match until struck, retains the hidden fire, so lust remains dormant till called into being by an exciting cause. [Acton, in JEFFRIES, p.43]

At the same time that the individual prostitute was reviled as a threat to hearth and home and the sanctity of marriage, prostitution itself was seen as a necessary evil – it was the price society must pay for maintaining the integrity of the bourgeois family and protecting the innocence of true women. The prostitute herself may have been (in Lecky's phrase) 'the supreme type of vice', but she was also:

> ultimately the most efficient guardian of virtue. But for her the unchallenged purity of countless happy homes would be polluted, and not a few who, in the pride of their untempted chastity, think of her with an indignant shudder, would have known the agony of remorse or despair. On that degraded and ignoble form are concentrated the passions that might have filled the world with shame.[22]

Far from receiving social recognition for this valuable service, however, individual prostitutes were subject to social opprobrium and measures of control which deprived them of dignity and human rights. The problems associated with prostitution from the state's point of view were largely those of control and public perception. It was important that respectable citizens should not be outraged by the sight of prostitutes or importuned by them, so laws were often aimed at restricting their access to public spaces.

In nineteenth-century Germany control of prostitutes was regionally administered and took a variety of forms, largely centred on restricting their freedom of movement and attempting to keep them free from disease. Control of the spread of VD was based on regular medical examination of registered prostitutes together with enforced 'cures' if they were found to be infected. Salvarsan, an effective if highly toxic cure for gonorrhoea, was only discovered in 1910, so treatment prior to this was experimental – often involving mercury – dangerous and largely ineffective.[23] The system, known as *Reglementierung* [regulation] dates back to Napoleonic law and was in place throughout continental Europe.

The most widespread system of regulation, known as *Kasernierung* [limitation by district], restricted registered prostitutes to certain streets, whereas the system in Hamburg, known as *Bordellierung* [limitation to brothels], effectively entailed state-run brothels under the supervision of the *Sittenpolizei* [vice squad]. In Bremen around 1900, registered prostitutes were not just restricted to certain streets but were also forbidden to visit the theatre, leave the designated streets in pairs, ride in open carriages or walk on the city walls. They could not visit each other in their rooms, certain windows had to be painted over to prevent the women from making a display of themselves and they had to be medically checked and bathed twice a week.[24] While the basis of the regulations was a pragmatic acceptance of prostitution as a necessary if morally opprobrious outlet for a natural urge, the authorities were concerned to render the process as invisible and separate from the rest of city life as possible.

In nineteenth century Britain, the Contagious Diseases Acts [CD Acts] applying to garrison towns had been passed in 1864 to safeguard the health of soldiers and their families. In 1866 pressure from the Continent to develop a unitary system of control led to calls for the extension of the Acts to other towns in Britain: i.e. also to towns with a non-military population. It was not until this date that Josephine Butler, previously engaged in rescue work with prostitutes in Liverpool, became aware of the Acts and of the proposal to extend them to other British towns.

The Contagious Diseases Acts – a nomenclature hitherto more usually associated with controlling the spread of disease in livestock – allowed the compulsory examination by speculum of any women suspected of prostitution. Any woman refusing to sign the consent form for this examination was in breach of the law and had to appear before a magistrate to defend her character. More often than not, she was ordered to submit to examination in any case. Refusal at this stage was a punishable offence and the woman, on no more solid ground than the suspicion of a government agent, could be imprisoned for up to 30 days. If she still refused her consent, she could be imprisoned again indefinitely until she did submit. If found to be diseased, she would be admitted to one of the Lock hospitals until cured, after which she would be registered as a prostitute and required to attend fortnightly medical examinations at which her continued good health would be certified if appropriate and she would be allowed to ply her trade. The intention was to stop the spread of venereal disease among the troops and their families by removing diseased women from circulation and ensuring a supply of 'clean' women for the use of the troops.

Although there already existed a group of Abolitionists who objected to the CD Acts, largely on the grounds that they were ineffective in preventing disease and immoral in that they amounted to state sanction of prostitution, Butler established the Ladies National Association for Abolition [LNA] in 1869. This campaign took the form of raising public awareness of the Acts, which had been passed in great secrecy – in the middle of the night after minimal debate – to reflect the delicacy of the subject matter. Butler's campaign soon succeeded in mobilising public opinion against the Acts. The movement worked closely with the newly enfranchised working-class men, whose wives and daughters were most at risk, establishing their own organ, *The Shield*, to publicise the campaign, as none of the mainstream press would touch the issue. The LNA raised the issue at electoral campaigns, in one instance successfully blocking the election of a Liberal candidate in Colchester solely on the Abolition issue. In 1870 a Royal Commission was set up to examine evidence on both sides of the argument and Butler was called upon to give evidence. Extension of the Acts was prevented for fear of adverse public reaction, but the Acts remained on the statute books and applied, as before, to garrison towns. Butler's aim was total repeal, and in 1871 she presented a petition against the Acts supported by signatures from a quarter of a million women. But it was not until 1883 that the motion, 'This House disapproves of the compulsory examination of women under the Contagious Diseases Acts' was passed, thus finally making the Acts unworkable. Actual repeal of the acts in the UK came in 1886 (though they continued to apply in India and other British colonies).

The mere fact of a woman addressing such issues in public was seen as morally dangerous and degrading and, although the person and motivation of Butler were highly respectable, response to her campaign portrayed her and other female campaigners as worse than the women they sought to protect. Butler herself was described by one journalist as 'an indecent maenad, a shrieking sister, frenzied, unsexed, and utterly without shame' and it was often suggested that the women campaigners were strangely drawn to their sordid subject matter.[25]

The CD Acts, just like the continental legislation which had inspired their introduction, were a clear expression of society's double moral standard since they reflected an acceptance of male vice and the necessary existence of a class of women to service this vice. The unequal treatment of the prostitute and her client was justified in the following terms:

> we may at once dispose of any recommendation founded on the principle of putting both parties to the sin of fornication on an equal footing by the obvious but not less conclusive reply that there is no comparison to be made between prostitutes and the men who consort with them. With the one sex the offence is committed as a matter of gain; with the other it is an irregular indulgence of a natural impulse.[26]

The LNA objected to the CD Acts on a number of grounds. First, they were unconstitutional: only women were punished for a crime committed by both sexes. A woman could be arrested on the flimsiest of grounds, forced to choose between enduring what the campaigners saw as a humiliating violation – in itself a worse punishment than would be meted out to a convicted felon – or serving a prison term. Thus a woman could be criminalised, robbed of her good name and punished simply on the uncorroborated 'suspicion' of a policeman – a far cry from the presumption of innocence and the right to a fair trial enshrined in the law for all other groups. Secondly, they were ineffective, curing women while leaving men free to infect prostitutes and wives alike. The regular examinations gave rise to the illusion that sex with registered women was 'safe' whereas there was no guarantee at all that a woman might not be infected soon after her examination. Both sides used available statistics to argue the efficacy or inefficacy of the Acts in reducing the incidence of VD. Thirdly, the regulation and registering of prostitutes amounted to the state sanction of vice and lowered moral standards in public life, causing men to lose all sense of right and wrong. Equally, the degrading nature of the examinations by male doctors served to destroy what sense of shame and modesty the prostitutes may have retained. Once registered as a prostitute, a woman found it very difficult to re-enter respectable society. Effectively, argued Butler, the Acts sanctioned and encouraged the creation of a slave class of women whose sole purpose was to service the lusts of men.[27]

Butler refused to accept the argument that the prostitutes were innately degraded and thus distinct from the category of virtuous women. She argued that there was a strong class interest involved, because the women of the working-class were to be made sexually available to middle-class men. Although the CD Acts were hardly a direct threat to women of her own class, Butler felt that they were degrading to *all* women and ultimately to the whole of society:

> Sirs, you *cannot* hold *us* in honour so long as you drag our sisters through the mire. As you are unjust and cruel to them, you will become unjust and cruel to us. [WALKOWITZ, p.81]

She argued, with Acton, that a man used to treating and viewing women as sexual playthings could not treat any women with respect. This is the crux of her argument. She refused to accept the sacrifice of one class of women as the price of protection for her own class. She refused to accept the notional separation of women into angels and whores and she recognised the economic basis of much prostitution: 'the absolute dependance [sic] on men to which so many women are reduced, means either beggary or *shame*.'[28]

Butler's campaign called into question the models of sexuality on which the Acts were based. She went into battle against male immorality, turning the tables on those who portrayed men as the victims of rapacious prostitutes:

> [We] shall regard all men (however pure in their own conduct) as depravers of society, who hold the loathsome and deadly doctrine that God has made man for unchastity and woman for his degraded slave.[29]

The justification of 'separate sphere' ideology rested to a great extent on the acceptance of male fitness to legislate on behalf of men and women, and on the demonstrable fairness and rationality of their rule. Butler's campaign called this into question, challenging the social order as an expression of the natural order 'determined to prove that it is not a law of nature, though these men have declared it and ratified it by an act of parliament, that women must be preyed upon by men.'[30]

Looking back on the campaign five years later, the annual report of the LNA for 1877 reflected that the Acts were based on

> an acceptance of the doctrine that women are inferior to men, that men's interests are paramount, and that, where necessary, women must be entirely sacrificed to those interests, that women are unfit and unentitled to regulate their own lives, which must be ordered by men in the interests of men.[31]

Butler's campaign was ultimately successful in England after 20 years of campaigning, first blocking the extension of the Acts in 1869, then achieving a parliamentary majority in favour of repeal in 1883, followed by repeal of the acts in 1886. As well as the ability to arouse the anger and outrage of middle-class women against the Acts, part of her success was due to the willingness of the working-class male to use his vote to put pressure on parliament and get the subject taken seriously as a political issue.

The progress of Butler's ideas on the continent.

In 1874 Butler turned her attention to the continent. In response to a proposal, made that year at the Triennial Medical Congress in Vienna, that a world-wide league should be established to oversee the system of regulation, the Abolitionists felt that they should liaise with their supporters on the continent. Butler had been aware of the systems of regulation in place in Europe since early in her campaign against the CD Acts and indeed supported her arguments with reference to the unhappy consequences of these systems. In 1872 she published *The New Era*, in which the system of regulation in Berlin is described and criticised.[32] Following Butler's short European tour from November 1874 to February 1875, it was decided that European contacts should be used to co-ordinate a campaign against regulation in continental Europe. The British Branch of the British, Continental and General Federation for the Abolition of Government Regulation of Prostitution [referred to below as: the Federation] was duly founded on 19 March 1875, with a European journal, *Le Bulletin Continental*, being established in December of that year to report on the progress of the campaign.

Abolitionist ideas were warmly received in Switzerland, Italy and France, but not in Germany. Private letters and allusions to Germany in *Le Bulletin Continental* and elsewhere show how infertile Butler considered the soil for Abolitionist ideas in Germany. The Fourth Annual Report 1878-1879 contains the following description of the situation in Germany:

> The regime of political repression there prevents, for the present, any organisational public work in favour of our principles, but has not prevented the appearance of some very remarkable isolated protests, which continue from time to time to be published against the system of regulation.[33]

Some ten years later, Butler writes, '[o]ur progress in Germany is very slow indeed, owing to the subjection in which women are held in that country.'[34]

Early attempts to discuss Abolitionist ideas within the women's movement in Germany failed and it was not until 1889, some 14 years later, that the first German branch of the Federation was founded. In order to understand why this is the case, we need to look briefly at the situation of women in Germany.

The *Allgemeiner Deutscher Frauenverein* [ADF] was founded in 1865, with the twin aims of increasing opportunities for education and employment for middle-class girls and women. The ADF set out to work within the boundaries of convention and the law, accepting that marriage and child-rearing was the highest calling for women, but arguing that unmarried women should have the possibility of useful, respectable employment in suitable professions and be able to support themselves on their earnings. The ADF remained extremely cautious in its methods and restricted in its aims owing to a number of legal barriers, some of which remained in place until the beginning of the 20th century, and because of a social climate which was anything but receptive to liberal ideas. The defeat of liberalism after the unsuccessful revolution of 1848 reinforced Germany as a conservative, hierarchical society with no tradition of equal rights for men, let alone women. Men's privileges as citizens were based on their willingness to fight for their country, not on the concept of inalienable human rights. It was only after the establishment of the Second Empire in 1871 that 'Germany' existed as a unified political entity, and the fact that this unity had been achieved through a series of military victories served to cement the military values permeating German society.

In 1888 Auguste Schmidt refused an invitation to join the International Council of Women with the words:

> In Germany we have to work with great tact and by conservative methods. [...]. The difference between our position and that of our American sisters is largely due to the fact that you live in a republic, we in a monarchy [...] in a land centuries old, where the ideas and habits of thought are [...] incrusted in the people.[35]

As well as restricted legal and political rights similar to those in force in nineteenth-century England, German women faced additional legal barriers. The political disabilites encoded in the *Preußisches Vereinsgesetz* [Prussian Law of Association] applied through much of Germany, although there was some regional variation.

> Politischen Vereinen ist die Aufnahme von Frauenpersonen, Schülern und Lehrlingen verboten. Auch dürfen solche Personen nicht an Versammlungen und Sitzungen teilnehmen, bei denen politische Gegenstände verhandelt werden. [*Preußisches Vereinsgesetz,* 1850-1908]
>
> [Political Associations are forbidden to accept as members female persons, schoolboys or apprentices. Further, such persons are not allowed to attend gatherings or meetings at which political subject matter is debated.]

Even where this law was not applicable (Hamburg, Bremen, Baden and Württemberg) there were stringent laws on public order or public decency which could be invoked to restrict women attending public meetings to suitable topics. In addition to this, the *Sozialistengesetz* [Law on Socialists] (in force 1878-1890) outlawed membership of any Socialist parties or the spreading of Socialist ideas, thus effectively preventing any co-operation between working-class and bourgeois women.

It was small wonder that Butler referred to Germany as a land where enlightenment could not reach, and complained about the insufferable arrogance of German men:

> The German men are very insolent – unconsciously so perhaps – they regard me as an inconvenient, unmanageable intruder into the Federation, an old woman who sets her own opinion against the whole of the German male wisdom. I wish someone would tell them that I founded the Federation in 1875. They are so ignorant and refuse to learn.[36]

Despite the difficulties, there were early attempts to promote public discussion of Butler's ideas. In 1875 at the ADF conference, Lina Morgenstern attempted to place the Federation's abolitionist aims on the agenda, but this was overruled. In 1880, despite opposition from the ADF who feared conflict with Bremen's strict decency laws, Gertrud Guillaume Schack attempted to set up an unofficial branch of the Federation in Bremen, disguising its nature under the name *Deutscher Kulturbund* [German Cultural Association] and organising lecture tours to German cities, where she often spoke to working-class women. In these meetings she openly espoused Abolitionist ideas, opposing the German system of regulation. Her analysis demonstrated the economic roots of prostitution, leading some working-class women to band together and agitate for higher wages. Because of the seditious effects of her lectures, Schack was regularly prosecuted and prevented from speaking under various rulings: breach of the peace, contravention of decency laws, laws of association or the *Sozialistengesetz*. The *Kulturbund* was forced to disband in 1885.[37]

Pre-1870 the regulation of prostitution had been small-scale and local. After 1870, and prior to the reform of the Civil Code in 1900, the relevant paragraphs of the Imperial Criminal Code overrode these local regulations. This code was largely based on Prussian law, so Sections 361/6 and 180 had been in force in Berlin and other areas under Prussian control since the late 18th century. Section 361/6 ordered the compulsory examination of any woman suspected of being a prostitute, while Section 180 stated that anyone countenancing and furthering prostitution was liable to imprisonment. As the police had in effect been controlling prostitution by the methods described earlier, this contradiction laid them open to accusations of pandering.

Before 1890 it had been impossible to discuss sexual issues openly, since both convention and the law prescribed silence on the subject between the sexes in private as well as in public. After 1890, the lapsing of the *Sozialistengesetz* coupled with the forced departure of Bismarck signalled a new freedom to express interest in social issues. Of the many *Sittlichkeitsvereine* [Morality Associations] which sprang up at this time, several were concerned with the control of prostitution and pornographic material and with generally raising moral standards in public life. With the rapid growth of cities under industrialisation and a rise in the numbers of women driven to prostitution by the lack of alternative sources of income, prostitution became more visible and less easy to control.[38] The middle-classes, already fearful of the new class of urban proletariat, came to see prostitution as a major social problem which symbolised the moral decadence of the cities. In 1891 a vicious murder, committed by a pimp and by a prostitute named Heinze while they were attempting to rob a church, brought hysteria against prostitutes to a head. Calls for the suppression of prostitution, supported by the Kaiser himself, led to the proposed amendment of Section 180. The debate was taken over by the moral lobby who attempted to extend the law to condemn all forms of vice, including censorship of entertainment, art and literature. The proposed legislation became known as the *Lex Heinze* and, although never actually passed, served as a focus for debate in parliament and press throughout the 1890s, ensuring that the issue of prostitution was very much part of public consciousness.

The Morality Associations, united in the *Allgemeine Konferenz der deutschen Sittlichkeitsvereine* [Congress of German Morality Associations], were dominated by men, particularly Protestant clergymen, and women were excluded from membership. Yet a number of equivalent organisations were founded by women. Among these were the *Verein Jugendschutz* [Association for the Protection of Youth] founded in 1888, *Verein Frauenwohl* [Women's Welfare Association] in 1889 and *Frauenverein Reform* [Women's Association for Reform] in 1895.

From the early 1890s onwards, the views of Hanna Bieber-Böhm, founder and president of the *Jugendschutz*, remained unchallenged, largely because of continued reluctance to discuss such a sensitive and therefore dangerous subject. Even a radical organisation such as the *Verein Frauenwohl*, where Bieber-Böhm was a member of the executive committee until 1899, was at first unwilling to discuss the issue. As a result, there was no counter-position to Bieber-Böhm's and the *Frauenwohl* endorsed her campaign. The petition she presented to the Berlin police chief in 1895, although it called for an end to state regulation of vice on moral grounds, shows how far removed from the Abolitionist standpoint these views were. Bieber-Böhm was heavily influenced by Pastor Weber, President of the *Konferenz der deutschen Sittlichkeitsvereine*.[39] Like Weber, Bieber-Böhm saw prostitutes themselves as the root of the evil, accepting Lombroso's theory of their innate depravity. Like Weber, she believed that they must be reformed or punished and she called for draconian measures against all prostitutes, deportation of all foreign prostitutes, suppression of erotic literature and art along with compulsory registration of anyone found to be sexually diseased. The measures thus called for, apart from the extension of compulsory registration to include diseased men as well as women, showed none of the commitment to equity and gender solidarity that was central to the Abolitionist view.

In 1894 the *Bund Deutscher Frauenvereine* [BDF: Federation of German Women's Associations] was founded as an umbrella organisation for all the various women's groups which had sprung up throughout Germany, ranging from conservative housewife circles to professional associations, some of which had become relatively radical in their demands for access to education and the professions. With this huge range of interests to cater for and the legal restrictions preventing political discussion, the BDF tended to be highly conservative. Despite this, Bieber-Böhm managed to persuade the BDF to adopt her views on the regulation of prostitution on the grounds that it was entirely appropriate that women should attempt to raise standards of morality in public life.

Despite the early receptiveness to Bieber-Böhm's ideas in the *Frauenwohl*, exposure to Abolitionist ideas during the 1890s soon led to a radical challenge on this issue. By the end of the decade, key figures within the movement had been converted to Abolitionism; Käthe Schirrmacher during a period of study in Paris, Anita Augspurg while studying law in Zurich, and Minna Cauer, President of the *Frauenwohl* were soon convinced. Together these women pressed for the adoption of more advanced ideas, shifting the emphasis of their work from social welfare to social reform.[40] In contrast to earlier German timidity towards the international women's movement, the Radicals were characterised by their openness to ideas from abroad. From 1895 onwards, *Die Frauenbewegung*, edited by Minna Cauer, reported on developments abroad, and in 1896 the Radicals organised an international conference in Berlin which was attended by 1700 delegates.

By the end of January 1899, Bieber-Böhm had been replaced by Anita Augspurg on the committee of the *Frauenwohl*, and her views on prostitution had been rejected in favour of Butler's standpoint. The *Frauenwohl* was now effectively an Abolitionist association. In 1898-9 the first branch of the Federation on German soil was founded in Berlin under the leadership of Anna Pappritz, and in 1904 local groups joined to form a German branch under the joint presidency of Katharina Scheven, Käthe Schirrmacher and Anna Pappritz. In 1898 Germany sent a delegation to the meetings of the Federation for the first time, and the names Pappritz, Schirrmacher, Bieber-Böhm, Cauer and de Tscharner appear in the list of those attending the 29th anniversary meeting of the Federation in London in 1899.

With the election of Marie Stritt to the presidency of the BDF in 1899, it became possible to challenge the dominance of Bieber-Böhm's views on prostitution. Stritt had met Butler during a visit to London in 1899 and was swiftly persuaded by her arguments. Under Stritt's presidency Abolitionists were given a sympathetic hearing, and in 1902 the BDF rejected the principle of the prosecution and regulation of prostitution, passing a resolution which called for the abolition of Section 361/6 of the Criminal Code.

German campaigners were deeply indebted to Butler's analysis and were inspired by the success of her campaign in Britain. They adopted many key elements of Abolitionist thought, not least of which are the striking degree of empathy and identification with the prostitutes, a rejection of the double moral standard and its expression in *Reglementierung*, and an analysis which placed sexual exploitation at the heart of man's oppression of women.

It was through involvement with women's morality organisations and rescue work that middle-class women came into contact with working-class women and 'fallen' women for the first time. Like Butler in Liverpool in 1860, they were absolutely horrified at men's brutality to women. Lida Gustava Heymann, the radical leader of the the Hamburg campaign, arrived at the same conclusion as the British women that, far from the two classes of women being separate as they had always been told, men's sexual licence with prostitutes, especially as it was sanctioned by the state and condoned by the popular view of man's sexual nature, brutalised and degraded the client as well as the prostitute. These men then brought their moral corruption and distorted attitudes to women into their married relations:

> Durch den Vekehr mit den reglementierten Prostitutierten erwerben sich die Männer Ansichten über das Sexualleben, die für die sittlich intakte Frau physiologisch und psychologisch ein Faustschlag sind.[41]
>
> [Through intercourse with regulated prostitutes, men form views of sexual life which, to the morally intact woman, constitute a psychological and physiological slap in the face.]

The campaign against the system of regulation in Hamburg, which by dint of its system of *Bordellierung* was most vulnerable to attack under Section 180, involved a wholesale assault on men. Their moral character was held up for public scrutiny through the discussion of scandalous rape cases against innocent victims, showing how the moral climate had been lowered by the state sanction of male vice.[42]

Even more clearly than in Britain, the battle lines were drawn up on gender lines. Abolitionism came to be seen as a female standpoint while support for regulation was male. Anna Pappritz, reporting on the Conference of the *Gesellschaft zur Bekämpfung der Geschlechtskrankheiten* [Society for the Control of Sexual Diseases] in 1903, recognised that this was indeed the case in Germany, although this was mainly due to the stupidity and self-interest of the men:

> Wenn, wie auf dem Kongreß und in zahlreichen Berichten über den Kongreß vielfach behauptet wurde, die Frauen geborene Abolitionistinnen, die Männer aber geborene Reglementaristen seien, so ist das ein Urteil, das gerade nicht gegen die Frauen spricht, denn der Abolitionismus vertritt weite und gerechte sozialpolitische

Gesichtspunkte, während der Reglementarismus eine engherzige und ungerechte Klassen- und Geschlechtsjustiz befürwortet.[43]

[If, as has frequently been maintained at the Congress and in numerous reports on the it, women are born Abolitionists and men are born Regulationists, then that verdict does not speak against women, for Abolitionism represents broad and just socio-political viewpoints, while Regulationism supports a narrow-minded and unfair form of justice based on class and gender interests.]

The male view of the women's standpoint was that it demanded an unrealistic and medically inadvisable standard of chastity for both sexes, ignoring 'natural' biological differences. The existence as well as the 'naturalness' of these differences was challenged by Pappritz, who suspected that they were simply comfortable for men rather than the expression of a law of nature:

So behaupteten sie immer wieder und wieder, daß die physiologischen Bedingungen der Geschlechter ganz verschiedene seien, der Geschlechtstrieb des Mannes verlange nach der Vereinigung mit dem Weibe, die Frau aber kenne diesen Trieb gar nicht (!!!), bei ihr wäre der Geschlechtstrieb nur Sehnsucht nach dem Kinde! [...] Und das sagen Männer, Ärzte, Naturforscher, Physiologen, deren Forscheraugen das heilige Buch der Natur erschlossen ist, die ihren Geheimnissen mit allen Mitteln der Wissenschaft nachspüren durften; sie begehen die Majestätsbeleidigung an der heiligen Schöpferkraft der Natur, zu behaupten, daß diese zwei Kategorien der Weiber schuf, 'perverse Naturen' zur Befriedigung der 'außerehelichen Bedürfnisse' des Mannes und 'mütterliche Naturen' zur Fortpflanzung der Art innerhalb der Ehe.[44]

[They [the men] claimed again and again that the physiological conditioning of the sexes is quite different, the man's sex drive having as its object union with the woman, whilst sexual drive is unknown to women (!!!), in her the sexual drive is simply a yearning for a child! [...] And that is the view of men, doctors, scientists, physiologists, to whose scientific gaze the Book of Nature is opened, who have been permitted to seek out its secrets with all the resources of Science; these men dare insult the holy creative force of Nature by claiming that she created two categories of women: 'perverted natures' for the satisfaction of the extra-marital needs of men, and 'motherly natures' for the reproduction of the species within marriage.]

In a neat reversal of the ideology of *Geschlechtscharakter*, Pappritz attacks men for their irrationality through their adherence to this outdated, ineffective mode of controlling VD, accusing them of being blinded by their own interests and having no broader grasp of wider social issues:

Der Standpunkt der Herrenmoral hat durch seine Jahrtausende währende Gültigkeit eine so suggestive Macht und Wirksamkeit auf das Gedankenleben des Mannes ausgeübt, daß alle Gründe der Logik, ja die Evidenz der Thatsachen an diesem Bollwerk zerschellen. [*Herrenmoral*, p.13]

[The standpoint of 'gentlemen's morality' has, through a reign of many thousands of years, exercised such subtle power and influence over the intellectual life of the male that all logical arguments, even the evidence of the facts cannot overcome the barrier of their prejudice.]

Just as Butler had used her knowledge of what happened in practice on the continent to oppose the extension of the CD Acts, so Pappritz used evidence from Britain and other countries where regulation had been abolished to support her points and underline the illogicality of male arguments.

Despite the force and vehemence of the German campaign, it remained impotent due to lack of female influence and significant male support. The lack of a tradition of co-operation between the classes was even stronger in Germany than in England, as the working-classes were seen as the natural class enemy of the bourgeoisie, an attitude underlined by the *Sozialistengesetz.* Yet even if these class antagonisms had been more fully overcome, the working-class men who had proved such powerful allies of Butler in England lacked political influence in Germany due to the differential weighting given to the votes of the propertied classes. In fact, measured in terms of legislation, the women's campaign had no effect at all, as the next legal change came at the start of the First World War and aimed at even harsher controls on women and the provision of a pool of prostitutes to cater for the masculine needs of the troops. Legislation in line with the Abolitionists' demands was not introduced until the more liberal years of the Weimar Republic, only to be reversed in 1933 when the Nazis came to power.[45]

Yet the importance of the campaign against the state regulation of prostitution cannot be measured by what it achieved in legislative terms, nor can the movements be dismissed as the forerunners of sexual repressiveness and state intervention in private morals, although these were undoubtedly unlooked-for consequences of Butler's campaign in Britain. Identifying these campaigners as 'radical' is not unproblematic, as they did perpetuate the myth of female moral purity, positioning women in both countries as the helpless victims of men and thus denying them any possibility of historical agency. Butler's appeal to working-class men to rise up and protect 'their' women – although pragmatic and effective – reinforced the idea of female dependence on male strength. Despite her own impatience with 'the fatuous idea that you can oblige human beings to be moral by force',[46] Butler's involvement in the White Slave campaign and initial endorsement of the National Vigilance Association made the Criminal Law Amendment Act of 1885 possible, 'a particularly nasty piece of omnibus legislation' [WALKOWITZ, p.85] which undoubtedly did allow a greater level of state interference in private morality, disproportionately affecting women. Pappritz, too, despite her curdling condemnation of men, supported marriage as a way of forcing men to take responsibility for the consequences of the sexual act, which she saw as the maintenance of wife and children. She was therefore opposed to contraception, which she saw as the removal of a powerful brake on men's sexuality and a means of making women even more sexually available to men.

In Germany as in Britain, the women became politicised as a result of their involvement in the campaigns. Their disillusionment with men, their refusal to accept the double moral standard or the arbitrary separation of women into the categories of Madonna and whore as being a 'natural law' undermined the ideology of 'separate spheres'. The sense of sisterhood served to blur class distinction, even leading to bourgeois German women declaring common cause with their class enemies on this issue. They identified men as being weak, irrational, selfish and ultimately dangerous to women both morally and physically, and they sought to reduce their influence as far as possible. Some women even equated marriage with prostitution, showing how a marriage made from economic necessity was morally no different from selling oneself on the streets.

In both countries the campaign also raised public awareness of the dangers of venereal disease to the health and fertility of women and their offspring. Although these had been known in medical circles since 1872, public awareness had been suppressed as doctors colluded with infected men to hide the symptoms of the disease, while lying to infected women about the nature of their illness. Once the link between sexual licence and female infertility, illness and the congenital blindness of infants was known, many women began to fear marriage and to mistrust even further the medical profession which had placed the sexual needs of men above the health of women and children. Prostitution, justified on the grounds that it preserved the purity of the home and protected the virtue of innocent wives, was now revealed to be the source of infection, suffering and death to just those wives and children.

In both Britain and Germany, women's eyes were opened to the moral failings of men and the injustice of the legal, political and social system which was based on the ideology of separate spheres. In both countries their response was radical and far-reaching. As part of the moral mission of women, they began to demand women's involvement in the public sphere in areas where men's moral character disqualified them. Thus women demanded access to education and to medical training so that girls should be spared the corrupting influence of male teachers and the shame of examination by male doctors. They demanded political influence, economic independence and legal reform so that women should no longer be delivered over to the 'protection' of men or faced with the choice between 'beggary or *shame*'.

Notes and References

[1] The previous studies principally referred to in this paper are, in chronological order of publication: Richard J. Evans, *The Feminist Movement in Germany 1894-1933* (London: Sage, 1976; <*cited as*: EVANS (a)>); Richard J. Evans, 'Prostitution, State and Society in Imperial Germany', in *Past and Present*, no.70 (Feb. 1976; <*cited as*: EVANS (b)>); Ute Gerhard, *Verhältnisse und Verhinderungen. Frauenarbeit, Familie und Rechte der Frauen im 19. Jahrhundert.* (Frankfurt am Main: Suhrkamp, 1978; <*cited as*: GERHARD>); Judith R. Walkowitz, 'Male Vice and Feminist Virtue: Feminism and the Politics of Prostitution in Nineteenth Century Britain', in *History Workshop Journal* Vol 13, 1982, pp.79-93, <*cited as*:

WALKOWITZ>); Louise Newman (ed.) *Men's ideas/women's realities: Popular Science, 1870-1915* (Oxford: Pergamon Press, 1985, pp.77-86; <*cited as*: NEWMAN>); Sheila Jeffries (ed.), *The Sexuality Debates* (New York, London: Routledge & Kegan Paul, 1987; <*cited as*: JEFFRIES>); Elisabeth Meyer-Renschhausen, *Weibliche Kultur und soziale Arbeit. Eine Geschichte der Frauenbewegung am Beispiel Bremens 1810-1927* (Cologne, Vienna: Böhlau, 1989; <*cited as*: MEYER-RENSCHHAUSEN>); Susan Kingsley-Kent, *Sex and Suffrage in Britain 1860-1914* (London: Routledge, 1990; <*cited as*: KINGSLEY-KENT>.

[2] Michel Foucault, *The History of Sexuality Volume I* (London: Penguin, 1990) p.116.

[3] *ibid.*, pp.120-127.

[4] See KINGSLEY-KENT, pp.47 ff. See also Barabara Ehrenreich and Deirdre English, *For Her Own Good. 150 Years of the Experts Advice to Women.* (New York: Anchor Press/ Doubleday, 1978), pp.108ff.

[5] See WALKOWITZ for a detailed discussion of tensions between the feminist goals of women's empowerment and the aim of social purity, which often ended in the suppression of vice, frequently to the detriment of individual women.

[6] Karin Hausen: 'Family and role division: The polarisation of sexual stereotypes in the nineteenth century – an aspect of the dissociation of work and family life', in Richard Evans and W.R. Lee (eds), *The German Family* (London: Croom Helm, 1981), pp.51-83, (p.56).

[7] J.H. Campe, *Väterlicher Rath für meine Thochter, Ein Gegenstück zum Theophron. Der erwachsenen weiblichen Jugend gewidmet* (Braunschweig, 1789) extracts of pages 5-24; 182-191, quoted in GERHARD, p.375.

[8] J.G. Fichte, *Grundlage des Naturrechts*, 1796. English translation first published in 1889, available as: 'First Appendix to the Science of Rights. Fundamental Principles of the Rights of Family', in *The Science of Rights Translated from the German by A.E. Kroeger* (London: Routledge & Kegan Paul, 1970; <*cited as*: FICHTE-KROEGER>.

[9] See GERHARD for a full discussion of the laws affecting women in nineteenth-century Germany.

[10] Quoted in KINGSLEY-KENT p.35.

[11] See GERHARD, p.373.

[12] J.G. Schlosser, *Briefe über die Gesetzgebung überhaupt und den Entwurf des Preußischen Gesetzbuches insbesondere* (Frankfurt, 1789), quoted in GERHARD, p.87.

[13] John Ruskin, 'Of Queens' Gardens', in *Sesame and Lilies* (London: George Allen, 1891; first published in 1865), p.115.

[14] Lorenz von Stein, *Die Frau auf dem Gebiet der Nationalökonomie* (Stuttgart, 1886) extracts, pp.1; 16-25; 33-55; 90-118, quoted in GERHARD, pp.311-324, p.311.

[15] William Acton, *Functions and Disorders of the Reproductive Organs* (London: John Churchill, 1857), quoted in JEFFRIES, p.61. Lucy Bland notes that the original parenthesis read 'happily for them', but that this was replaced by the wording 'happily for society' in the fifth edition published in 1871 – see Lucy Bland, *Banishing the Beast. English Feminism and Sexual Morality 1885-1914* (London: Penguin, 1995), p.55.

[16] Henry Maudsley, 'Sex in Mind and Education', 1874; quoted in NEWMAN, p.81.

[17] See NEWMAN, p.77.

[18] See Nancy F. Cott, 'Passionlessness: An Interpretation of Victorian and Sexual Ideology, 1790-1850', in *Signs*, vol.4, 1979, pp.219-36.

[19] William Acton, *Functions and Disorders*, quoted in JEFFRIES, p.61.

[20] C. Lombroso and G. Ferrero, *Das Weib als Verbrecherin und Prostituierte. Anthropologische Studien, gegründet auf eine Darstellung der Biologie des normalen Weibes*, translated by H. Kurella (Hamburg, 1894).

[21] William Acton, 'Prostitution Considered in its Social and Sanitary Aspects' (1870), quoted in JEFFRIES, pp.42-56, (p.42).

[22] William Lecky, *History of European Morals* (1869), quoted in KINGSLEY-KENT, p.62.

[23] For an overview of 19th century medical knowledge and the treatment of venereal diseases see Allan M. Brandt, *No Magic Bullet. A Social History of Venereal Disease in the United States since 1880,* (Oxford: OUP, 1987; first pub. New York, 1985), pp.3-51.

[24] See MEYER-RENSCHHAUSEN, pp.315-316.

[25] See KINGSLEY-KENT, p.10.

[26] Report of the Royal Commission upon the Administration and Operation of the Contagious Diseases Acts (London 1871), I, 17. Quoted in Keith Thomas, 'The Double Standard', in *Journal of the History of Ideas* vol. 20 (Lancaster, Pa., and New York, 1959), pp.195-216, (p.198).

[27] Writing in *The Dawn*, (November 1894, p.2) Butler makes the analogy between the campaign for the abolition of slavery and the abolition of regulation of vice clear, pointing out that '[i]n the slave states of America slavery could never have been successfully combatted if it had been made penal to be a slave and to labour as a slave. There is much analogy with the present case. If we bring women and girl prostitutes within the penalities of the law for the sin they are committing or have been, as is often the case, forced to commit, we shall only add one more injustice to the great mass of injustice and oppression which now exists.'

[28] Josephine Butler, *Sursum Corda* (Liverpool, 1871) p.33, quoted in KINGSLEY-KENT, p.69.

[29] *Sursum corda*, p.36, quoted in KINGSLEY-KENT, p.71.

[30] Josephine Butler, *The New Era* (Liverpool, 1972), pp.51-52, quoted in KINGSLEY-KENT, p.75.

[31] The Ladies National Association, Eighth Annual Report 1877, p.26, quoted in Kingsley Kent, p.77.

[32] Josephine Butler, *The New Era* (Liverpool, 1872).

[33] Fourth Annual Report of the British, Continental and General Federation for the Abolition of Government Regulation of Prostitution 1878-1879, p.26; Fawcett Library, London.

[34] *The Dawn,* vol.1 (May 1888) p.4.

[35] See EVANS (a), p.30.

[36] Josephine Butler, private letter, 3.5.1895, Fawcett Library, London.

[37] For a fuller account of Guillaume Schack's activities, see MEYER-RENSCHHAUSEN, p.275 ff. In the Fifth Annual Report of the Federation, 1879-1880, Schack was given great credit for her isolated bravery and pioneering work in an unenlightened country: 'The energy and courage of the Countess Guillaume Schack are beyond praise'.

[38] Evans gives the following figures for population growth of major German cities: Berlin grew from a population of 172,000 in1850 to 2,000,000 in 1910; Hamburg from 130,000 to 1,100,000. See EVANS (b), p108.

[39] Writing in 1894, Butler criticised Weber's stance, pointing out that his declared commitment to the equal treatment of men and women in fact aims at the harsh punishment of prostitutes who do not submit to being 'rescued' along with pimps and procurers, while continuing to

ignore the role of the man in the transaction. Butler concludes: 'M. Weber is a man of great energy, and his authority is considerable in his Association. He is aiming decidedly at what is good, but seems to be very much impregnated with a kind of theocratic spirit, and has his share of the almost universal inheritance of German men – *contempt for women*.' See *The Dawn*, Nov. 1894, No.25, p.5. Writing privately a year later she comments: 'I have not the strength to tell you of the complications arising from the influx of German male influence into our work.' (Fawcett Library, correspondence 3.5.1895).

[40] See EVANS (a), p.44 ff.

[41] Lida Gustava Heymann, 'Die rechtliche Grundlage und die moralische Wirkung der Prostitution', in *Die Frauenbewegung* 9. Jg 1903, pp.162-164, p.163, quoted in MEYER-RENSCHHAUSEN, p.305.

[42] For a full discussion of the Hamburg campaign against *Bordellierung*, see EVANS (a).

[43] Anna Pappritz, *Herrenmoral* (Leipzig: Verlag der Frauen-Rundschau, 1903; <*cited as*: *Herrenmoral*>), p.18.

[44] *Herrenmoral*, p.14. Pappritz goes on to question why, even if the sex drive of women were merely a yearning for a child, men's needs should be met while those of unmarried women should be left unfulfilled and why women who *did* give in to their desire for children outside wedlock should be seen as 'unnatural' and punished by society: *Wenn aber thatsächlich die Frau nur die 'Sehnsucht nach dem Kind' hätte, dürfte sie nicht mit dem gleichen Rechte Erfüllung dieser Sehnsucht fordern, mit dem der Mann die Befriedigung seiner Triebe verlangt.*

[45] See EVANS (b), pp.127-128.

[46] Josephine Butler, quoted in WALKOWITZ, p.87.

Three letters to Jethro Bithell, from the correspondence held in the Brotherton Library Bithell Collection [1]

Jethro Bithell has been out of fashion for a while. Just as tastes in literature change down the years, so one generation's critical certainties do not command automatic respect from the next – and Bithell's literary judgments are a case in point. His high opinion of Carossa (nicely illustrated in the introduction to the third of the letters here edited) by contrast with his negative response to German Expressionism[2] is a good example: who, though, reads Hans Carossa nowadays? On the other hand, in the context of Modern European Language Studies generally – and most certainly in the field of German Literature – posterity is bound to judge Bithell as having been one of Britain's most prolific and influential scholars this century. Eloquent testimony to his range and productivity is borne by his *Translations from the Minnesingers* (1909) which gained him early entry into *Who's Who*, his compendium *Germany, A Companion to German Studies* (1932)[3], his magisterial *Modern German Literature 1880–1950* (1939, [3]1959) and the three *Anthologies of German Poetry* which he published during his retirement – not to mention his dictionary, several other verse anthologies and his publications in the field of language teaching.[4] As a teacher and writer he was very influential, and his circle of literary acquaintance was enormous.

Born into a Lancastrian farming family in 1878, Bithell attended Owens College in the Victoria University, Manchester, graduating with first class honours in Modern Languages in 1900, and he completed his MA in 1903. After graduation he continued his studies briefly at the universities of Munich and Copenhagen. His first academic appointment was to a Lectureship in Modern Languages at Salford Technical College. Soon, however, he was offered an appointment as Lecturer in German at his home university (1904), and he remained in Manchester for a further six years until, in 1910, he took up the post of Head of the Department of German at Birkbeck College, London. He was promoted to a Readership in 1921, and he 'retired', aged 60, in 1938. The challenge of teaching German Language and Literature within Britain has never lacked a certain *frisson*, but, given the implications of two World Wars fought during their lifetime against our German cousins, it was a peculiarly difficult challenge for Bithell's generation. We can only admire his – and their – commitment and perseverance. It is a most fitting tribute to Bithell's work as Teacher that his name is memorialised in the annual Bithell Lecture and in the Bithell Dissertation Series, both supervised by the London University Institute of Germanic Studies.

After his death in 1962 Bithell's prolific correspondence and manuscripts (concerned almost exclusively with modern European literature – French, Belgian, Dutch and Flemish no less than German and Austrian) were divided between the Institute of Germanic Studies (London University), and the University of Leeds. The gift to Leeds owes everything to the friendship Bithell shared with Alexander Gillies who, during his years as Professor of German at Leeds (1945-1973) was also for periods Germanic Editor of the *Modern Language Review* and General Editor of the *Blackwell's German Texts Series*, in both of which Bithell published. During the earlier years of Gillies' Headship at Leeds Bithell acted as External Examiner.

The Leeds Bithell Collection consists mainly of letters received in the course of Bithell's compilation of the following works: *Contemporary German Poetry* (1909; – see the first letter edited below); *Contemporary Belgian Poetry* (1911); *Contemporary French Poetry* (1912); *Emile Verhaeren* (1914, translated from the biography by Stefan Zweig); *Contemporary Belgian Literature* (1915); *Contemporary Flemish Poetry* (1917); *Modern German Literature* (1939); and *An Anthology of German Poetry, 1880 - 1940* (1941; – see the second letter edited below).[5] Among the main correspondents are Felix Braun, Richard Dehmel, Else Lasker-Schüler, Gregoire Leroy, Albert Mockel and Emile Verhaeren.

Editorial principles

The paragraphing and orthography of the originals are preserved (including the use of upper and lower case).

Hyphenation is used only where found in the original.

Punctuation has been adjusted according to modern conventions, when appropriate.

Underlinings have been retained except for the titles of books in Werfel's letter, where they are replaced by single quotation marks; these are used throughout in place of double quotation marks.

Alfred Mombert to Jethro Bithell (6th September 1909)

edited by Susan Bollinger

Alfred Mombert was born into a wealthy Jewish family in Karlsruhe on February 6th, 1872. He studied Law in Berlin, Heidelberg, Leipzig and Munich before establishing himself as a lawyer in Heidelberg in 1899. He withdrew from the legal profession as early as 1906, however, and devoted himself to writing poetry, studying the natural sciences and philosophy, and travelling.

Mombert has said of his writing that he strove to unite all the sounds of the cosmos in his poetry, to create a picture of the heights to which human feelings can aspire and the depths into which they can fall.[6] In October 1940 Mombert, who had served in the German army during the First World War, was arrested along with 6,500 Jews from Baden and deported by the SS to an internment camp in the Pyrenees. He was by this time already a sick man. Thanks to the efforts of Hans Carossa and Hans Reinhart, who interceded on his behalf, he was transferred to an internment sanatorium in Idron in April 1941 and finally allowed to leave Germany for Switzerland in October of the same year. He died on April 8, 1942 in Winterthur.

In 1909 Jethro Bithell was completing work on a volume of contemporary German poetry in translation, the precursor of similar anthologies in other languages and noteworthy in that it contains some of the first translations into English from Rainer Maria Rilke's work.[7]

Bithell planned to include a selection of Mombert's verse and, for this purpose, he had sent Mombert sample translations of some of the poems he wished to include.[8] The letter transcribed here is Mombert's reply.[9] Mombert refers in particular to one of his works, *Der himmlische Zecher*, in which, according to Bithell, 'the quintessence of Mombert is offered by himself'.[10] *Der himmlische Zecher* was first published in Berlin in 1909, in four books, to which a fifth was added in 1922 (Leipzig) and the final selection, compiled shortly before Mombert's death, was published in 1951 (Wiesbaden).[11] Many of Mombert's manuscripts were destroyed in the Second World War.

Description of MS 386/199

The letter is written on both sides of a single sheet of writing paper measuring 22 x 29.5 cm. The paper is cream in colour and bears the watermark 'Necker Bank Post'. The letter had been folded in four originally, and obviously refolded, and there is slight discoloration on the folds and signs of wear, including a slight tear on the right-hand side. There is a smudge at the bottom right-hand corner of the first page, and the nib of the pen has scratched occasionally, causing some blurring of one or two letters. Mombert writes in *Kurrent* (but Roman script for quotations in English) in a distinctive hand which is legible for the most part, causing hesitation in only one or two instances. There is an irregular margin at the left-hand side of the paper, 2 cm. wide at the beginning of the text and 3 cm. wide by the bottom of the first side. The first line of the text measures 18 cm., the last line on the first side 19 cm. The letter continues on the reverse, where the discrepancy in margin width is not quite so great.

TEXT

Recto:

Heidelberg, 6 IX 09

Sehr geehrter Herr Bithell!

Freundlichen Dank für die Übersendung der Übersetzungsproben, die ich anbei zurücksende. Sie scheinen mir ganz gelungen.[12] Da Sie den 'himmlischen Zecher' kennen, wissen Sie, auf welche Seite meiner lyrischen Produktion ich den Nachdruck lege, und daß ich kein Verfertiger 'schöner Gedichte' bin. Vielleicht gelingt es auch Ihrer kleinen Auswahl, dem englischen Leser eine Ahnung von dem religiösen-philosophischen Gehalt meiner Dichtung zu geben.

Zu Ihren Fragen übergehend:

Unter 'webt mit seinem Schädel' ist das taktmäßige Nicken mit dem

Kopfe zu verstehen, wie es häufig bei alten, idiotisch gewordenen Personen vorkommt. Auch Pferde, die den Kopf auf und abwärts bewegen,

Verso:

nennt man 'Weber'.[13] Ob die von Ihnen versuchte Wendung 'making a shuttle of her head' verständlich sein wird, ist mir fraglich. Vielleicht haben Sie für die genannte Kopfbewegung ein anderes Äquivalent in Ihrer Sprache. Das ganze Gedicht ist ein Rembrandtsches Helldunkel-Gemälde, wobei auf die Betonung der mysteriösen Licht-Quelle alles ankommt. Die Bezeichnung 'das Licht' (wohl auch 'the light') reicht vom Talglicht bis ins Mysterium; ich glaube daher, daß Ihr Zusatz 'Candle' in der Überschrift unbedingt wegzulassen ist; ferner scheint mir auch der Ausdruck 'penny dip' an dieser nachdrücklichsten Stelle des ganzen Gedichtes viel zu nah bezeichnend, beschreibend. Freilich müßten Sie dann den Reim opfern, mit dem Sie allerdings sehr schöne Wirkung erzielen.

Ganz gut ist es vielleicht, wenn Sie 'Schlafend trägt man mich' an den Anfang stellen – oder ans Ende![14]

Mit freundlichem Gruß

[Mombert]

Franz Werfel to Jethro Bithell (4 April 1940)
edited by John Hogg

In April 1940 Jethro Bithell was in retirement. He had left his post as Reader in German at Birkbeck College in London two years previously and was spending his retirement writing books and articles, and acting as an external examiner for various schools and universities.

The reason for Bithell's brief correspondence with Werfel (1890–1945) in early 1940 relates to the preparation of his *Anthology of German Poetry, 1880-1940* – as is confirmed by the first sentence in Werfel's letter, approving Bithell's particular selection of his verse (*Ich beuge mich Ihren Gründen und stimme der von Ihnen getroffenen Auswahl gerne zu*).[15] The remainder of the letter contains explanations for certain poetical nuances and a brief list of his published poetry collections – presumably the information which Bithell had asked for.

Werfel was writing from his temporary home in France – Moulin Gris – a converted lighthouse in Sanary-sur-Mer, a Provençal fishing village. In 1940 Sanary was swollen with German and Austrian émigrés including Wilhelm Herzog, Ludwig Marcuse, Robert Neumann and Friedrich Wolf, to name but a few.[16] An Austrian Jew and opponent of Nazism, Werfel had been living and working in France since the *Anschluß* of March 1938. His early volumes of poetry, *Der Weltfreund* (1911), *Wir sind* (1913) and *Einander* (1915), condemning wars and the politics which led to them, had made him one of the leaders of that modern movement in which the spirit of youth, protesting against the hypocrisy and dehumanising tendencies of pre-war society, found expression. To attempt to continue his work from within the Greater German *Reich* would have been impossible.

The postscript, advising Bithell to contact Otto Pick in London for further information, points to Werfel's uncertainty regarding the immediate future.[17] His position in Francc, and that of his wife, Alma, was precarious. The previous September, following the German invasion of Poland and the French declaration of war, Werfel had been interviewed by the police. No further action was taken, but the writing was on the wall. The Werfels left Sanary following the capitulation of Belgium in May 1940. Travelling with Heinrich Mann and his wife, they made their way to Portugal and thence sailed to the USA, reaching New York in October.

Description of MS 386/189

The letter comprises a single sheet of plain, unlined paper with dimensions 27 cm. x 21 cm., i.e. slightly shorter than standard A4 (29.5 cm. x 21 cm.). The paper is thin, of poor quality, and has no watermark. The handwriting on the reverse is visible through the paper. The MS, dated April 1940, has yellowed over time and has several minor creases extending from top left to bottom right. The overall condition, however, is good.

The hand-written area on the front of the MS has dimensions of approx. 25 cm. x 18-20 cm. – the varying width arising from a variable left margin (3-4 cm. for lines 1-20, 1.5 cm. for lines 21-25). There is no appreciable right margin. The reverse of the MS has a hand-written area of 13 cm. x 16 cm., located in the upper half of the page. Right and left margins are 2.5. cm each. There is a top margin of approx. 2 cm.

The handwriting (written with a pen using dark blue ink) has a cursive ductus, legible throughout. It exhibits, however, some marked inconsistencies: upper case letters P, L and S vary significantly (cf. *Portofino/Prag, Landschaft/Litanei* and *Strom/Sie*). There is no evidence of either erasure or palimpsest. One word in the second paragraph, which appears to read *nach* between *bis* and *in*, has been crossed out.

TEXT

Recto:

écrit en allemand[18]

Sanary (Var)
Moulin Gris
4/4 40

Dear Mr Bithell

Ich beuge mich Ihren Gründen und stimme der von Ihnen getroffenen Auswahl gerne zu. Ich bitte Sie aber, keine Angst zu haben, wenn ein oder das andere Gedicht etwas schwieriger erscheint. ('Litanei von den Zimmern der Verstorbenen'[19]). Aus meiner eigenen Jugend weiß ich, daß gewisse Dunkelheiten in einem Gedicht die Wirkung verstärken. 'Der

Held'[20] ist nicht ironisch gemeint, sondern als Gegensatz zum Kriegshelden. Dieses Gedicht aber bleibt heute besser fort.

Zu: 'Elegie an einen Jugendgefährten'.[21] Die Heimatstadt ist Prag. Hundertmastig = Hunderttürmig. Der bescheidene Strom ist die Moldau mit ihren kleinen Dampfschiffen, Schleppern und Frachtkähnen, die bis in die Nordsee fahren, zur Freude der Knabenphantasie. Der Freund ist im Weltkrieg gefallen. Deshalb nenne ich mich selbst, der den Weltkrieg überlebt hat, einen Renegaten des Todes. Die Landschaft des Gedichtes ist die italienische Küste bei Portofino.

Die Titel meiner Gedichtbücher: 1911 *Der Weltfreund*, 1913 *Wir sind*, 1915 *Einander*, 1916 *Gesänge aus den drei Reichen*, 1919 *Der Gerichtstag*, 1922 *Beschwörungen*, (1920 *Arien* nur in bibliophiler Ausgabe), 1926 *Gedichte* als erster Band der *Gesammelten Werke*, 1935 *Schlaf und Erwachen* (in drei Teilen).

Verso:

Die gegenwärtige Adresse von Alfr[ed] Wolfenstein[22] kenne ich leider nicht.

Mit bestem Dank und Gruß

Ihr

[Franz Werfel]

Wenn Sie etwas Näheres über meine Gedichte erfahren wollen, so wenden Sie sich bitte an Herrn Otto Pick, 35 Russel Road, London W14, der ein Prager Dichter ist und einer der besten Kenner zeitgenössischer Lyrik.

Hans Carossa to Jethro Bithell (9th May 1949)

edited by Claire Harder

Hans Carossa was a direct coeval of Bithell's – born in 1878 in Tölz, Southern Bavaria. Having studied medicine and practised in Passau and Munich, he volunteered as an army medical officer in 1914 at the outbreak of the First World War. Carossa's first publication to make any impression was a volume of war reminiscences drawn from the Romanian campaign entitled *Rumänisches Tagebuch* (1924).[23] Most of Carossa's work has autobiographical reference – such as his *Eine Kindheit* and *Verwandlungen einer Jugend*, published together in 1933. In 1941 Carossa accepted the presidency of the National Socialist 'Europäischer Schriftstellerverband'. His account of this in *Ungleiche Welten* (1951) deals frankly with this point in his career and the whole period of Nazi rule. In his later years Carossa, never a prolific writer, produced only a few stories. He died aged 78 in 1956.[24]

Amongst the Bithell holdings at Leeds are three items of correspondence from Hans Carossa.[25] Bithell's contact with German authors such as Carossa began during the course of the compilation of his study: *Modern German Literature* (1939) and his *Anthology of German Poetry, 1880-1940* (1941). Carossa himself wrote many letters during his lifetime to friends, colleagues and fellow-authors including Hermann Hesse, Hugo von Hofmannstahl, Alfred Mombert and Rainer Maria Rilke – which reflects the varied cultural and philosophical range of his personal writings. This correspondence is extensively documented in a three volume collection, *Briefe / Hans Carossa,* published by Carossa's daughter, Eva Kampmann-Carossa.[26]

Although the correspondence between Carossa and Bithell held in Leeds is brief, Carossa's letter of 9th May 1949 is valuable for the information it reveals about their personal and professional relationship. Carossa had three main reasons for writing: to thank Bithell for the introductory chapter to his Blackwell edition of *Verwandlungen einer Jugend,* likewise for his tribute in the volume *Gruß der Insel,* and also to thank him for his representations on behalf of the writer Ernst Bertram. Carossa also refers to family-members: his wife, their son Hans Wilhelm, and their daughter Eva (Kampmann-Carossa, future editor of his letters).

Bithell's admiration for Carossa is exemplified in his tribute in *Gruß der Insel,* the volume compiled by the Insel Verlag to commemorate Carossa's seventieth birthday.[27] In his essay 'Carossa in England', Bithell discusses Carossa's importance in the curricula of English Schools and Universities. Amongst the chosen texts was *Eine Kindheit* which, Bithell states, had a powerful effect on English students because, when reading this contemporary text, they felt that they were becoming involved with important contemporary issues: Goethe's works represented nothing more than museum pieces to them, but Carossa's stories were alive and real. Bithell goes on to comment that the students were curious to find out whether Carossa had survived the war:

> [sie] waren hell begeistert, als ich zum Beweis von Carossas leiblicher Gegenwart in einer zerrütteten Welt ihre Schulbücherei um einen Briefumschlag bereicherte, der in seiner eigenen wohlbekannten, noch immer festen und kühnen Handschrift meinen Namen trug (*Gruß der Insel*, p.38).

Bithell is eager to emphasise that Carossa's works are in no way sympathetic toward Nazism: 'In Carossas Schriften läßt sich keinerlei Spur nazistischer Doktrin finden' (*Gruß der Insel*, p.40), and he praises him for his Englishness:

> Carossas Einstellung zum Krieg und seinen Auswirkungen ist wiederum ganz und gar englisch [...] Ganz offenbar englisch ist Carossas Art, von den Beziehungen der Geschlechter zu sprechen. Nach der hektischen Sensationslust und zuweilen auch dem Schmutz in deutschen Romanen, die in den vergangenen dreißig Jahren der großen Masse der englischen Leser als die Auslese der deutschen Literatur vorgelegt wurden, fühlt man sich erleichtert, wenn man bei Carossa eine englische Zurückhaltung und Zartheit in der Behandlung der Beziehungen zwischen Mann und Frau findet (*Gruß der Insel*, pp.43-44).

As well as including Carossa in his studies of modern German literature, Bithell also prepared student editions of *Eine Kindheit* and *Verwandlungen einer Jugend*.[28] Carossa's letter of 9 May 1949 clearly demonstrates the personal and professional respect and admiration which were shared by Jethro Bithell and Hans Carossa.

Description of MS 386/33/1

The letter comprises one piece of light blue stationery with writing in dark blue ink on both sides. The letter is still in very good condition with only minimal fading where it has been folded into quarters. The letter's legibility has not been affected by smudging or ageing of the ink, and any problems of decipherment can be attributed to Carossa's use of *Kurrent* and somewhat sloppy handwriting. The final paragraph of the letter is particularly difficult to decipher as the writer has condensed several sentences into a very short space in order to avoid using another page. This difficulty is also exacerbated by the scribbled deletion of one word towards the end which adds confusion to the clarity of the text.

The page measures 29.5 cm x 21 cm, and all of the space has been used except for an approx. 2 cm left-hand margin (on both sides).

MS 386/33/2

The envelope is of the same light blue stationery as used for the letter and is written in the same dark blue ink. The envelope is also in good condition with only minimal signs of ageing around the edges. The envelope measures 16 cm x 11 cm. There are three stamps in the right hand top corner – two have the value of 5 *Pfennigs* and one of 20 *Pfennigs*. The two postmarks are faint but appear to read 'Schalding 10/5/49'. The name Rittsteig bei Passau is imprinted on the flap.

ENVELOPE:

Front:

Professor
Jethro Bithell
Trevergy, 17 Mennaye Road

England Penzance Cornwall

Reverse:

Hans Carossa
RITTSTEIG
BEI PASSAU
Post: Schalding, Nieder-Bayern
U.S.A. - Zone

TEXT

Recto:

Rittsteig bei Passau, 9. Mai 1949

Sehr verehrter, lieber Herr Professor Bithell,

vor drei Tagen kam die deutsche Ausgabe der 'Verwandlungen einer Jugend', von Basil Blackwell aus Oxford gesandt und während ich mit großem Vergnügen Ihre knappen treffenden Anmerkungen (Notes) lese, wird mir wieder so recht bewußt, daß Ihr Beitrag im 'Gruß der Insel', der eine so außerordentliche Freude und Überraschung für mich war, noch immer unbedankt geblieben ist, d.h. keine schriftliche Danksagung gefunden hat. Es wird Sie kaum verwundern, wenn ich Ihnen gestehe, daß mich in Ihrer wohlwollenden und eingehenden Abhandlung kein Satz tiefer bewegt hat als jene einfache-klare auf Seite 42: [']Wenn man als Engländer C.[Carossa] liest, hat man das unbedingte Gefühl, daß er einer von unserer Art ist.'[29] Wie sehr ich empfinde, was dieses Wort im Munde eines Engländers bedeutet, werden Sie merken, wenn Ihnen einmal das Buch in die Hände gelangt, das mich noch immer beschäftigt; es ist darin auch viel die Rede von unserem ländlichen Leben während der Kriegszeit.[30] Mein Sohn hielt mich damals von Tag zu Tag über die englischen Berichte auf dem Laufenden, und es ist keine Übertreibung, wenn ich sage, daß im Spätsommer 1940, als unsere Zeitungen wie von einer selbstverständlichen Sache von der bevorstehenden Landung in England sprachen, wir tatsächlich mit größter Sorge auf die neuen

Verso:

Meldungen warteten. Daß ich mir mit dem neuen Buch Zeit lasse, mich nicht zu einer vorzeitigen Veröffentlichung drängen lasse, dafür setze ich gerade bei Ihnen ein Verständnis voraus; wie oft, bei Stellen, an denen mir besonders viel liegt, habe ich Sie mir als Leser gewünscht! Es erfordert ein ungewöhnliches Verantwortungsgefühl, über Erlebnisse aus der jüngsten Vergangenheit zu berichten; es soll doch möglichst *sine ira et studio* geschehen und ein plastisches Bild von allgemeiner Gültigkeit werden. Erlassen aber kann ich mir diese Aufgabe nicht; es müßte auch meinen Freunden sonderbar vorkommen, wenn ein Autor, der so gern von seinem eigenen Leben erzählt, gerade über diese ereignisreichsten Jahre schweigend hinwegginge.

Unsere Eva, die übermorgen in München ihre englische Dolmetscherprüfung macht, würde gewiß einen eigenen Brief für Sie beilegen, wenn sie wüßte, daß ich an Sie schreibe. Wir haben, im Verein mit meiner Frau und meinem Sohn, während des vergangenen Winters oft von Ihnen gesprochen; wenn ich nicht irre, war auch einmal von einer größeren Arbeit über Robert Browning die Rede, von der ich nur leider nicht weiß, ob es eine Übertragung ins Deutsche gibt.[31]

Herzlich danken möchte ich Ihnen auch für Ihr warmes Eintreten zugunsten Ernst Bertrams.[32] Zum Glück ist Mr.Birley[33] ein durchaus gerechter, wohlwollender Mann, der auch z.B. Bertrams Nietzsche Buch kennt und schätzt. Seit längerer Zeit darf Ernst B.[Bertram] jedenfalls wieder publizieren und ich hoffe, das Übrige wird ebenfalls bald in Ordnung kommen. Die stärksten Widerstände gehen leider von deutscher Seite selbst aus; das ist bei uns immer so. Nun verzeihen Sie, bitte, daß der Ausdruck meiner Dankbarkeit und meiner Freude so spät zu Ihnen kommt! Mit allen guten Wünschen für Sie, für Ihr Wirken und Ihr ganzes Haus grüßt Sie Ihr Hans Carossa.

Notes and References

1 This study is indebted to the account of Bithell's work and of the Leeds Bithell Collection given by John S. Andrews, 'Jethro Bithell (1878-1962)', in *University of Leeds Review*, vol. 8, 1962-3, pp.146-153 <*cited as*: ANDREWS>.

2 Bithell was particularly dismissive of Georg Trakl: 'It is only necessary to read a few poems [... to gain ...] an impression of the motley disorder of the world presenting itself as the reality it is to the heightened poetic hearing and vision of a madman; there is no sense in it save to the senseless [...]', *Modern German Literature 1880-1950* (London, 1959), p.421.

3 With four more editions to 1957. (The volume which bears the same title nowadays is edited by Malcolm Pasley, 1972.)

4 *German Life and Letters* vol.XI, 1958, *Jethro Bithell Anniversary Number*, lists Bithell's publications, p.255f. In his 80th birthday tribute for Bithell in the same volume, Professor Willoughby wrote in generous terms, recording that Bithell's former students and colleagues knew him 'as a forceful, inspiring teacher and as a meticulous and wide-ranging scholar'. L. A. Willoughby, 'Jethro Bithell: A Biographical Note' (*GLL*, vol.XI, 1958, p.253).

5 Sixty-six poets are represented in this anthology, including Mombert and Werfel.

6 See the Introduction to vol.III of *Alfred Mombert, Dichtungen* (München, 1963).

7 *Contemporary German Poetry – Selected and translated by Jethro Bithell* (London & Felling-on-Tyne: Walter Scott Publishing Company, 1909). See ANDREWS, p.150f.

8 Fifteen of Mombert's poems are included, with 'Sleeping they bear me' in final position (see *Contemporary German Poetry*, pp.147-157).

9 The Brotherton Library Bithell Collection contains three Mombert items: (A): a letter (31 Aug. 1909), in which Mombert declares his willingness to authorize Bithell's translation of some of his poetry and requests copies. (B) the letter (6 Sept. 1909) transcribed here. (C) a postcard (13 Oct. 1909) received the following month. The Collection also includes some of his unpublished MS notes on Mombert. (The Bithell Bequest Papers held by the Institute of Germanic Studies include correspondence from 1935–1964, but there is no reference to Mombert.) None of this correspondence is mentioned in 'Alfred Mombert, Briefe 1893–1942.' Ausgewählt und herausgegeben von B. J. Morse, in *Deutsche Akademie für Sprache und Dichtung*, Bd 26/36 (Heidelberg, Darmstadt: Schneider, 1961).

10 Jethro Bithell (ed.), *Germany: A Companion to German Studies* (1932), p.285.

11 Alfred Mombert, *Der himmlische Zecher. Ausgewählte Gedichte* (Berlin: Schuster & Loeffler, 1909). The final selection to appear under this title comprised:

Erstes Buch:	*Land und Meer. Gluten. Forschung*	Fünftes Buch:	*Plejaden-Gott. Vogelsang. Seliges Alter*
Zweites Buch:	*Weib. Inbrunst. Schöpfung*	Sechstes Buch:	*Traum. Farben-Lichter. Spiel der Welt*
Drittes Buch:	*Dämon. Gesetz. Ballung*		
Viertes Buch:	*Wunder der Stunde. Seelen-Glanze. Fahrten Sfairas*	Siebtes Buch:	*Äther und Gestirne. Schweben. Der himmlische Zecher.*

Alfred Mombert, *Der himmlische Zecher*, in sieben Büchern. Große Ausgabe (Wiesbaden: Insel-Verlag, 1951).

12 These 'Proben' are no longer held with the letter.

13 Bithell had selected *Das Licht* for his proposed compilation of German poetry in translation. *Das Licht* forms part of Mombert's poem *Tag und Nacht* (1894). It includes the lines: *'s ist Dämmerzeit. Ich steh am Fenster // und schau' ins Pfründnerhaus hinüber. // An jedem*

Fenster ein Mütterchen. // Das Eine webt mit seinem Schädel. // Das Eine ringt die welken Hände. – Alfred Mombert, *Dichtungen*, 3 vols (München: Kösel-Verlag, 1963).

[14] This comment is added at the bottom left of the sheet as a form of postscript. The line 'Schlafend trägt man mich' introduces Mombert's poem *Schlummerlied* (from Book One of *Der himmlische Zecher*). It opens: *Schlafend trägt man mich // in mein Heimatland. // Ferne komme ich her, // über Gipfel, über Schlünde, // über ein dunkles Meer // in mein Heimatland.*

[15] The selection of Werfel's poetry comprises: *An den Leser, Kindersonntagsausflug, Menschenblick, Katharina, Elternlied, Erster Schultag, Gebet um Sprache, Fremd sind wir auf der Erde alle, Warum mein Gott, Nebel, Gesang von den großen Toten, Der Schmerz, Blick der Kreatur.*

[16] See Lore B. Foltin, *Franz Werfel* (Stuttgart, 1972), p.92.

[17] Otto Pick (1887-1940), lyric poet and story writer, was a close friend from Werfel's student days in Prague. Ironically in the light of Werfel's PS, he was already deceased by the date Werfel wrote this letter.

[18] In Werfel's hand.

[19] From the anthology *Schlaf und Erwachen*. Published in: Franz Werfel, *Gesammelte Werke. Das lyrische Werk*, hrsg. von Adolf D. Klarmann (Frankfurt a.M.: Fischer, 1967).

[20] From the anthology *Einander*.

[21] The first verse of the Elegie reads: *Freund! Wir hatten die Schule geschwänzt // Im Kastanienschatten des alten Wirtsgartens // über der hundertmastig schwankenden Stadt. // O wie groß war die Heimat! Den Ozean // zauberten wir in ihren bräunlichen Nebel, // und der bescheidene Strom trug unsern hoch-bordigen Stolz.* – From *Schlaf und Erwachen*.

[22] Alfred Wolfenstein (1883-1945), poet and novelist, was a German Jew who fled to Paris in 1938, using false papers to prevent detection by the Gestapo. Six of his poems appear in Bithell's Anthology of German Poetry, 1880-1940.

[23] Republished in 1935 as *Tagebuch im Kriege*.

[24] See Volker Michels, *Über Hans Carossa* (Frankfurt am Main, 1979).

[25] These are (*pace* ANDREWS, p.152): (A): MS 386/32/1+2 (with envelope): letter 15/9/47 from Carossa to Bithell (Rittsteig bei Passau to Penzance). (B): [edited here] MS 386/33/1+2 (with envelope): letter 9/5/49 from Carossa to Bithell (Rittsteig bei Passau to Penzance). (C): MS 386/34: postcard 14/9/51 from Carossa to Bithell (Rittsteig bei Passau to Penzance).

[26] *Briefe / Hans Carossa*, hrsg. von Eva Kampmann-Carossa, (Frankfurt am Main: Insel, 1978-1981), vol.1: 1886-1918; vol.2: 1919-1936; vol.3: 1937-1956.

[27] *Gruß der Insel an Hans Carossa* (Wiesbaden: Insel-Verlag, 1948) <*cited as*: *Gruß der Insel*>.

[28] In the 'Blackwell's German Texts' series, 1942 and 1949 respectively.

[29] This refers to a paragraph in Bithell's essay in *Gruß der Insel*, in which he talks of his own introduction of Carossa to an English reading public with his Modern German Literature, first published in 1939. Bithell attributes his interest in Carossa's work partly to his similarity to English writers: 'Wenn man als Engländer Carossa liest, hat man das unbedingte Gefühl, daß er einer von unserer Art ist. Da ist zunächst einmal sein Optimismus; denn seine Lehre vom Heilen und die wissenschaftliche Grundlage seiner Philosophie, wonach Wachstum und Fortchritt nicht aufgehalten werden können, gipfelt im Optimismus dem wissenschaftlich begründeten Optimismus Goethes – oder, was das anlangt, Hegels' (*Gruß der Insel*, pp. 42-43). Bithell continues by comparing Carossa's style to that of Robert Browning (see note 31 below).

[30] It seems most likely that Carossa is here referring to *Ungleiche Welten*, which he had planned to finish in 1948 but which had to be delayed until 1950 and was eventually published in 1951.

[31] Carossa's interest in Robert Browning could have been awoken by Bithell's comments comparing Carossa and Browning in his essay 'Carossa in England' in *Gruß der Insel*: 'Der englische Schriftsteller, mit dem man Carossa instinktmäßig vergleicht, ist Robert Browning; abgesehen von persönlichen Berührungspunkten (beide an eine kranke Frau gebunden, beide etwa vom gleichen Gesichtstyp), gelangt beider Optimismus am Ende zu dem gleichen Grundsatz: 'Ein Mensch in der Welt der Menschen zu sein' ' (*Gruß der Insel*, p.43).

[32] Ernst Bertram (1884–1957) was a professor of German Literature in Cologne from 1922 until 1946, when he was dismissed during the process of denazification. He was a poet and also wrote scholarly works on Nietzsche, Stifter, and Heinrich von Kleist, among others. There is a reference to Bertram in Bithell's introduction to *Verwandlungen einer Jugend*, where he writes of his article, 'Lichtgeheimnis', in *Das Innere Reich* (1937), and of Bertram's description of Carossa as a 'sun-worshipper' on account of his doctrine of light (Lichtlehre). See Bithell, *Verwandlungen einer Jugend*, p. xvii.

[33] i.e. Sir Robert Birley, appointed as Adviser to the Deputy Military Governor in 1947. He played a leading role in the denazification of German education, i.e. the elimination of all Nazi and militarist doctrines, which included a thorough purge of teachers and textbooks. His opinion of the work of a denazified author such as Ernst Bertram would therefore have been vital. See Arthur Hearnden, *Red Robert – A Life of Robert Birley* (London, 1984).

The Contributors

Susan BOLLINGER completed the Leeds University BA in German Language & Literature in 1966 and has recently been awarded the Leeds MA in Anglo-German Cultural Relations. She lives in Munich where she has been a Lector in the English Department at the Ludwig-Maximilians-Universität since 1970. Her special interests are British cultural studies, Anglo-German cultural relations, and translation. She also works as a freelance translator.

A graduate of Queen's University, Belfast and of Cambridge University, Fred BRIDGHAM taught in the English Department at the Westfälische-Wilhelms-Universität, Münster before taking up an appointment in German at the University of Leeds where he is now Senior Lecturer and co-ordinator of the Departmental MA programme in Anglo-German Cultural Relations. His publications include *Rainer Maria Rilke: Urbild und Verzicht*, and *The Friendly German-English Dictionary*. He is currently preparing a book on Kleist.

Brought up and educated in Ireland (a Dublin University Foundation Scholar), Richard BYRN taught briefly at Dean Close School, Cheltenham before joining the Leeds University Department of German in 1964. His teaching and research interests lie in Medieval Studies as well as Anglo-German literary relations. With K.G. Knight he co-edited the present volume's predecessor: *Anglo-German Studies*. His principal intellectual interest is in the way religious truth is reflected in literature, medieval or modern.

A native of Hamburg, Ingo CORNILS has lived in the USA as well as England. He is currently Senior Teaching Fellow in the Leeds University Department of German and Director of the University's Language Centre modules. His Ph.D thesis compares English Romanticism and Science Fiction. His principal recent publications deal with aspects of modern romanticism, the German Student Movement, and German Science Fiction.

Joyce CRICK was Senior Lecturer in the German Department at University College London. She has written on Schiller and Coleridge, Thomas and Heinrich Mann, Bertolt Brecht, Christa Wolf, and Günter Grass. The present article is a by-blow from her bilingual edition of Coleridge's translation of Schiller's *Wallenstein* for the Princeton *Collected Coleridge*. She is currently working on a new translation of Freud's *Die Traumdeutung* (the 1st edition) for Oxford University Press's 'World Classics'.

A native of Dundee and a graduate of St Andrews, Sydney DONALD's interest in Dürrenmatt dates back over two decades to his Ph.D thesis on 'das Groteske' in Dürrenmatt's work. More recently he has published a commentary on *Der Besuch der alten Dame* and on Dürrenmatt's treatment of the Minotaur/labyrinth theme. He taught in the English Department at Erlangen University before taking up his appointment at Leeds where he is now Head of the Department of German and also Treasurer of the British Universites' Standing Conference of Arts and Social Sciences.

Claire HARDER studied German & History of Art for her BA at Leeds University, followed by the MA in Anglo-German Cultural Relations. For the past three years she has worked in the Liddle Collection, the Frist World War archive in the Brotherton Library. In her involvement with three major publications and the Collection's journal, her knowledge of German and her editorial skills have been a particular asset. Her interest and career are now moving into Second World War experience.

An occasional translator of German philosophy and poetry, Raymond HARGREAVES has published on a number of German literary subjects from the eighteenth century to the present day, with some bias towards modern German poetry. A Leeds University Modern Languages graduate, he studied for a couple of years at the University of Münster before returning to Leeds, where he remained until his retirement from teaching in 1992.

John HOGG studied German & Economics and Anglo-German Cultural Relations at the Universities of Sheffield and Leeds before taking a PGCE and becoming a teacher of modern foreign languages at Queen Elizabeth's Grammar School in Horncastle, Lincolnshire. He enjoys literature with an Anglo-German connection and holiday travel that adds colour and depth to his spheres of interest.

Diane MILBURN studied at the Universities of London, Leeds, Mainz and Strasbourg and taught in Ingolstadt. After completing her Leeds University doctorate on *The Deutschlandbild of A.R. Orage and the New Age circle* she held a temporary Lectureship in the Leeds German Department and has continued to contribute to the MA programme in Anglo-German Cultural Relations. She currently works as a full-time translator.

An Oxford University graduate of German & Philosophy, Ingrid SHARP is a Lecturer in German at the University of Leeds. Her main research interest is in women's history, ranging from the birth and development of the women's movement in Germany to gender and culture at the *fin de siècle* and the position of women in the German Democratic Republic. Author of a number of articles on gender-related topics, she is currently researching the influence of Abolitionist ideas on the regulation of sexuality in Germany, 1898-1933.

ANGLO-GERMAN STUDIES

edited by R. F. M. BYRN and K. G. KNIGHT

THE LEEDS LITERARY AND PHILOSOPHICAL SOCIETY LTD

APRIL 1992

'In its concentration on mainstream authors, *Anglo-German Studies* substantially enhances an already rich body of critical work in Anglo-German literary relations.' – *The Modern Language Review*.

'This volume offers a series of stimulating, sometimes amusing, sometimes alarming insights into Anglo-German literary relations. All but one are concerned with the translation, reception, and interpretation of English literary culture in Germany ... Let us hope that the Leeds German Department will perhaps one day produce a volume with an emphasis complementary to that of the present one.' – *Notes and Queries*.

'Its interest resides in the strength of the individual contributions.' – *Revue de littérature comparée*.